Popular
Politics

Population Politics

Virginia D. Abernethy

with a forward by Garrett Hardin
and a new introduction by the author

Transaction Publishers
New Brunswick (U.S.A.) and London (U.K.)

New material this edition copyright © 2000 by Transaction Publishers, New Brunswick, New Jersey. Originally published in 1993 by Plenum Press.

Library of Congress Catalog Number: 99-23301
ISBN: 0-7658-0603-7
Printed in the United States of America

Library of Congress Cataloging-in-Publication Data

Abernethy, Virginia
    Population politics / Virginia D. Abernethy ; with a foreword by Garrett Harden and a new introduction by the author.
        p. cm.
    Includes bibliographical references and index.
    ISBN 0-7658-0603-7 (paper)
    1. Population policy. 2. Fertility, Human. 3. Demographic transition.
I. Title.

HB883.5. A23   1999
363.9—dc21   99-23301
                                                                    CIP

To my children

Seize today, plan for tomorrow

Nature is ruthless when it comes to matching the quantity of life in any given place at any given time to the quantity of nourishment available. So what have you and Nature done about overpopulation? Back here in 1988, we were seeing ourselves as a new sort of glacier, warm-blooded and clever, unstoppable, about to gobble up everything and then make love—and then double in size again.

KURT VONNEGUT

It doesn't take man long to use up a continent.

ROBERT FROST

America is sauntering through her resources, and through the mazes of her politics with an easy nonchalance; but presently there will come a time when she will be surprised to find herself grown old—a country, crowded, strained, perplexed—when she will be obliged to pull herself together, husband her resources, concentrate her strength, steady her methods, sober her views, restrict her vagaries.

WOODROW WILSON

Contents

II.   WHY GROWTH FLIES OUT OF CONTROL

III.   THE BIG PICTURE:
POLITICS, INCENTIVES, AND STRATEGIES

Introduction to the Transaction Edition

Reflection upon events since completion of a book is a luxury that an author is seldom offered. Uppermost on my mind and a matter that touches on many others is the tension between national sovereignty and its chief nemesis, globalism or one-world. Trends in world and U.S. population and the environment bear on how this tension will play out.

In the half-dozen years since first publication of *Population Politics*, possibilities barely apparent at the time have become clearer. Other of history's twists and turns have been unexpected. For the future, the greatest certainty I have is that this edition, the paperback I have long wanted, will meet impassioned foe no less than friend.

THE HOT-BUTTON ISSUES

Population, immigration, national sovereignty, and carrying capacity are not unemotional topics. They entail choices affecting conservation and environmental protection as well as the tug of war with policies that advance globalism–one-world.

The concept of carrying capacity is itself sometimes controversial, because it refers to the number of individuals who can be supported without degrading the natural, cultural, and social environment, that is, without reducing the ability of the environment to sustain the desired quality of life over the long term.

The standard carrying capacity question is, "How many people can be supported in a given area—or nation—over an indefinitely long term?" Alternately, the question of how many people a particular region can support can be inverted so that it is about the amount of productive land required to sustain a defined population indefinitely, wherever on Earth that land is located (Rees, 1992; Rees and Wackernagel, 1994). This becomes a study of load per person in a population with a particular standard of living. Ecologists William Rees and M. Wackernagel call it the "ecological footprint."

Focus on the ecological footprint of a Canadian, an American, a Bangladeshi, or whomever, leads to recognition that the load factor changes if a person moves; a Bangladeshi coming to Canada quickly adopts local consumption attitudes. Ecological footprint also recognizes that load is distributed far beyond where a person actually lives. Urban dwellers occupy less space, but the offset is the considerable energetic cost of transporting their food, building materials, and other consumer goods in, and their wastes out, of the city.

The phrase, "ecological footprint," also evokes the image of humans pressing heavily upon the Earth, through both numbers and consumption, as well as the capacity of wealthier nations to trade for whatever is wanted, from wherever it is. Each American imposes a variety of demands and costs on the world environment, so the ripple effects of U.S. population growth are felt far beyond U.S. borders. An example is the burning of fossil fuels that release carbon dioxide into the atmosphere; the fact is, between 1970 and 1990 the United States increased its use of energy by 25 percent, and population growth caused 93 percent of that increase (Holdren, 1991). The American Dream envisions raising everyone, so the more Americans there are, the greater the demand upon the resources and the waste-assimilative capacity of Earth.

Nevertheless, conservation is a positive value for most Americans, and many graciously accept the increasing burden of environmental regulation, even while recognizing that the

need for regulation is a direct consequence of the nation's growing population. Moreover, some people in the United States live
modestly, involuntarily or not. A reduction in the general standard of living would almost certainly weigh first and most heavily
on those who already are poor. Public policy might profitably
take into account how many Americans can live well, without
destruction of the United States' and others' carrying capacity.

Perspectives on the United States' demographic future are
complicated by environmental, economic, and social considerations. If not the "third rail" in politics, demography is at least a
matter of some delicacy because of Americans' ethnic diversity
and the loyalties this inspires. It is nonetheless inescapably—
mathematically—true that if the population continues to grow
at the current rate of approximately 1 percent annually, it will
double every seventy years. Is this population growth a sign of
economic health and vibrancy—or might it push us to the brink
of indescribable enormity?

Does the United States' population grow because most
Americans want it so, or is it due to the immigration policy of a
government and industrial/media elite over which the people
have lost control? Why is the United States the only developed
country in the world with steady population growth, when all
others are fast approaching a stable—even declining—population? Is this growth an appropriate source of national pride, or
should one worry? These are questions raised in *Population Politics*. Politically, they remain heated. Scientifically, trends are
clearer and, for the United States, alarming.

THE POPULATION BOOM

U.S. population growth is best understood in the context of
wider developments. As foreseen in *Population Politics*, the world's
total fertility rate is falling rapidly from the high levels it reached
after World War II. The decline in fertility (an estimate of the
total number of children the average woman in a population will

have if she continues childbearing at the rate observed at a particular moment in time) is occurring for reasons explained here and first explored in an earlier book, *Population Pressure and Cultural Adjustment*.

Before getting to this, let us go back one step to what may be learned from history, sociobiology, and anthropology. During most of human experience, perceptions of strictly limited resources were the rule. Only rarely, through technological innovation, conquest, populist revolution with redistribution of wealth, or immigration, did most people escape from familiar environments where the ebb and flow of resources were well understood. During the very long periods of almost no change in technology or opportunity, the human population—as though in lockstep—barely grew. Innovations and large population movements—a reprieve from known limits—came along slowly at first, only once in several millenia, but by the Middle Ages the pace was picking up.

The era of industrial, navigation, and energy revolutions abruptly shattered the perception that carrying capacity is strictly limited. New technologies and expectations that first arose around the Mediterranean and Western Europe were soon exported to the far reaches of the globe. Aided by science, cultural understandings of "limited good" collapsed. An escape of this magnitude is a condition known in biology as "ecological release," and it is invariably followed by rapid growth of the affected population.

Indeed, when people perceive new economic opportunity, they usually increase the number of children wanted and the actual number born. For example, French and English colonists in America had much larger families than did their close relatives who remained in the intensively farmed landscape and relatively closed economic environment of the Old World.

With no change in mortality rates, a higher birth rate, alone, leads to population growth. With better child survival (because of improved nutrition and public health), higher fertility leads still more quickly to births outnumbering deaths in small, older generations. The process gathers momentum when each generation of young women is larger than the one before. At present, the largest number of ten- to nineteen-year-olds ever alive at a single time—nearly 1 billion—will deliver the largest number of births ever recorded, unless this cohort's fertility rate falls below replacement level (Population Reference Bureau, 1998). Momentum explains why populations may keep on growing for sixty or seventy years after the fertility rate has declined to replacement level.

A few historical examples of rising and falling fertility rates appear in *Population Politics*. Since 1993, excellent demography has turned up other cases that show how changing economic expectations lead to altering family size targets. The proposition that perceived opportunity causes people to adjust family size is becoming richer and more interesting.

A CHANGE IN EXPECTATIONS

It seems clear that the optimistic perceptions of economic opportunity that were dominant after World War II began to shift sometime between 1965 and 1980, one by one, in countries throughout the world. Limits are, in fact, closing in, and the sense of tightening constraints is the main reason that fertility rates are now falling nearly worldwide. Most people want children, but not more than they think can be raised well. People weigh resources and economic opportunity against an accustomed standard of living, the lifestyle wanted for themselves and their family, and aspirations including education for their children.

Absolute destitution may be rare in most continents, but in the context of today's rapidly growing populations, limited and marginally less economic opportunity is being encountered almost everywhere. In addition, the consumer ethic makes most people feel poor: whatever one has, it could be more. In wealthier consumer cultures, wants regularly exceed income—witness the explosion of consumer debt in the United States. Even Middle Eastern oil-producing countries have felt a pinch brought on by a decade of low oil prices. Their shrunken government revenues have forced retrenchment in once-lavish education, healthcare, and other social subsidies that, for decades, supported high family-size targets. Families are now cast relatively on the own resources, and fertility rates are on the way down.

New United Nations (UN) projections for the next two centuries count on fertility declining to a rate at least as low as where parents just replace themselves. In a society with low mortality rates, replacement level fertility is about 2.1 children per woman. After two or three generations where parents just replace themselves, deaths balance births and the population stops growing.

In 1997, the UN suggested that population growth would stop early in the twenty-third century, and that by then the total world population would number approximately 7.7 billion, compared to about 6 billion in 1999. This was the UN's "likeliest" scenario among an array of scenarios that allow for both faster and slower approaches to population stabilization — and eventual decline. All such demographic projections change frequently.

In fact, population may be stabilizing much faster than the UN projects. Six years ago I was confident that a dawning sense of ecological limits would reduce fertility rates, but the speed of this perceptual shift has been a surprise. In fact, some continents are seeing very rapid deterioration in natural, social, economic, and political conditions, and people are responding by dramatically reducing ideal family size—the number of children that they want to have. Family planning assistance is expanding, fortunately, so humane methods for limiting family size within marriage are usually available. Without modern contraception, the total number of births is usually limited by postponing marriage and the first birth, an adjustment being seen in many countries.

Nor did I anticipate—and was intent on denying, in fact—that rising mortality would contribute to stabilizing world population. But signs of this are about, even if not yet recorded in official demographic statistics. The more frequent famines, the floods due to deforestation up-river, the rise in infectious disease, the killing in intertribal and inter-ethnic warfare, and even some mothers' resignation as young children die, take a toll. No country wants to shout it out. But I think it is true, and it will slow population growth rates even faster than would be expected from the fertility decline alone (Abernethy, 2000).

As late as 1979, world population was growing at the rate of about 2 percent a year. The growth rate now is about 1.3 percent. One can plot the points, by year, and see that the rate of growth is slowing rapidly. Kenneth E.F. Watt has derived the mathematical equation that describes this flattening of the growth curve and, using the equation to project forward, concludes that world population will have stopped growing by approximately 2021. This is just 22 years from now and a full two centuries earlier than the UN's 1997 "likeliest" projection for an end to growth. Watt's analysis will appear early in the year 2000 in the *Encyclopedia of Human Ecology*.

Optimists will bet on a scenario somewhere between the Watt and the UN projections. The UN likeliest scenario projects population stabilizing too late, probably, to save the open space, the forests, and the quality of water resources on which natural bio-diversity and a decent quality of human life depend. The Watt scenario can come to pass only with tragically increased prevalence of almost every cause of mortality imaginable.

THE UNITED STATES' CONNECTION

What, in this context, should one make of population growth in the United States? The United States is growing at approximately 1 percent annually, faster than any other industrialized country in the world and on course to double in 70 years if current trends persist. The vast majority of current U.S. population growth comes from the annual flow of immigration and the descendants of immigrants who arrived after 1969. If the current level of immigration continues, these sources will account for virtually all growth through year 2050, because the native-born population is contributing little to the U.S. population increase.

Black Americans have reached replacement level fertility, and the non-Hispanic white population has had a below-replacement fertility rate for 25 years. The U.S. population would be quickly stabilizing were it not for immigration.

The composition of the population is also changing because of immigration. In 1995, Hispanics were 10.3 percent of the population but accounted for 18 percent of all births in the United States. Of these, 70 percent were of Mexican heritage. Hispanics are on track to become the largest minority group and are expected to surpass blacks within 7 years. In 1998, Hispanics surpassed blacks as the largest under-age-18 minority group (Holmes, 1998).

Without immigration, native-born blacks would slowly become a larger share of the whole. With immigration, they will soon cease to be the largest minority and could conceivably become the smallest. With anything close to as high as the 1990s level of immigration, non-Hispanic whites will cease to be a majority shortly after mid-century. In parts of the United States this demographic reversal is imminent. Commenting, for example, on his study of mental health disorders among immigrants, Sergio Aguilar-Gaxiola states that "Forty-one percent of the residents of Fresno County," California, are Spanish-speaking (Taylor, 1998). This is population replacement of historic proportions and is described in some quarters as a demographic Holocaust.

Using 1995 (instead of 1969) as its benchmark, the 1997 National Research Council Report to the National Academy of Sciences suggests that immigration and the descendants of immigrants will account for approximately 95 percent of U.S. population growth occurring at mid-century. The NRC Report also points out certain fiscal, economic, and social correlates of the present immigration stream. For example, Mexico is the single largest source of immigrants to the United States, and the average educational achievement of Mexican (and other Central American) immigrants is eighth grade. The United States' information-age economy has no good place for these workers.

The contribution that immigrants could potentially make appears to vary by ethnic group (Harrison, 1992).

THE FISCAL EFFECTS OF IMMIGRATION

The mismatch of immigrant skills and labor market characteristics is one reason that poverty rates and the number without healthcare insurance stay stubbornly high—in fact, the poverty rate of the foreign-born population is nearly 45 percent higher than that of native-born Americans. This poverty rate inevitably makes immigration a fiscal burden for state and local government. After subtracting taxes that immigrants pay, households headed by a native-born man or woman are left with a significant bill for the education, law enforcement and justice, healthcare, infrastructure and other systems and services used by the foreign-born and their children.

The fiscal burden is acutely felt in states, such as California, that have a large concentration of immigrants. The National Research Council (NRC) finds that each native-headed household in California pays, annually, an additional $1,178 in state and local taxes to support the immigrant population.

Economist Eben Fodor is making it his life work to demonstrate the fiscal costs of growth at the community level. Taking Portland, Oregon, in 1997 as his type case, Fodor shows that each new residential unit imposed approximately $32,754 costs for additional infrastructure. Each additional person created demand for a $15,721 investment in public facilities. Established residents who would not need the new infrastructure if it were not for growth are taxed to pay for it, even though the population growth sometimes changes a community in ways that established residents deplore (Fodor, 1997; Carrying Capacity Network, 1998).

Fodor is often misunderstood and required to repeat that his calculations do not address the increased cost of operating facilities; he estimates only the cost of building added capacity for the larger population, including schools, roads, sanitation and water systems, recreational facilities, energy plants and other community necessities and amenities.

Other communities can estimate their cost of growth by comparing their average land and building costs with Portland's. An extrapolation from data compiled by the National Association of Homebuilders suggests that San Francisco's cost for each additional resident is nearly $20,000 whereas the marginal cost per added person in Ocala, Florida, is approximately $5,000 (Carrying Capacity Network, 1998). Many newcomers are not, of course, immigrants. However, they may have, in a sense, been pushed. Demographer William Frey (1995) documents the large, continuing flows of native-born black and white Americans out of high immigrant-impact states into communities where they expect taxes to be lower and cultural compatibility, greater.

At the federal level, according to the 1997 NRC Report, immigrants do not run a deficit. This, however, is an accounting fiction. They are "excused" from a pro-rated accounting charge for national defense (which is, of course, distributed among all others), and they are not charged for the net liability accruing on their Social Security accounts.

SOCIAL SECURITY AND IMMIGRATION

Social Security is a re-distributive program, meaning that retirement benefits paid out by the program are proportionately higher to low-wage earners than to those who contributed the average amount or more during their working years. Therefore, the larger the ratio of low-paid to higher-paid workers, the sooner the Social Security system goes broke. Rice University economist Donald Huddle calculates that under current terms of Old Age and Survivors Insurance (OASI), "a low-wage male married worker beginning coverage in 1995 and retiring at age 65 in 2038 will receive $4.15 for every dollar contributed to the system in present value 1995 dollars; a high earning married [male] worker will receive $2.05 and the average married [male] worker will receive $3.10 for every dollar contributed over their lifetime" (Huddle 1998, pp. 535–6).

It is increasingly clear to all that the Social Security system as presently constituted is not likely to "be there" for the retirement of baby-boomers. One of the fixes under consideration is an across-the-board reduction in benefits. Under reduced benefit formulas that have been placed before the Social Security Board of Trustees, the program would continue to pay out proportionately more to low-wage earners than to middle and high-wage earners, relative to their contributions. The present-value liability incurred on behalf of low-wage earners would continue to exceed their contribution, and this deficit would be made up by middle and high-income participants in the system who would receive no more than, and probably less, than their lifetime contributions.

Now consider that about 70 percent of immigrants have less education than does the average American. Combined with English-language deficits, the result is that immigrants tend to be low-wage earners. Inevitably, "the more immigration which occurs, the deeper into insolvency the system falls" (Huddle, 1998, p.534). That is, the immigrant account is dominated by unskilled, non-English-speaking workers, and its accruing deficit is speeding the bankruptcy of the nation's Social Security system.

The same conclusion is reached through cash flow analysis, that is, comparison of contributions made versus benefits received in a given year. Focusing on the 1993 cash flow for a broad range of Social Security programs, Huddle calculates that the immigrant sector had a $2.7 billion deficit for the year. "By comparison, the native-born population of the United States had a $19.0 billion surplus in 1993" (Huddle, 1998, p.533).

THE ECONOMIC EFFECTS OF IMMIGRATION

Turning from fiscal to economic considerations, immigration's vaunted $1 to 10 billion per year contribution to Gross

National Product hides the reality that immigration changes the distribution of income. In fact, employers gain $140 billion while American wage-earners lose $133 billion, annually, due to the wage depression and displacement of American workers caused by immigration. In the nation as a whole, "…44% of the decline in the relative wage of high school dropouts between 1980 and 1994 can be attributed to the large influx of less-skilled immigrants who entered the United States during that period" (National Research Council, 1997, p.228).

One needs look no farther to see a major cause of the polarization of America into rich and poor! More than ever, the present high level of immigration is breaking faith with Americans, and those hurt first and worst are our own poor, the very Americans that forty years of social policy have sought to protect.

Further, the 1996 welfare reform legislation assumes that, when welfare benefits end, entry-level positions for those just entering the labor market will be available. This confidence may be misplaced so long as immigrants and their family networks capture entry-level positions over ever-wider areas of the United States.

Miami, Florida, is at the leading edge. Here, the pay scale is one of "the lowest of any major city"; wages "have gone down in the last decade"; and "working-class blacks, Hispanics and whites are locked in a bitter struggle over jobs." The city is said to be "the nation's capital of multiculturalism, a showcase for the demographic bouillabaisse the country seems destined to become." Not English nor any other language is a lingua franca; communications between ethnic groups are breaking down; and the city is becoming "more volatile and dangerous" (Sugarman, 1998, pp.16–17).

THE NATIONAL DISCUSSION OF IMMIGRATION

These facts notwithstanding, sincere humanitarians and certain subversive multiculturalists argue that the United States cannot, must not, reduce immigration. Regarding multi-culturalism, Martin L. Gross "contends that a 'new Establishment' of opinion-makers and style-setters has bought a destructive myth about America. That the greatest nation on earth is a structure of evil, an engine of exploitation and victimization. This re-writing of history has unleashed forces that could bring society crashing down, even though 90 percent of Americans know better" (Markowitz, 1998). No rational point will sway the multiculturalist who sees American culture as, simply, bad, deserving of being derided and, as soon as possible, replaced.

The open-minded humanitarian, however, might consider immigration from three perspectives. First, immigration floods the labor market (debasing the value of labor) and overwhelms the educational system, so hurting poor and middle class Americans—hurting them badly. (And does one not owe prior allegiance to fellow Americans?) Second, that maintaining, here, a safety valve for other countries' population growth allows couples in these immigrant-sending countries to delay the reductions in fertility that could save them from suffering, later, the much worse fate of rapidly rising mortality. And third, that the U.S. environment and social fabric are not immune from harm that results from exceeding the carrying capacity. This means that our ability to help internationally while still maintaining an adequate standard of living domestically could end in a hurry.

U.S. CARRYING CAPACITY

Environmental resources are the national life support system, and the degradation of these resources is exposed in many small, separate signs. For example, San Diego announced in 1998 that city water needs would soon be met by recycling wastewater. The process entails purification, allowing one year for "settling," and re-purification. Then it is "ready" to drink. (After you, please.) In Nashville, a city of nearly one million, traffic starts to build on local roads as well as freeways at 6:30 A.M. Los Angeles is jammed two hours ahead of Nashville, or maybe there is no hour when commuting at the speed limit is possible.

Nationwide, about 3 million acres (more than half of it arable land) is lost annually to erosion, roads, and other construction. Agriculture is at risk not only because of vanishing topsoil, but because underground reservoirs of water, vital to irrigation, are being depleted 25 percent to one -and-a-half-times faster than the replenishment rate, depending upon the site. The topsoil loss cannot be reversed in 500 years, and refilling the underground water reservoirs, the aquifers, takes thousands of years (Pimentel and Pimentel, 1996;1997; Pimentel et al. 1998).

Moreover, U.S. oil production in the lower 48 peaked in 1970, and now more than 60 percent of oil for domestic consumption is imported. The decline in U.S. (including Alaskan) oil production is permanent. Geologists Richard C. Duncan and Walter Youngquist point out that,"from 1991 through 1997, it decreased every year, averaging minus 2% per year for that period"(Duncan and Younquist, 1998).

Production in most other oil-producing countries, including Mexico, Venezuela, Indonesia, Norway, Great Britain, and Russia is peaking or already has done so. By the turn of the century, just five Middle Eastern countries will account for 30 percent of all oil production, a proportion that inevitably will rise (Campbell, 1998a; 1998b). Social stability in the countries that have oil depends in part upon their ability to access export markets and foreign exchange; trade is a shared interest. Lest their oil be lost to us, U.S. foreign policy should avoid destabilizing Middle Eastern governments. But even under the best case scenario, oil will become more expensive as its depletion is increasingly recognized, and this will severely impact U.S. agriculture, industry, and transportation.

Population growth is the principal cause of the ever-rising demand for energy in the United States. Between 1970 and 1990, total energy use in the United States increased by 25 percent, and population growth accounted for 93 percent of that increase

(Holdren, 1991). Even in the period of economic expansion that characterized the mid-1990s, population growth accounted for more than half of the increase in U.S. energy use. But most citizens are kept deliberately ignorant, it seems, of the linkages between population growth, energy use, the decline in the real wealth of the nation, and the habitability of their communities.

WHY FEW PEOPLE THINK ABOUT POPULATION GROWTH

In 1997, Michael Maher addressed the news blackout at the source. Selecting newspaper stories where no mention was made of local population growth as a contributing or root cause of threats to open space, bio-diversity, community services, and environmental quality, Maher asked the reporter why population was ignored. Answers included, "didn't know," "limited [column] space," "interviewees didn't mention population," and usually-unspoken pressure from editors to gloss over the population connection. It is not politically correct to suggest that people, too many people, could ever be a problem in the United States.

Censure by all that is politically correct reaches new extremes when immigration is the underlying cause of population growth. Thus, scarcely mentioning immigration, U.S. Secretary of Education Richard Riley announced an enrollment crisis in American education in a special report entitled, The Baby Boom Echo. Released on August 21, 1996, it states, "Twenty-five years after the baby boom generation set a national record for school enrollment…it is fitting that the children of the baby boomers are doing the record breaking." The problem with the report's title and conclusion is that the recent large and rapid increases in the school population are not primarily the result of children born to baby boomers. Riley's attribution is disingenuous. The baby boomers have below replacement level fertility; they are not reproducing themselves. On the contrary, Hispanic immigrants average nearly 4 children per woman.

THE OBSTRUCTIONIST ACTIVITIES
OF THE U.S. GOVERNMENT

The U.S. government's culpability in this population/immigration debacle is not limited to obfuscation of facts, failure to reduce legal immigration numbers, and upper-level administrative undermining of dedicated Immigration and Naturalization Service (INS) front-line officers who try to curtail illegal immigration. The government also appears to condone the criminal activities of immigrant-advocate activists, while at the same time failing to protect the civil rights of American citizens. Several short examples are illustrative.

In Santa Barbara, California, prior to the 1994 and 1996 elections, Barbara Coe, an American citizen and sixtyish grandmother, posted signs (at her own expense) that stated, "It shall be unlawful for any alien to vote in any election held solely or in part for the purpose of electing a candidate for the office of President, Vice President, Presidential elector, Member of the Senate, Member of the House of Representatives...." The language on Coe's "Only Citizens May Vote" signs was taken from Section 216 of California's voting rights law. Nevertheless, several FBI agents appeared at her home after the 1994 election and grilled her for three hours. They wanted to know, Why had she? For whom was she acting? What did she mean by it? Coe experienced this questioning as harassment and notes that no government apology for the episode was ever forthcoming.

For the 1996 election of federal representatives, Mrs. Coe distributed fliers with the identical language and was scrupulous in keeping them at least 100 feet away from any polling place. Nevertheless, she "was threatened with legal action by the Justice Department of Orange County, the Orange Country Registrar's Office and immigrant advocacy groups for 'intimidating voters' on Election Day" (Larson, 1996, p.1). One state Senator said that she belonged in jail!

If former U.S. Congressman (B1) Bob (blue eyes) Dornan had had the foresight to back up Coe's 1994 warning, he might not, in 1996, have been defeated by some 950 votes. At least 600 of those going to his opponent, soon-to-be-Congresswoman Loretta Sanchez, proved to have been cast illegally. Orange County, it should be noted, was at that time 49 percent Hispanic.

A different kind of incident occurred outside the Westwood (Los Angeles) federal building. On July 4, 1996, a multi-racial and multi-ethnic gathering of citizens celebrating Independence Day, carrying American flags and demonstrating against immigration was confronted, then physically attacked, by a much larger group of mostly-Hispanic immigrants organized by La Raza Unida (the united race). The attackers carried Mexican flags, posters showing severed "gringo" heads, banners cum hammer and sickle, and words including "Fight for Communism; Power to the Workers" and "Este Puno Si Se(unreadable) Los Obreros Al Poder." This group chanted epithets against the United States and such slogans as "Viva, Aztlan." (Heads up, America. Aztlan is the name of the irredentist nation that is to be formed out of present-day California, Arizona, New Mexico, Texas, and southern Colorado). The episode ended sometime after the Hispanic attack turned physical—while several police looked passively on—and a few elderly Americans with bloodied heads were carried away on stretchers. A video-tape is and was available from the California Coalition for Immigration Reform (CCIR). No attacker was ever questioned or charged with assault.

At Blythe, a small town on route I-10 very near California's border with Arizona, the CCIR rented a large billboard on which to post, "Welcome to California, the Illegal Immigrant State" and "Don't let this happen to your state." Mario Obledo, a lawyer engaged in radical pro-immigrant activism, took offense. He announced in a press release that, "on Saturday, June 27, 1998," the billboard would be set on fire. The sheriff of Blythe telephoned Obledo—not to say that this act would be vandalism and illegal—but to warn him of a nearby natural gas plant that would likely ignite and go "boom." Not renouncing his plan and perhaps relishing possible escalation, Obledo spoke to the Sacramento Bee of an explosion that would annihilate Blythe, surpassing the devastation of the Murrah Building by Timothy McVeigh. Four days before the scheduled climax, the Martin Media billboard company folded its tent. Under pressure from Burger King and Best Western, to whom they also rented sign-space and which had been threatened with boycotts by Obledo and company, Martin Media removed CCIR's sign

Perhaps Obledo feels immune from the law. On January 15, 1998, President William Clinton awarded him the Presidential Medal of Freedom for enhancing "the character and condition of America." He was honored specifically for "'pioneering' civil rights work...performed on behalf of the radical, Ford Foundation-funded Mexican American Legal Defense and Education Fund (MALDEF), for which he served as general counsel in the 1970s" (Grigg, 1998, pp. 19-20). Obledo later served California Governor Jerry Brown as Health and Welfare Secretary, an opportunity useful for cementing ties with alleged mobster Jimmy Coppola, Communist Cuban dictator Fidel Castro, and Community Concern, which has been linked to multiple murders and convictions for attempted murder and narcotics trafficking. Currently the leader of the politically powerful Coalition of Hispanic Organizations, representing more than 50 Latino groups, "Obledo is virtually untouchable." With impunity he not only threatens to set fire to private property but also proclaims, "'It's inevitable that Hispanics or Mexican-Americans are going to control the institutions of the state of California in the not-too-distant future. If people don't like that, they can leave" (The Triumph of Immigration, September, 1998).

A documentary audio-tape called "Takeover of America," which consists of speeches by leaders of MEChA, the political organizing arm for Aztlan, has been compiled by CCIR. Pronouncements on this tape include Jose Angel Gutierrez, Professor at the University of Texas (Arlington) saying, "We have an aging white America. They are dying. They are sh.... in their pants with fear. I love it." When Aztlan is achieved, promises another MEChA spokesperson, "All non-Chicanos will be expelled."

Apparently oblivious, many city and county governments

in the United States have laws that prohibit employees from turning in illegal aliens. In June, 1997, such a law in San Joaquin County, CA cost Tamara L. Lowe her job in the district attorney's office. Her responsibilities included coordinating data from criminal histories maintained by law enforcement agencies, motor vehicle records, and credit reports. In this connection, she became aware that convicted heroin smuggler and deportee Miguel Angel Segovia, a Mexican national, was again working in the United States while also seeking county child support for his two young children, who lived with their mother. Lowe alerted agents of the INS Border Patrol who showed up to arrest Segovia. Lowe was fired at the behest of a county supervisor, Steve Gutierrez, who alleged a "breach of confidentiality" in Lowe's dealing with the "client," Segovia. After one year, during which she was forced into bankruptcy, Lowe received a favorable ruling from an arbitrator and was reinstated.

None of these accounts is funny. It is none other than egregious that a county employee was punished because she helped federal law enforcement officers and in so doing violated county law that instructs employees to ignore criminal behavior they observe. In other cases, citizens' First Amendment free speech rights were at issue. The voter warning was legal. Carrying the American flag and patriotic signs and protesting immigration is legal. The CCIR sign is legal. In these cases, which unfortunately are not isolated instances, Americans who acted legally were not given protection against illegal acts and threats of illegal acts by legal and illegal immigrants.

As of fall, 1998, the CCIR sign was to go back up on another stationary billboard. Soon to be revealed was whether it would again become a target for thuggish elements that often do not honor Constitutional protections under the law, except when opportunistically invoked to help their causes.

Citizens may well wonder why U.S. authorities sometimes take minimal action to stop transgressions against civil rights and law breaking. The answer appears to be that little action may be taken if the perpetrators are effectively a protected class—

non-native-born Americans and even illegal aliens. Note in this
connection that FBI crime statistics differentially report the ethnic group of victims and perpetrators. Victims may be black,
white, Hispanic or other; but the perpetrator classification drops
"Hispanic." Therefore, most Hispanic perpetrators of crimes are
classified as "white," which inflates the categories of white-on-
Hispanic and white-on-black crime.

CONSTITUTIONAL MANDATES

The Constitution gives the federal government the over-
arching responsibility to protect the United States from invasion. Citizens are waiting, and find it increasingly difficult to
respect a government that seems more intent on coddling others than in guarding and supporting its own. Mexican
irrendentism in the United States is becoming bolder, artfully
finding protection under the Bill of Rights that seems sometimes
to be differentially applied, disfavoring citizens. U.S. govern-
ment-endorsed multiculturalism, and a 1997 Mexican law that
allows Mexicans to retain all rights of citizenship even after becoming naturalized citizens of another country further facilitate
the disuniting of America.

NATIONAL SOVEREIGNTY

When will the United States government again put America
first?
Perhaps the answer is "not soon," because the concept of
national sovereignty has fallen on evil times. Advocacy for erasing national sovereignty, that is, for globalism, has a long history. Some boosters of globalism try to deflect objections by
asserting its inevitability. For instance, "On 17 February 1930, a
leading member of the Council on Foreign Relations, James P.
Warburg, told a U.S. Senate Committee: 'We shall have world

government whether we like it or not...by consent or by conquest.' In 1976, Professor Saul Mendlovitz, director of the World Order Models Project, said there is '...no longer a question of whether or not there will be a world government by the year 2000.'" Former Senator Alan Cranston (D–California), past president of United World Federalists, prefers the stealth strategy. He "told Transition, a publication of the Institute for World Order, that: 'The more talk about world government, the less chance of achieving it, because it frightens people who would accept the concept of world laws'" (de Courcy, 1998, pp. 34–35).

University of Chicago professor Martha Nussbaum is one who believes in breaking down national boundaries because nation-states perpetuate disparities in wealth. She teaches that "the concept of national citizenship is too exclusive and 'morally dangerous.' Justice and equality, she claims, require 'allegiance to the worldwide community of human beings'" (Erasing Self-Rule, 1998, p.16). Rick Swartz, "an ex-leftist who is perhaps the foremost pro-immigration political strategist in the country," explores similar themes. He quotes, for example, the Book of Leviticus, "'If a stranger sojourn with thee in your land, ye shall not vex him. But the stranger that dwelleth with you shall be unto you as one born among you, and thou shalt love him as thyself: for ye were strangers in the land of Egypt'" (Miller, 1998, p. 36).

Americans are powerfully moved by such sentiments. A 1997 poll conducted for the Public Broadcasting Station (PBS) by Princeton Survey Research Associates found that more Americans wanted immigration to stay at present levels than wanted it reduced or stopped. The same poll found, nevertheless, that "big majorities of Americans think immigration over-burdens the welfare system, causes taxes to rise, hurts job opportunities for the native-born, and fosters racial and ethnic conflict" (Miller, 1998, p.36). Californians, who have the greatest experience with immigration, would probably share the latter opinions and endorse more restrictive policy.

Indeed, a 1994 California referendum known as Proposition 187, to deny various state social services, healthcare, and education benefits to illegal aliens, passed with 59 percent of the vote, including one third of Hispanic and majorities of white, black, and Asian voters. As it was about to take effect, federal judge Claudia Pfaelzer blocked its implementation, and as of fall, 1998, the matter sat on appeal with the U.S. Supreme Court.

Other California referenda may also have received a push from the backlash against immigration, although other issues were primary. Affirmative action was ended in 1996 with the strong support of black millionaire Ward Connerly, who considers the system demeaning and destructive to blacks. For many Americans, the justice-based rationale for affirmative action collapsed under the weight of the many South American, Asian, and even African foreigners claiming minority-based entitlements as soon as they voluntarily walk, drive, fly, or swim into the country. Affirmative action was not intended for them, but for the descendants of those who came involuntarily and paid their dues in America under the horrific nineteenth century condition of slavery.

A further California referendum, in 1998, supposedly ended bilingual education. This reform is intended to let schools focus more effectively on teaching American children and assimilating immigrants, although a provision still allows parents to have their children excused from immersion in English instruction. But because it passed with the strong support of millionaire and immigration-advocate Ron Unz, some Californians suspect a Trojan horse. In addition to ending bilingual education, the bill designates some $50 million annually of public funds, for ten years (i.e., one-half billion dollars), for adult education to be provided by community-based immigrant organizations. Conceivably, these funds could be redirected toward political organizing and advocacy for more immigration.

THE POLITICS OF IMMIGRATION

In the United States, population politics is accurately described as immigration politics. If present trends persist, the least foreseeable differences for the nation are that the population will approximately double by mid-century, and the values and governance of the country will begin to resemble the Mexican model.

In addition, abuse of the carrying capacity will escalate with population pressure and loss of incentives to promote conservation. That is, if it becomes obvious that environmental efforts are doomed to be overwhelmed by population growth—because no community is able to limit entry—very few will be motivated to make the commitment and present sacrifice entailed in conservation. This would be a great loss, because ample data suggest that the most effective conservation takes place at the local level with local support.

In the absence of local commitment, most conservation, if any, would have to be mandated centrally and implemented through bureaucratic regulation—meaning bigger government and, some would say, a loss of liberty. An alternative is private capture of resources, with conservation implemented through denying public access. This is the British model of huge, managed estates, private shooting parks, and long stretches of river with fishing rights reserved to the owner.

A multicultural country might also disintegrate along the lines of Kosovo, Yugoslavia, as new ethnic majorities demanded independence. Serbs were the 60 percent of the Kosovo population as late as World War I, but immigration and the high Albanian fertility rate radically altered the region's demographic profile. By 1998, ethnic Albanians accounted for 90 percent of the population, and this majority claimed legitimacy bestowed by the new demographic facts "on the ground."

No more in the United States than in Kosovo would one expect peaceful secession, because some Americans would surely resist letting their country fragment. If the world government longed-for in some circles has eventuated (a probability that can be disputed), international sanctions might follow. Perhaps fortunately, the future is largely hidden.

To my mind, these reflections are connected by the preeminent importance of one's native land and the loyalty one feels toward all its people. The urgency of considering the carrying capacity and cultural integrity of the United States is underscored by worldwide news that one can read daily. The United States is a model having nearly universal appeal, and it stands ready to give assistance. But to continue helping, the United States must itself remain strong, united, and free.

VIRGINIA DEANE ABERNETHY

November 11, 1998
Nashville, Tennessee

REFERENCES

Campbell, Colin (1998a). The Future of Oil and Hydrocarbon Man. Houston and London: Petroconsultants, sales@petroconsultants.com

Campbell, Colin (Nov. 1998b). Personal communication. San Mateo, California.

Carrying Capacity Network (1998). The Cost of Growth. Washington, D.C: Author.

deCourcy, Joe (1998). Globalists v. the Nation State. The St. Croix Review, 31 (2), 34–38.

Duncan, Richard C. and Youngquist, Walter. (October 2, 1998). Letter to the Editor, Science, 282.

Erasing Self-Rule. (June, 1998). Middle American News, p.16.

Fodor, Eben V. (1997). The real cost of growth in Oregon. Population and Environment 18 (4), 373–388.

Frey, William (1995). Immigration and Internal Migration "Flight": A California Case Study. Population and Environment 16 (4): 353–375.

Grigg, William Norman (August 31, 1998). California's Acceptable Terrorist. The New American, pp. 20–21.

Harrison, L.E., (Summer, 1992). America and Its Immigrants. The National Interest, 37–46.

Holdren, John P. (1991). Population and the Energy Problem. Population and Environment 12 (3): 231–256.

Holmes, Steven A. (Feb. 12, 1998). Hispanic Births in U.S. Reach Record High. New York Times, p.1.

Huddle, Donald L. (1998). Post-1969 Immigration and the Example of the Insolvency of the Social Security System. Population and Environment, 19(6), 533–539.

Larson, Ruth (Nov. 17, 1996). Immigration Reformer Threatened by Justice. Washington Times, p.A1.

Maher, T. Michael. (1997). How and Why Journalists Avoid the Population-Environment Connection. Population and Environment 18(4), 339–372.

Markowitz, Jack (September 27, 1998). Great Guilt Trip Unravels Nation. , Tribune Review, editorial page, Greensburgh, PA.

Miller, John J. (October, 1998) The Politics of Permanent Immigration. Reason, pp.34–40.

National Research Council (1997). The New Americans: Economic, Demographic, and Fiscal Effects of Immigration. Washington, D.C: National Academy Press.

Pimentel, David and Pimentel, Marcia (1997). Land, Energy, and Water. Revised edition. Boulder: University of Colorado.

Pimentel, David & Pimentel, Marcia (Eds.). (1996). Food, Energy and Society. Niwot, CO: University Press of Colorado.

Pimentel, David, Giampietro, Mario, and Bukkens, Sandra G.F. (1998). An Optimum Population for North and Latin America. Population and Environment 20 (2), 125–149.

Population Reference Bureau (October, 1998). Speaking Graphically. Population Today, p.6. Washington, D.C: Author.

Rees, William E. (1992). Ecological footprints and appropriated carrying capacity: What urban economics leaves out. Environment and Urbanization 4, 121–130.

Rees, W.E. and Wackernagel, M. (1994). Ecological Footprints and Appropriated Carrying Capacity: Measuring the Natural Capital Requirements of the Human Economy. In A-M Jansson, M. Hammer, C. Folke, and R. Costanza (Eds.). Investing in Natural Capital: The Ecological economics approach to sustainability, pp.362–390. Washington, D.C: Island Press.

Sugarman, Ellen (October 5, 1998). A Miami Vision of Our Future? Insight, pp.16–17.

Taylor, John G. (October 5, 1998). Mental Disorders Can be a Trap for U.S. Immigrants. The Fresno Bee, p. A1.

The Triumph of Immigration: Kiss California Goodbye (September, 1998). Middle American News, p. 10.

Zuckerman, Ben (1999). The Sierra Club Immigration Debate: National Implicationss. Population and Environment 20 (5), in press.

Foreword to the 1993 Edition

Nearly two hundred years have passed since Malthus published his celebrated essay, and the controversy is as spirited as ever. Since "facts" in the simplest sense have not been enough to produce consensus, we suspect that psychological resistances are involved. Indeed they are, as the reader of this volume will soon see.

Psychoanalysts tell us that we never wholly free ourselves of the expectations of infancy: passively we hope that somebody or something will take care of us. In the early months of life such expectations are realistic, but as we grow and mature we find that we must take ever more responsibility for our own lives. But always there remains a residual expectation that *my* problems will be taken care of by some external power. For some, the beneficent power is a personal God who answers prayers. Others hold that an impersonal Providence will eventually set things straight. In our culture, most adults cherish a childlike belief in the equation *Providence = Science* (with a capital S!).

The evidence assembled by Virginia Abernethy clearly shows that faith in impersonal, beneficent forces can be misplaced. Contraception, a gift of Science, can reduce fertility, but the problem of population control ranges far beyond the techniques of birth control. Better technology is always welcome, of course, but improvements in reproductive control will not, by themselves, keep the human race from "trashing" the environment that supports it.

In the classical Greek theater, when the plot got out of

control, the playwright "solved" this problem by introducing a *deus ex machina*—an indefensibly godlike gimmick that straightened out the mess by fiat, as it were. In the search for easy solutions to overpopulation, demographers in the 1930s produced their own *deus ex machina*, which they called the "demographic transition." Inherent ambiguity conferred long life on this verbal invention. Sometimes the term stands for the merely descriptive assertion that fertility and prosperity are inversely related. Unfortunately, it is more often taken to mean that excessive fertility cures itself whenever prosperity is conferred on a population. Among professionals the second version of transition theory had a considerable following for about forty years, but since 1975 it has been trumpeted almost exclusively by politicians, journalists, and the philanthropic bureaucracy. (Is it cynical to note that these three groups stand to gain in power by supporting this "optimistic" superstition?)

Simply put, the *benign* demographic transition theory asserts the anti-Malthusian proposition that an increase in well-being *decreases* fertility. Abernethy was not the first to attack this myth, but so competently does she marshall the compelling evidence against it that she may well be the last. The problem of restraining population growth is far more difficult than most people suppose. This conclusion inclines many population buffs toward pessimism.

The pessimism is understandable but not necessary. What *is* necessary is that we stop relying on Providence—stop hoping to find solutions to population problems in the heart of the atom or the fine structure of DNA. Since it is human behavior that produces population (and population problems), we must take seriously the ancient Greek advice to "Know thyself." The inner nature of human beings is at least as complicated *and as promising of wonders* as molecules of deoxyribonucleic acid. The behavior of men and women must be studied with as much objectivity and concern as were previously devoted to the purely physical world. The ill-defined "population problem" is produced by the complexities of human behavior; *there* is where we must look for solutions. *There* is where Abernethy looks.

Scientific inquiries are facilitated by diversity in the material to be observed. There are about 180 separate nations in the world, which means that there are about 180 distinguishable population problems. Controls that are effective in one culture may be ineffective in others; intelligent observation of a variety of nations can suggest possible alternatives for our own. (In passing, note that many of the blessings of "diversity" evaporate when we try to meld many cultures into one. Recurrent violence in the Balkans and in the Near East indicates that the most dependable outcome of "multiculturalism" is the violence of civic disorder, a quite unacceptable method of population control.)

Virginia Abernethy, trained in anthropology and economics, is a splendid guide through the jungle of human reproduction. Her beacon is the star of Terence: this pre-Christian Roman playwright, who began life as a slave, boasted that "Nothing human is alien to me." Such should be the attitude of all who seek solutions to the human problems created by exponential growth. In the end, the means used must be highly selective (and probably different in different cultures), but in looking for the end we must allow ourselves to be informed by what other cultures have done, and how they have learned from their mistakes. The challenge of population control is like no other that humanity has faced in the past. Previous successes in meeting other challenges should give us courage to tackle this one. We cannot, godlike, wish it into nonexistence.

GARRETT HARDIN

Emeritus Professor of Human Ecology
Department of Biological Sciences
University of California, Santa Barbara
Santa Barbara, California

Preface to the 1993 Edition

The preface is sometimes written last, is the port in a storm, is the welcome chance for retrospection and speculation. By way of a backward look, the ideas developed a dozen years ago in my book *Population Pressure and Cultural Adjustment* are still in the ring and now make their reappearance. The central theme has been supported by new findings—owing to historians, epidemiologists, economists, and anthropologists—and much of their work is reported here. Most important, I was optimistic then and, despite our ever-closer approach to disaster, still find grounds for optimism today.

My refrain is that population growth is the most serious threat that we, as a species, have ever encountered but that, with correct information, we can deal with it. The greatest obstacles to making needed corrections are bad data, and good data badly *interpreted*. Interpretation is the weak spot because it entails accepting (1) that too many humans *are* the problem, and (2) that high fertility—which created the crisis—stays high so long as individuals and families believe that they can afford lots of children.

The good news is that the first point has gained wide currency. Most official environmental statements now indict population pressure as the root cause of stress. Increasingly, as well, the media pick up on the link between population size and the spreading environmental mess. This insight represents a sea change, one that seemed to get under way, in fact, while this book was in progress. The role of human population growth in natural resource shortages and environmental degradation had to be proved when I began writing. I do not think it has to be proved to most readers any longer.

My second point, however, may still bring people to the barricades because it touches on our fondest hopes for our fellow man. And, not inconsequentially, it challenges a core misunder-standing promulgated by demographers. Since the 1930s, many experts have said that modernization and lower infant mortality would produce fertility *declines* in the third world, accomplish-ing a "demographic transition." By 1975, although more than one prominent demographer was saying that the demographic transi-tion model had failed, others kept fiddling with the concept, giving it artificial life support. Ironically, acceptance of the model by policymakers and scholars in other disciplines has never been greater. The idea that socioeconomic development is the way to control worldwide population growth is appealing and continues to hold sway.

It is my conclusion that the demographic transition model is wrong. Attempts to implement it usually harm the very countries one tries to help. Most efforts are flawed because they signal, intentionally or not, the comforting but tragically misleading message that no real environmental constraints exist.

Families which expect a trend of expanding opportunity have *more* babies, not fewer. So any policy which conveys a message that we live in a world of abundant resources and few constraints has blundered—and blundered badly.

Most people perceive that the message of abundance is wrong. Larger populations, or even the present size matched with current standards of living, are not sustainable—not in the United States and not in India, Egypt, or China. But international aid and liberal immigration policies undercut perceptions of real scarcity and a finite environment. Many people are encouraged to believe that the industrialized world is willing to share its territory and give away large amounts of wealth; they reason, unsurprisingly, that they and their children can look forward to real opportunity. Some national leaders conclude (and many couples act as though) very large populations and high fertility rates are affordable.

History shows that rapidly growing national populations cast most citizens into poverty. This axiom is true today in America—as will be shown—so how can it not be true in countries that start with less capital, lower productivity, and fewer natural resources?

Many people contributed directly and indirectly to the writing of this book, and I wish to thank them all. I have received articles, been encouraged, had helpful criticism, and much, much more. I have been buoyed up. Without such good fellowship and good minds, this book would have been very different and might not even have been at all. I particularly thank my husband Greg; my daughter Elena; my friends Al, Bill, Cordy, both Davids, Ieda, Joan, and Norma; and ever-patient and skilled Lynne Lindsey, who somehow saw it all through.

We humans, we Americans, have a chance to protect our future.

Let's not blow it.

VIRGINIA ABERNETHY

Nashville, Tennessee

FRAMING THE ISSUES

1

Growth
Why We Love It

From the founding of Jamestown, the country that was to become the United States of America needed more people. Natural resources and space were abundant; technology emerged as needed; but westward expansion and economic development were held back for *want of people*. Labor—to clear and hold the land, farm, teach, lay ties, fight, pour the molten steel, build—depended on strong-minded men and women. Courageous, inventive, and proud natures flourished in the new land. People became more productive and *better* here, the Land of Opportunity.

Historians suggest that perceptions of abundance and opportunity shaped the national character. In *People of Plenty* (1954), David Morris Potter introduces his subject with the writings of early travelers:

> Sir Thomas Dale, Governor of Virginia in 1611, said of his colony: "Take foure of the best kingdomes in Christendome and put them all together, they may no way compare with this countrie either for commodities or goodnesse of soil." Hector St. John de Crevecoeur, writing in the 1780s, pictured America as a land of plenty for men of every occupation and every social objective: "There is room for every body in America: Has he any particular talent, or industry? He exerts it in order to procure a livelihood, and it succeeds. Is he a merchant? The avenues of trade are infinite. Is he eminent in any respect: He will be employed and respected. Does he love a country life? pleasant farms present themselves; he may purchase

what he wants, and thereby become an American farmer. Is he a labourer, sober and industrious? he need not go many miles, nor receive many informations before he will be hired, well fed at the table of his employer, and paid four or five times more than he can get in Europe. Does he want uncultivated lands? thousands of acres present themselves, which he may purchase cheap. Whatever be his talents or inclinations, if they are moderate, he may satisfy them. I do not mean, that every one who comes will grow rich in a little time; no, but he may procure an easy, decent maintenance, by his industry. Instead of starving, he will be fed; instead of being idle, he will have employment; and these are riches enough for such men as come over here."

Labor transformed the natural abundance into wealth, and population growth soon came to be equated with prosperity. A city that was growing could be confident that its citizens were becoming wealthy, and their prosperity attracted new growth. In contrast, population loss meant that a major industry and, with it, the city were failing. At some point, economic development began to be seen as nearly interchangeable with size, whether of national economies or metropolitan areas. Urbanization was equated with modernization. Still today, most American regions and cities are proud to grow. They are fulfilling the promise of manifest destiny.

FIRST DOUBTS

Sometimes now, though, one hears a different tone. Is the ring of optimism gone? In its place, does one hear disquiet? For now, let us just register that there *are* critics. Economist John Culbertson (1990) observes that growth

is represented as providentialistic, that is, guided by Nature so as to benefit mankind, and therefore unquestionably beneficial. . . . Getting a sufficiently rapid rate of so-called growth is asserted to take care of poverty, overpopulation, the environment, and other matters. . . . [But] the so-called economic growth . . . is not an answer to excessive population increase. In many societies, excessive population increase will prevent—and has prevented in recent as well as earlier experience—improvements in living standards. It tends to bring about conditions in which efforts at environmental preservation are futile.

Planners for tributaries of the Chesapeake Bay know well that dense residential settlement in surrounding counties is the root cause of environmental stress. For example, the Patuxent River Policy Plan (1984) states: "The driving force behind the increasing sediment and nutrient pollution problems of the river is population growth." Efforts to clean up and mitigate environmental effects are overwhelmed by more development. The volume of nutrient-loaded waste from sewage-treatment plants is so huge that, "in periods of low flow, the Patuxent at its mouth is over 50 percent treated effluent."

Insult piles on injury when taxes for established residents rise just to pay for the infrastructure that accommodates more growth. Expansion of sewers, roads, and water services for new development around the Patuxent Basin is a major cost to local communities; even where developers build the roads, maintenance is a community expense. The Patuxent Basin experience is standard. Nationwide, taxes get higher as communities get bigger.

ECOLOGICAL ECONOMICS

The loss of amenities and higher taxes to pay for growth reflect pressures foreseen by economist Herman Daly of the Environmental Division of the World Bank. Daly (1991) points out that limits are inherent in the productive (nonservice) sector of the economy:

The concept of optimal population has an honorable place in the history of economic thought. But it no longer occupies any place at all in modern standard economic theory. The belief today is that

the concept is of no interest because the niche which the human
population occupies is itself expandable by human action. . . . The
limiting factor in determining the size of the human niche has
traditionally been manmade capital.

But recently we have entered a new era in which the limiting
factor is remaining natural capital. . . . When what was previously
limiting ceases to be, and what was previously superabundant
becomes limiting, then behavior has to change if it is to remain
economic.

America's natural abundance masks Daly's home truth that
the Earth and nature simply are finite, and therefore that the
productive sector of the economy—the part that grows food,
builds houses and infrastructure, creates real wealth—cannot
grow infinitely. The conclusion that the scale of the human
economy (numbers of people × resource use per capita) is
overwhelming nature and diminishing man's niche evokes biologists' understanding of "carrying capacity": *The number of individuals who can be supported without degrading the physical, cultural and
social environment, that is, without reducing the ability of the environment to sustain the desired quality of life over the long term.*

A new phrase, "green accounting," captures the idea that the
depletion of natural capital impoverishes a society in the long
run. This system adjusts gross national product (GNP) or gross
domestic product (GDP), the grand total of economic activity, by
subtracting the value of natural capital that has been *used up* once
and for all. Robert Repetto of the World Resources Institute (WRI)
developed green accounting to recalculate economic growth in
Indonesia, in order to expose the direct effects of its extractive
industries. Lester Brown (1990) summarizes: "Considering only
oil depletion, soil erosion, and deforestation, [Repetto] showed
that Indonesia's economic growth rate from 1971 to 1984, originally reported at 7 percent, was in reality only 4 percent. The
conventional [accounting] system not only sometimes overstates
progress, it may indicate progress when there is actually decline."
President of WRI Gus Speth attributes the miscalculation of true
benefits to archaic accounting practices. Interviewed by *Science*
(Accounting For, 1991), he stated that the "national accounting

framework followed worldwide [is] a 'relic of the 1930s—when no one was worrying about resource depletion—that fosters the illusion that countries can prosper by destroying their natural resource base.'" Repetto's discount factors are actually modest. For example, his calculation does not include the burden of global pollution associated with industry. Yet the "sink" functions of the Earth and atmosphere (i.e., their ability to absorb pollution) are looking more and more like the ultimate limiting factor on growth. So second-generation models of environmental accounting may include pollutants such as greenhouse gas and ozone-destroying emissions.

THE ENVIRONMENT LOSES

GNP (or GDP) numbers are never more misleading than when one is counting the economic activity involved in cleaning up after an environmental disaster: With conventional accounting, the dollar amount of the material and labor used to clean up the *Valdez* tanker spill, the multiple 1990 Gulf of Mexico spills, and Kuwait *add to GNP*. There is no negative number that tallies bird and fish kills; the loss of soil, air, water, and ocean-floor quality; or the never-to-be-recovered oil.

Deteriorating environments are all about us. In December 1991, a panel under the auspices of the National Academy of Sciences (NAS) called for a large-scale program to restore the nation's environmentally damaged lakes, rivers, and wetlands in order to forestall permanent and widespread ecological damage. The panel concluded that "Without an active and ambitious restoration program . . . our swelling population and its increasing stresses on aquatic ecosystems will certainly reduce the quality of human life for present and future generations" (Hebert, 1991).

The NAS conclusions are punctuated almost daily by fresh accounts of environmental wastage—changes which often have an immediate effect on the food supply. For example, oceanographer Theodore Smayda warns of a worldwide "epidemic" of harmful algal blooms. As reported in the *Wall Street Journal* (Stipp, 1991), the blooms spread in 1991 to the rich fisheries of the Georges Bank (off the eastern coasts of Canada and New England) and to the California, Oregon, and Washington coasts. The toxic red tides affect anchovies off California and razor clams off the more northern states, making these foods dangerous for human consumption and, indeed, killing seabirds which feed on them. Shellfish are also threatened by contamination from sewage runoff. Fecal coliform bacteria are putting an increasing number of shellfish beds off-limits to fishing: Harvesting was banned or limited in just over 20 percent of beds in 1965, but by 1990 the prohibition extended to 37 percent of U.S. shellfish beds. As recently as 1985, only 31 percent were off-limits. One concludes that the beds are deteriorating at an accelerating rate.

Sewage is the clear culprit in fecal coliform bacteria, and Smayda suggests that coastal pollution in general and possibly global warming account for the red tides. The changes are overwhelmingly anthropogenic, manmade, a function of human numbers and technology. Regarding the projected steady climb in the coastal population, The National Oceanic and Atmospheric Administration warns of " 'an almost inexorable trend that threatens to destroy the harvest of wild or natural shellfish' in U.S. waters" (Stipp, 1991).

Biologist Larry Harris of the University of Florida is another who singles out population growth as the root cause of environmental loss. Florida's population grows by 4 percent annually, while 50 percent of the native forest already is "liquidated." Liquidation continues at the rate of 1 percent per year. Florida has plenty of wildlife—"weed" species that live in proximity to humans—but has lost most of its native fauna.

A THREAT TO PROSPERITY

These scientists along with economists Culbertson, Daly, and Repetto are not alone, nor are they the first to warn that

population growth worldwide—including in the United States—
is a threat to prosperity. Classical economist David Ricardo, a
contemporary of Thomas Malthus, saw that continuing population growth leads to impoverishment because scarce natural
resources are an absolute constraint on economic growth.

A coalition—including Californians for Population Stabilization; Sierra Club, Population Committee; Population-Environment
Balance; Zero Population Growth, west coast coordinator; and the
Ministry for Population Concerns—adds a footnote to history. In
an October 28, 1991, letter to the California Office of Planning
and Research, the coalition states: "Your attempt to use growth
management as a means of strengthening the California economy
flies in the face of the cold, hard facts that growth may well be the
cause of our economic woes."

Indeed, companies are moving headquarters and plants out
of California because of high taxes, traffic congestion, crime, and
other signs of a deteriorating quality of life. For the first time since
records have been kept, the period July, 1990, through June, 1991,
saw "more young people from the age of 30 to age 44 [leave]
California for other states than moved in" (Rheinhold, 1991). For
the first time ever, as well, the outbound flow of all Americans
matches the inbound number. The strains of "California! Here I
Come!" are sounding dim.

Neighboring states are beginning to see that their quality of
life will be the next to be spoiled; hence the bumper sticker "Don't
Californicate Oregon." It is not that Californians are not nice
people. The trouble is that they are starting to move and there are
so many of them.

Population stabilization was the target spelled out in the 1972
recommendations of the President's Commission on Population
Growth and the American Future (the Rockefeller Report). Citing
renewable and nonrenewable resources, pollution, and quality of
life, the commission found that "continued population growth—
beyond that to which we are already committed by the legacy of
the baby boom—is definitely not in the interest of promoting the
quality of life in the nation." The report continues, "Neither the

health of our economy nor the welfare of individual businesses depend on continued population growth. In fact, the average person will be markedly better off in terms of traditional economic values if population growth slows down." Further, the commission warned that all social and environmental problems would become more difficult to solve, more "intractable," with further population growth. Were they prophetic?

In 1972, we numbered just over 210 million. In 1993, the United States holds about 50 million people more. Our numbers grow by 58,000 a week, or over 3 million a year. That is an annual growth rate of more than 1.1 percent, and the social, environmental, and urban problems that the commission saw then are now worse. In 1972, was homelessness an issue? Access to health care by the middle class? Private debt? Stagnant real disposable personal income? Today, how many American families have a deepening sense of unease? How many fear that they will provide less for their children than they themselves received?

POLITICAL VALUES

Various observers note a growing sentiment that more than economics or usual business-cycle fluctuations is at stake. Core American values—reverence for country, liberty, self-reliance, family, and community service—all seem under attack. So also are the commitment and economic capacity to guarantee equal opportunity to all Americans. Education falters, the social fabric shreds, productivity barely grows, America falls further into debt, and our competitive position internationally weakens.

Organization is one of the linchpins of prosperity, and it depends on stability and security. But maintenance of order within a democratic framework ultimately depends on the consent and consensus of the governed. Without a core of common values, order depends upon coercion and the criminal justice system. Public safety in today's American cities comes at the cost of erosion in treasured liberties such as freedom from unreasonable search and seizure—the Fourth Amendment to the Constitution. And the shift toward greater state coerciveness will probably be irreversible so long as the numbers outside the law, or in disagreement with fundamental values, keep growing.

Well-meaning Americans might unite to defend their culture and society, but mainstream America is distracted by evaporation of the American dream, torn apart over abortion, and admonished to feel responsible, if not guilty, because we are still better off than many in the world. Internal population increase and explosive growth internationally are unquestionably contributing to changes in American values, opportunities, and goals. The sources of this growth also change America. A mini-baby boom cannot mask the fact that immigration accounts for about half of annual population increase in the United States, and that the socialization of adults into the language and culture of their adopted country presents new challenges. Change that is healthy when small in comparison to the system already in place can tend toward chaos when the proportions of old and new become unbalanced. The changes occurring in America are large-scale and rapid.

A dynamic society deals constructively with change and uses it for enrichment. Nevertheless, change that is beyond the capacity of a culture to absorb leads to disintegration of the political fabric. Sociologist Charles B. Keely (1989), an advocate for immigration, nevertheless questions whether "the center [can] hold." He writes that

> we seem incapable yet (still) of addressing the important issue of what holds this society together (and therefore needs attention and nurturing) in a way that allows for detached analysis. When raised, the question usually seems to have a bigoted tone. . . . [But] can the center still hold in this pluralistic society? How? Is immigration a threat to stability or a requirement if the American experiment is to have any credible chance of continued success?

THE ENGINES OF CHANGE

Population growth is the principal agent of change for the 1990s. Even though numbers are not a big point in this book, it helps to know two concepts: The first is the *rate of natural increase*, which is a percentage. The rate stays above zero so long as there are more births than deaths. With no migration, this figure tells the annual percentage growth of a population. Nicaragua, for example, is growing by 3.5 percent a year; this is their rate of natural increase.

The second statistic is the *total fertility rate* (TFR), the number of children a woman is expected to have over the whole span of her reproductive life. This is not a percentage. A total fertility rate of 2.1 (just over two children per woman) is said to be replacement-level fertility: Assuming low mortality, couples just

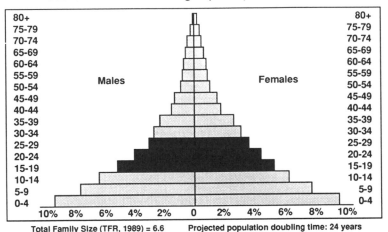

Figure 1a. Population pyramid for Nigeria. *Source*: United Nations, *World Demographic Indicators of Countries: Estimates and Projections as Assessed in 1980.*

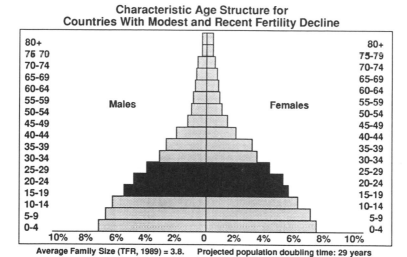

Figure 1b. Population pyramid for Mexico. *Source*: United Nations, *World Demographic Indicators of Countries: Estimates and Projections as Assessed in 1980.*

replace themselves with this number of births per woman. With replacement-level fertility, the rate of natural increase eventually goes to (or stays at) zero. Nicaragua is growing fast because the TFR is 5.8 and (since the population is very young) the death rate is lower than in the United States. The excess of births over deaths accounts for the natural increase of 3.5 percent a year.

The female sector is so critical in projecting future growth (since only women have babies) that a few demographers use a further statistic: the *total reproduction rate*. This rate estimates how many *daughters* a woman is expected to have during her reproductive career.

The fraction of the population age fifteen or under is also important. A large proportion in this age group indicates a recent combination of high TFR—four children or more per woman— and low child mortality. When as much as half of the population

**Characteristic Age Structure for
Countries With Dramatic Fertility Declines Beginning in the 1940s**

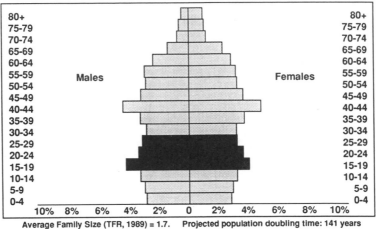

Figure 1c. Population pyramid for Japan. *Source*: United Nations, *World Demographic Indicators of Countries: Estimates and Projections as Assessed in 1980.*

is age fifteen or under, the reservoir of females just entering their childbearing years is correspondingly great. Even if the fertility rate then falls to replacement level, momentum for growth is built in so that population numbers keep increasing for forty years or more. If the fertility rate remains high (and assuming constant, low mortality), the population grows at a breakneck pace.

Half of the population age fifteen or under, combined with a high fertility rate and a low mortality rate, describes most third-world countries today.

Worldwide population growth is a frame of reference within which America can evaluate its own condition and future. What is going on beyond U.S. borders? What pressures can one expect? What choices do Americans have?

A Global Dilemma

In the population business, you'd rather be wrong.

The United Nations calls the 1990s the last possible decade for bringing fertility rates down so that the human population will not grow beyond the capacity of the Earth to sustain human life. The U.N. announcement shattered decades of complacency during which occasional small declines in the fertility rate were hailed as a trend. Professional demographers assumed that fertility would continue to fall until births about equaled normal deaths. They put their faith in economic development, but it backfired.

The U.N.'s conclusion that there is one last chance for a soft landing is optimistic. It portrays a rosier future than other experts now think likely. Many believe that the window of opportunity has closed and worry that even an immediate worldwide reduction in fertility cannot avert disasters of some kind. So many women and girls are alive today that, even if starting now each one limited herself to no more than two births, the number of people dependent on the Earth's resources would become too great to sustain.

MODERN BEGINNINGS OF RAPID GROWTH

About seventy years ago, the U.S. Public Health Service, followed by the Rockefeller Foundation in the 1930s and after World War II by the U.N. World Health Organization, determined to help poor countries reduce their high mortality rates. At nearly the same time, an interpretation of history was developing which almost certainly contributed to the runaway population growth seen from about 1950 right up to today. A few—but influential— demographers, including Frank Notestein of the Population Council, predicted that modernization, urbanization, and reduction in child mortality would cause a transition to small family size, that is, a "demographic transition" to low mortality *and* low fertility rates. This process was to be a repeat of what supposedly had occurred in the industrialized countries. That is, some social scientists looked at the completed demographic transitions in a few countries and assumed that prosperity, industrialization, urbanization, and declining infant mortality had preceded the transition to low fertility in Europe.

Historically this is dead wrong. In fact, the fertility transition occurred in the midst of desperate poverty and very high infant mortality. France was the leader in the shift to small family size. There, the pattern of very small family size was established a full fifty years before any decline in infant mortality. Industrialization and urbanization seem just as irrelevant: France was a predominantly agrarian country at the time of its fertility transition; and in countries that did industrialize (for which 1780 was a watershed year), the fertility transition did not come until four generations later. With so shaky a historical basis, predictions made for the third world were bound to fail. The poor results are as unsurprising as they are disappointing.

The next several chapters address concepts associated with the demographic transition and, especially, their application to foreign policy. Beliefs that decline in fertility follows modernization and declining infant mortality are pervasive. Demographic transition theory, so-called, still dominates public thinking about development, poverty, and population growth even though many demographers, historians, and anthropologists have tried to show how limited in value these ideas are.

Concepts based on flawed history are a poor basis for policy. Indeed, outside of Europe, English-speaking America, Australia,

New Zealand, and a few Asian countries, the two-child family has not caught on. Quite the contrary: Outpourings of international assistance and the better survival of children evidently mean to most people in the third world that a need to limit family size, which may formerly have existed, has vanished. A pattern repeated over and over again is that modernization and lower child mortality have led to more, not fewer, births. With mortality lowered by foreign public-health and medical interventions but with fertility still high, populations grow fast and then faster.

THE TRIGGER FOR RAPID GROWTH

Today's population explosion is the most extreme ever recorded but, in fact, episodes of rapid population growth have occurred throughout human history. The trigger has been some new opportunity, such as settled agriculture. Growth follows from beliefs that a constraint—either natural or political—has been lifted. The story of opportunity and high fertility pushing growth is told again and again in human history.

For example, more children can result from just settling down. Anthropologist Patricia Draper (1975) found that African Bushmen, the !Kung, reduced the interval between births from four years to about eighteen months (which increased their total number of births) when they abandoned nomadism for agriculture. The explanation is this: Nomads must space children. They do it even when infanticide is the only means available. Fortunately, the high-protein foods they usually eat are not suitable to mush up for infants, so mothers prolong breastfeeding. That in itself suppresses ovulation for an average of thirteen months. On the other hand, a settled people that grows cereals can cope with children born close together. High-starch gruels supplement breastmilk; breastfeeding is less essential and becomes less frequent. An unwanted effect is that ovulation resumes early and women conceive much sooner.

A different kind of opportunity preceded the explosive

"medieval increase" in population recorded for western Europe. In France, for example, the monarchy of Charles Martel was noted for beating back invaders on European soil,* easy access to land, and new food crops. The territory won back from the Hun and the Infidel now supported freemen instead of a subjugated people. Independence plus real opportunity were triggers set to raise fertility.

Backtracking slightly, European population had reached a low point around A.D. 543, after the breakup of the Roman Empire. Farms and irrigation systems lay abandoned (breeding malarial mosquitos) because marauding bands and armies made it dangerous to stay in the countryside. Attacks ceased only when Rome had been thoroughly sacked. By the sixth century, good land lay almost empty and uncultivated. Opportunities to reclaim fields abounded. Hard work yielded a good living. From the perspective of a subsistence farmer, this is prosperity.

The many abandoned farms promoted homesteading. Early marriage was a logical first step. Twelve-year-old brides were commonplace and triggered a fertility rebound. If opportunity means anything at all, the so-called Dark Ages were a good time to be young.

Lynn White, Jr. (1966) traces further recovery from depopulation to the introduction of new technology: simple items like beans and the stirrup. These Arab innovations were introduced into Europe in the seventh century and led to the greater utility of horses, their use as draft animals, better tillage, multiple cropping (beans mature quickly and put nitrogen into the soil), and much better nutrition (protein). Medieval Europe was literally full of beans.

Health status probably gained in the short run, but improvements were wiped out as population centers began to grow. Despite disease and malnutrition, however, growth gathered momentum around A.D. 1000, and the population of England, France, and other regions more than tripled within the next three

---

*"In 732 at the Battle of Tours Charles Martel defeated the Moor."

centuries. A now-crowded Europe quickly showed real signs of stress.

POPULATION PRESSURE IN MEDIEVAL EUROPE

Symptoms of population pressure included a rigidifying class structure, war, and famines that struck from the twelfth through the fourteenth centuries. Feudalism and serfdom tied people to land and to their niche in society; game, fishing rights, and other privileges were reserved to the nobility. Serfdom was the alternative to homelessness.

The legendary Robin Hood of the twelfth century has been romanticized, but reading between the lines one may conclude that the adventurers of Sherwood Forest were homeless, poached game in order to eat, and lived under the shadow of the gallows. The Sheriff of Nottingham was protecting property from common thieves. But 200 years earlier, Robin Hood and his followers would not have been landless: They might have been home-steaders, with no need to be thieves.

Along with shrinking opportunity for social mobility came war and conquest. Growing populations and severe hardship pushed invaders to new horizons where, frequently, they sub-dued the local population. The Vikings explored distant lands, attacking both France and Scotland. William the Conqueror, illegitimate and a third-generation Viking in France, spearheaded the 1066 A.D. Norman invasions of England.

The next waves of conquest took people *out* of Europe altogether. Over two centuries (1096–1291), the Crusaders left Europe in successive upwellings of religious fervor, and hun-dreds of thousands of men and children never returned. Most, probably, were slaughtered or enslaved. Others found a place to hide or conquer. The religious tide turned next against the Jews; their persecution reached a height in Spain, from which they and the remaining Muslims were driven by Ferdinand and Isabella, Los Reyes Catolicos, in 1492.

In other regions, nationalism emerged as a political force, and in 1337 England attacked France: *voilà*, the Hundred Years' War. In England, population-driven expansionist politics and enthusiasm for claims to French soil were high at first, but collapsed with the first wave of the Black Death. The pestilence hit Italy and then, by 1348, France and England. Populations were decimated in all of Europe. Life expectancy at birth fell to seventeen years. Labor was at a premium, again, in much-emptied kingdoms. A final onslaught of the plague swept Europe in 1430, coinciding almost to the year with the end of England's occupation of territory on the Continent.

Reflecting on this history, one may ask: Would serfs have stayed tied to an estate if they had had any place to go? Would the Crusaders, rag-tag or Knights Templars, have followed a religious calling from which most never returned if they had had good prospects at home? Would religious persecution have arisen? Does politics track population pressure? Chapters 16 through 20 explore just these effects in America.

OPPORTUNITY BREEDS EUPHORIA

The first topic, however, is how technological and political developments alter people's evaluation of their economic prospects and, thus, population trends. Long periods of stability on all fronts are broken by innovations as minor as the stirrup. Then prosperity sets off fertility. Call it the *euphoria effect*.

India is an example. Its population was nearly stable from 400 B.C. to about A.D. 1500. The population then began to grow, reaching a rate of 0.6 percent a year, with the restoration of peace from Mogul invasions and the stimulus of new trade opportunities. South India enjoyed particular prosperity under the Vijayanagara kings. The strongest of these, Krishna Deva Raya (1509–1530), is described by Spaeth (1991) "as an early advocate of free trade. He imported velvets and damasks from Aden and China, horses from Arabia, elephants from Ceylon, gold, silver—

and precious gems." European trade offered further opportunity and population growth accelerated after 1900. The real take-off came with independence, in 1947; the rate of growth accelerated in almost every decade after that, up to 1980.

Political change linked to lifting repression or to expectations of prosperity has often raised fertility. Cuba, for example, experienced a baby boom when Fidel Castro replaced the unpopular dictator, Fulgencio Batista, in 1959.

In Africa as well, trade, foreign aid, and independence from colonial powers coincided with rapid and still more rapid population growth. Again, euphoria promoted high fertility. Populations, which had been stable during the many centuries that societies remained relatively closed and technology changed little, now began to grow.

LOW FERTILITY IS THE HUMAN WAY

Low fertility has been the usual stabilizing factor because, for humans, *high mortality* is *not* the norm. Increased mortality appears mainly in densely settled regions toward the middle and end of a spurt of rapid growth. Paleontologists studying human remains agree that mortality has had, to date, only a weak effect on population size. Stability or growth has depended primarily on fertility rates. Human population growth was slow right up to modern times because *women almost never have all the children of which they are biologically capable.*

The baseline for the maximum number of children women *can* have is known as *natural fertility*, that is, births when no behavioral, social, or other obstacles stand in the way of conception and carrying a pregnancy to term. Rarely, and for brief periods, a few societies have reproduced at an average of ten children per woman, a level seemingly close to natural fertility. Comparing this baseline to actual fertility shows that few women have all the children that they are physically able to bear.

The number of births associated with natural fertility has

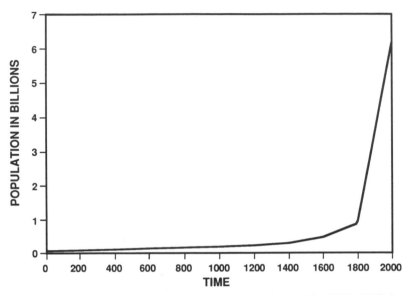

Figure 2. World population, 0 to A.D. 2000. *Source*: S. Umpleby (1988), "Will the Optimists Please Stand Up?" *Population and Environment* 10(2).

been inferred from studies of the Hutterites, a religious denomination of prosperous farmers living in Montana and in Alberta, Canada. In 1954, Eaton and Mayer reported a total survey of married and unmarried Hutterite women under forty-five years of age which indicated a gross reproduction rate of 4.0 *daughters* per woman. The same study showed that married women between forty-five and fifty-four years of age, a cohort that presumably was past childbearing, had averaged 10.6 children per woman. No known society has matched this total fertility rate (TFR) for more than brief periods—and these periods have been times of rapid culture change.

A completed family size of nearly eleven is huge by any country's standards. Our grandparents or great-grandparents on the farm averaged six or seven children—not as many as

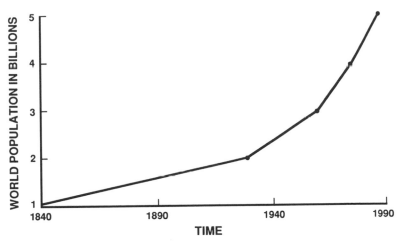

Figure 3. World population, A.D. 1840 to 1990. *Source:* D. B. Luten (1991), "Population and Resources," *Population and Environment* 12(3).

ten. Mid-nineteenth-century French farm families averaged two or three. At most times and in most places, births have not come close to the numbers racked up by Hutterite women. Even without modern contraception, average fertility has often been below, say, 3.0 or 3.5.

With medium to high child mortality, 2.5 or 3 children per woman is about the number at which generations just replace themselves. Replacement-level fertility is about 2.1 in mature industrialized countries. Replacement-level fertility and no in- or outmigration lets population size stabilize in balance with the resource base.

THE DISTANT GOAL

Many countries today are farther than ever from a balance between population and resources. As their populations grow, these countries become more dependent, or more destitute. Aid would have to rise just to keep their poverty from grinding deeper. It is a fact that international aid is being overwhelmed by the evergrowing numbers who need. Let's look at facts.

Up to half of the population in third-world countries is age fifteen or under. As successive waves mature and enter the labor force, productive opportunities are seized whether or not they are environmentally sound; yet the demand for jobs is never satisfied.

Central American families average six children each, for example, and a quarter of a million young people in the region (not counting Mexico) look for work each year. Including Mexico, Central America counts 125 million people and a population-doubling time of twenty-eight years. By the year 2020, Central America will have 200 million people, and the larger Caribbean region will have a population equal to that of the United States today. (Meanwhile—if immigration continues—many from the region will have moved here. The U.S. population is on track to double in sixty-two years; as recently as 1980, the doubling time was projected to be seventy years. If present immigration trends continue, the interval will shrink again.)

Would-be entrants into the labor force in overpopulated countries find neither land nor gainful employment, so they turn to service and piecework occupations including prostitution and crime. More and more attempt to farm marginal land that is highly vulnerable to erosion. Massive land hunger makes remaining forested or fertile resources difficult to protect. To stave off revolution, governments may elect to subsidize bread and become the employer of last resort—but this is not a longterm solution because governments themselves go bankrupt.

Poverty, political unrest, and environmental decline are inescapably linked to runaway population growth. Some problems become intractable as more and more people depend on Earth's limited natural capital. Unemployment, underemployment, pollution, and resource use above a sustainable level may not be the whole list!

Haiti, from which would-be immigrants regularly set sail for North America, presents one of the more harrowing scenes of overpopulation. Unemployment and poverty are unspeakable. The hills have long been bare of trees and soil; human activity has used them up. The population grows at about 3 percent per year, which means that it doubles in about twenty-three years. If the island were relieved of, say, one-half of its people, in twenty-three years the Haitians would again wedge themselves between the hard rocks of resource shortage and population overage.

The large array of problems in poor countries has, of course, more than one cause. Corruption and mismanagement in government, capital flight, foreign intervention, armed conflict (civil or foreign), and so-called capitalist agriculture may all contribute to poverty. Solutions in each of these areas might help to overcome present suffering. Nevertheless, third-world population growth, with its distinctive age structure and built-in momentum for vastly more growth, arguably is the common underlying cause of misery and a destabilizing force both within and between countries.

Technologies and social systems which are benign under conditions of low population density become devastating when numbers grow. Slash-and-burn gardening (swidden agriculture) is one system that has taken a bad rap; but it is, in fact, among the most ancient of agricultural practices and is a sustainable system when each family can utilize a large area (see Chapter 12 on conservation). Overpopulation destroys the environment by forcing overuse.

A SAMPLING OF SCENARIOS

Momentum for population growth, once begun, is hard to stop. For fifty years births have far outpaced deaths, and human numbers have grown faster during our lifetimes than ever before in history. The world population of 5.5 billion people in 1992 is growing by about 100 million a year. This is why the U.N.'s former "high" and "middle" projections for eventual population size have become the new "middle" and "low" projections, respectively. This upward revision follows several others made since 1950. *There is no sign yet of the expected leveling off of population growth*, and this goal has receded further into the future. A nongrowing population is not visualized until nearly the twenty-second century, and the most likely population total by the time growth levels off is now set at 14 billion persons.

The remarkable feature of U.N. and most other demographic projections is that they still portray gradually slowing growth, a leveling off, and a gradual fall in population size. This is a benign curve. It lets one think that falling fertility rates will account for most of the change in the growth trajectory. Historically, the projection is well grounded. But stabilization takes time, and never before has the human population spread so totally into all habitable corners of Earth with such devastating environmental consequences. This projection, today, is a truly extraordinary testimony to hope that humankind will be able to avoid terrible, terrible suffering.

The U.N. projection contains no hint that sharply rising mortality could reign in some human populations in the relatively near term, "a mortality ambush," warned Paul Demeny of the Population Council at a 1989 conference at the Hoover Institution. A curve describing the ambush scenario might show only a modest (but lasting) downward trend because local populations might be decimated serially, over an extended number of years. Alternatively, the present steep rise in numbers could be followed by a worldwide crash.

The climb-and-crash scenario describes a plausible future if only because animal populations that grow beyond the carrying capacity of their environment usually follow such a path. The longer overpopulation runs on, the more damage is done: More nonrenewable or very slowly renewable resources are used up; more harm is done to soil, water, and air quality; and species which help keep the ecosystem in balance and share this Earth with us are depleted or become extinct.

Life-support systems deteriorate from overuse and become less able to support life. That means that overpopulation in one period decreases the future number of people who can be maintained without aggravating the damage. The carrying capacity does not remain constant; it shrinks. The process seems to be occurring on our planet today, faster in some regions than in others. Humankind, through sheer numbers and the scale of human activities, may be already exceeding the Earth's carrying capacity. We are in danger of using up what was given us merely to use. If we are to fulfill our trust as stewards of Earth's goodness, we must become serious about it soon.

Biologists as well as soil, air, and water scientists are warning that one can expect episodes of famine that will kill millions; chronic malnutrition that leaves other millions vulnerable to disease; long-lasting floods as rainwater pours off deforested, eroded mountains; and social chaos in which millions more die or simply lack the stability for raising a child. These tragedies—which may seem independent—have to be seen actually as symptoms of one cause: overpopulation. Here, we will consider what is the responsibility and probable future of the United States in these circumstances.

THE BIOLOGICAL BASIS

Some biological facts are fundamental. For example, *every* living thing is descended from ancestors who reproduced. That is a truism, but it has important consequences. It means that the urge to reproduce is usually encoded in the genes. It is an inherited trait expressed in trying to produce offspring of one's own or helping to rear young relatives.

Certain species, including humans, have comparatively few offspring. For these species, the most successful reproductive strategy includes making strenuous efforts to guarantee the *survival* of each one born. Any other strategy wastes female reproductive effort, a potentially scarce factor. The young, themselves, emerge in a very immature state and need parental care to survive. When circumstances are favorable, parents are able to raise large families and, typically, they take advantage of the opportunity. But in undisturbed societies, one consistently finds that childbearing is avoided until childrearing is likely to be successful. The key to successful population policy is the part of the ancestral legacy which predisposes parents toward caution: Bear only those offspring that can be successfully reared.

Thus, the genetic imperative to reproduce (or assist in the rearing of kin—the auntie syndrome) appears to be tempered by the need to reproduce successfully, that is, to maximize the chances for offspring to survive and reproduce themselves in turn.

OVERVIEW

This book is about the urge to reproduce, the sometimes-cautious exercise of that function, and the pathological result of bad information: so many people on Earth that our very numbers may defeat our main goal. The discussion unfolds with a critique of belief in the demographic transition model. This pervasive concept feeds the indiscriminate rhetoric of development, foreign aid, and liberal immigration policy and, through these, drives up worldwide fertility. A look at the big picture, the linkage between population and environment, is followed by attention to American support for population growth over our nearly 400-year history. Americans today are ambivalent about the value of more population growth. Many working Americans and their families are victims of depreciation in the real value of labor, and crowding is increasingly seen as a factor affecting the cost of living and the quality of life. Indeed, moves to stabilize the U.S. population size began in the 1960s: Fertility rates fell and polls, then as now, showed that most Americans want small families and less, not more, immigration.

The United States will not renounce its international responsibility, but our commitment can be no greater than our resources, based on honest appraisals. The dilemma over how to help does not go away even if the problem of the enormity of scale is temporarily set aside. The quandary is: How does one help without belying the underlying fact that natural (not manmade) limits constrain everyone? A compassionate response builds on careful evaluation of which policies do good and which, although they may appear beneficent, do harm. Our actions and policy should be consistent with our longstanding traditions, our particularly American values. Much of the world around us is not so far from chaos, so one must help and at the same time try to remain realistic. In this high-risk period of human history, let us consolidate, work, and pray for grace.

WHY GROWTH FLIES OUT
OF CONTROL

II

Belief as Part of the Problem

Reducing fertility so that population growth can stop is the essential element for improvement in people's well-being. Mortality rates in the third world declined decades ago, but fertility remains stubbornly high. Foreign aid and development policy extending over fifty years are related to just this: how to stabilize population size in the third world through *both* low mortality *and* low fertility.

THE DEMOGRAPHIC TRANSITION MODEL

An idea that economic development leads to fertility decline appeared in the 1930s. The concept arose from the observation that industrialized, "developed" countries had low fertility rates whereas third-world countries had higher rates. The observation was true as a snapshot of that moment in time. The problem came from ignoring history and concluding that one condition led to the other, that is, that industrialization, urbanization, modernization, and declining infant mortality cause lower fertility.

The model expanded as social scientists talked to each other. Confident predictions focused on certain characteristics of industrialized countries which were said to lead—after a time lag, length unspecified—to lower fertility. Socioeconomic development, including rising literacy and reduced child mortality, was expected to trigger the transition from large family to small family size. The assumptions about the direction of cause and

33

effect became the rationale for medical and public health interventions and development assistance for the third world. Specifically, modernization, land redistribution, education, industrialization, and reduction in child mortality have been pursued in
part because of the belief that these developments will bring
down fertility.

Later in this chapter the actual sequence of declining fertility
and infant mortality will be discussed. To anticipate slightly, new
data show conclusively, for both Germany and France, that the
fertility transition came before or at least coincided with declining
infant mortality. Thus, even in the cradle of the demographic
transition, the sequence is close to being opposite of what
theorists have assumed.

Demographic transition concepts not only ignore history but
have failed to predict actual developments. Demographer Michael Teitelbaum (1975) writes of the idea in these words:
"Ironically, its explanatory power has come into increasing scientific doubt at the very time it is achieving its greatest acceptance by non-scientists."

The model has indeed captured the imagination of well-
meaning, compassionate people. They do not want to let it go.
Demographers Ansley Coale and S. Watkins (1986) are among
those who demonstrate that Europe itself did not follow the path
indicated by demographic transition theorists; however, they
justify continued support of international development assistance
by introducing intricate attitudinal and informational pathways
which, one is asked to believe, lead to timely use of contraception. As recently as spring, 1990, the president of the National
Academy of Engineering, Robert M. White (1990), editorialized,
"History shows that without economic development (sic) there is
no hope of changing the population patterns that are the root
cause of global pressures." Vice-President Albert Gore is another
who repeats the prevailing wisdom. See his 1992 book, *Earth in
the Balance*.

But if well-meaning people want to help, they had best take a
fresh look. What *is*, is often not the same as what one *wants*. Self-

deception is unlikely to help anyone when it becomes the ground for policy. Concepts arising from the demographic transition in the industrialized world are what everyone wants to believe; and their application has almost cooked our goose.

FOREIGN POLICY OBJECTIVES

An important consideration for U.S. foreign policy has been that it should be constructive. The American people clearly support policies which enhance international wellbeing and, wherever possible, alleviate human suffering. Americans assume that our foreign policy—including international aid and our very liberal immigration law—has a constructive result.

However, any policy carries a risk of having unintended and unwanted effects. As we continue to give foreign aid, and as immigration into the United States continues to grow, it is time to make sure that their principal effects are constructive. At a minimum, our policies must not harm those very countries that we are trying to help.

An example of a harmful effect is *raising* the desired or actual family size of people in a third-world country. And yes, fertility rates have risen in recent times. An Indian woman was likely to have more children during the 1960s and 1970s than a similar woman whose reproductive years centered in the 1930s. The same can be said of the average African woman. Change in the wrong direction is still more marked when the focus is on smaller social units: The Shipibo of the Peruvian Amazon have gone from an average of about four births to eight or nine per woman.

Precision regarding factors that make fertility go up or down is essential because it is unforgiveable to inadvertently delay, through our policies, downward adjustment in fertility rates. We do not wish to be doing harm—instead of helping. Demographic transition concepts, if they are right, support doing what we are doing. If wrong, policy changes are in order.

Reasonable questions are: Does modernization really promote small family size? Does large-scale foreign aid help or hurt? *Or* do the promise of prosperity and prospect of emigration so affect fertility that any possible good done by the aid is overwhelmed by extra births—children who will all need resources to grow and jobs later, to live? Does helping the number who come to the United States as immigrants justify raising the expectations of the far greater number who will never have that opportunity? Do "pull" factors, such as jobs and benefits in the United States, promote high fertility among those who actually make the move *and also* among those who only think about the possibility? In sum, does the liberality of American and western policy give the impression that all our people have all they need? That resources are not a constraint?

If so, we create the impression that local limits are purely a distributional problem rather than absolute, and that there is no intrinsic need to exercise self-restraint. We dispel the environmentally correct image of limited good—the idea that the Earth's bounty is finite—which for centuries provided the incentive to live within the carrying capacity of one's lands and allowed man to exist in relative harmony with his environment.

The possibility that high fertility is linked to policies which dispel a sense of limits heightens one's interest in the demographic transition model. Its concepts link declining fertility to modernization, industrialization, lowering infant mortality, urbanization, and higher standard of living. As conditions improve or change in these directions, fertility is supposed to drop. If the model were correct, large-scale international aid and liberal immigration policies would be the right thing to do.

But if improving conditions dispel the sense of environmental limits, and *that perception is necessary to check fertility and bring needed political reform*, what then? Do some kinds of aid work at cross-purposes with humanitarian goals?

Most bad old theories never die; they just fade away. But some theories have so many policy applications that they have to be met head on. Concepts related to the demographic transition model are in the second class. Are they right or wrong? Choose: up or down?

Test each example—new ones and the few from Chapter 2—against the predictions of the so-called demographic transition theory. The predictions are

- Modernization lowers fertility.
- Urbanization lowers fertility.
- Prosperity lowers fertility.
- Education lowers fertility.
- Declining infant mortality lowers fertility.

Where one or more of these predictors change, fertility should change, too—in a particular direction—*if* demographic transition theory is right.

GROUNDS FOR DOUBT: SOCIOECONOMIC TRENDS

Some African countries that had very high fertility in the 1960s and 70s are now seeing declines. For example, Sudan's fertility rate dropped by 17 percent (to 5.0 births per woman) during the 1980s. This trend could have many explanations, but prosperity and modern family planning are nonstarters. A 1991 *Newsletter* of the Demographic and Health Surveys states: "The use of contraception, although increasing, is still very low (6 percent of couples) and probably has had little impact on fertility" (Fertility, 1991). Instead, *the decline is attributed mainly to later ages of marriage and first birth* among the population at large. Believers in a benign, orderly transition would have one look for socio-economic development and modernization as the underlying causes of later childbearing. But in reality, the Sudanese economy deteriorated markedly during the 1980s, people lost hope, and famine was widespread. Worse conditions should lead to *lower* fertility? Read on.

East Africa experienced both buoyant optimism and rising fertility in the 1960s. Conversely, deteriorating economic conditions and the AIDS epidemic devastated morale in the 1980s, and fertility fell between 14 and 20 percent in every country of the region. Also in the 1980s, Indonesia saw fertility decline and decline most among people on the worst crowded islands and farmers who live on the most eroded slopes, that is, among the most impoverished. Likewise, the worsening conditions of the 1980s coincided in Brazil with a 50 percent fall in the fertility rate. Observers attribute the drop in fertility to economic stagnation and rising infant mortality. Tibet is another country experiencing economic decline where childbearing is being discouraged: In a departure from earlier practice, mothers are not given rest from their ordinary labors during pregnancy or for care of a sick child, and while nursing, they are not given the extra foods believed to enhance milk production. Both fertility and child survival are headed down.

So much for needing development and prosperity in order to lower family size. Instead we see fertility declining as times get harder.

CHILD MORTALITY

Change in child mortality is another sign of the times. Falling infant mortality is a joyous trend and one wishes that achieving it would lower fertility. But Maurice King (1990) summarizes the international data this way: "The view that, if the child death rate declines sufficiently, the birth rate must decline also, and that there is a causal link between them is untenable if the data are examined closely. Indeed the opposite can occur." Insights into the process are all around us. In Haiti, the Save the Children Fund set out to learn if women who had lost children compensated by increasing their total number of births. The exactly opposite effect was found: Women who had never lost children had the most births; women who had an infant die were least likely to continue childbearing.

Indeed, studies on several continents failed to find that high child mortality leads to more births. Comparison of women in India who had lost young children with those whose family was intact showed no increased childbearing among the former. Research in Guatemala yielded similar results: Women who had lost children did *not* desire additional births as replacements.

Sometimes infant mortality signifies that parents cannot keep children alive. At other times it looks like parental neglect or covert infanticide. Epidemiologist Warren Hern (1991) quotes anthropologists John Early and John Peters, stating that they are among a growing number who "provide evidence that high fertility structures such as are found among the Mucajai Yano-mama 'are not tied to high mortality structures, as argued by some.'" On the contrary, some parents do away with children they do not want. Hern's own fieldwork in the Amazon shows that infanticide is an option parents consider.

Historical data, while inconclusive with respect to infanticide, shed light on the sequence of declining fertility and infant mortality. Fertility, it seems, often declines even while infant mortality stays high or rises. Heilig *et al.* with the Population Reference Bureau (1990) cite the conclusion of historian John Knodel, that declining infant mortality was *not* the cause of lower fertility in the first and second German Reichs. Reviewing the records from 1871 onward of the Reich's 71 administrative areas, Knodel (1974) states that "The decline in infant mortality could not have been an initiating cause of the fertility decline in most areas" because fertility began to fall at the same time or sooner than infant mortality.

Still stronger evidence that fertility fell *first* comes from France, the country which led Europe into the fertility transition. Catherine Rollet-Echalier (1990) finds that small family size was established by 1850, but the decline in infant mortality was not recognizable until the twentieth century.

PERCEIVED PROSPERITY RAISES FERTILITY

Now, what happens to fertility when fortune smiles? Do signs of opportunity or prosperity—better child survival being just one of them—promote a wish for lower fertility as the demographic transition model predicts, or for larger families?

The answer is larger families, without doubt. For example, Turkish sharecroppers received land as part of a mid-twentieth-century redistribution program. Aswad (1981) states that the new wealth was very quickly followed by a baby boom. Some who received land had so many children born after the land redistribution that their family size rose to twice the usual number for that part of Turkey. The new, higher average was 6.4 children per family. The eighteenth-century Irish and post-World War II American experiences are little different (see Chapters 14 and 15).

Again, a baby boom occurred in Cuba after 1959, when Castro replaced Batista. Díaz-Briquets and Pérez (1981) say the explanation is "straightforward. . . . The main factor was the real income rise among the most disadvantaged groups brought about by the redistribution measures of the revolutionary government. The fertility rises in almost every age group suggest that couples viewed the future as more promising and felt they could now afford more children."

In North Africa, Algeria's independence from France in 1962 encouraged optimism and had a marked effect on fertility. Thirty years later, 70 percent of the population was under thirty years of age, and the population growth rate in 1991 was 2.7 percent per year. Lemsine (1992) reported that 7.5 million of Algeria's 25 million inhabitants were unemployed, the disparity between rich and poor was rapidly increasing, and religious fundamentalism now threatened to negate women's hard-won civil rights.

In China after 1980, liberalization of the economy including privatization of farming brought prosperity to ordinary people and, by 1984, fertility had risen to 2.4 children per woman. Rural settings are difficult to monitor, so Chinese farmers and migrant workers were more successful than city dwellers in avoiding family-size rules. Farmers may also have expected to profit from their children's cheap labor.

The incentive structure in China has changed, however. Since 1989, most migration into Shanghai and Beijing has been banned. These cities (8 million and 11 million, respectively) and others where work permits are required prior to migration, no longer act as a safety valve for excess rural population. Families that expected to benefit from child labor are now asked to absorb adults. The result is that many millions of unemployed, homeless Chinese are roaming the countryside. James McGregor (1991) reports projections of 100 million to 200 million landless, unemployed peasants by the year 2000.

EMIGRATION MAY PROLONG HIGH FERTILITY

Incentives related to migration opportunities—or conversely, the need to absorb a nation's own youth—are insufficiently studied. Nevertheless, recent data from high-fertility countries in the Caribbean suggest that fertility *stays high because parents expect that some of their children will emigrate.* Anthropologist Ann Brittain (1991) reports a positive relationship between marital fertility and emigration, by district, in present-day St. Vincent and the Grenadines. She concludes that the "anticipated loss of children to migration may be an important factor in maintaining high reproductive rates." Brittain cites supportive studies, specifically Friedlander (1983), who found that those nineteenth-century English and Welsh districts which "had high rates of emigration showed much less reduction in marital fertility . . . than would have been predicted."

FILLING IN DETAILS: EGYPT

Egypt's experience of the last thirty years also shows fertility tracking perceived opportunity. Besides international aid, petroleum resources, and the Aswân High Dam for generating electricity, Egyptians could take heart from certain geopolitical developments of the 1970s: (1) the OPEC-engineered oil shock, which increased the value of Egypt's own petroleum exports as well as

Suez revenues; (2) private bank lending of recycled petrodollars, and when private sources curtailed lending—in the early 1980s— assistance from the International Monetary Fund and the World Bank; and (3) the Camp David Accord, which returned the oil-producing Sinai peninsula to Egypt and brought it $2.5 billion a year in subsidies from the United States (Egypt's share of the more than $6 billion a year in direct U.S. aid that was intended to further the Israeli-Arab-Palestinian peace process). Such re-sources allowed Egyptian primary- and secondary-level educa-tion, health care, and access to modern contraception to become among the best in the third world. These amenities are supposed, according to demographic transition theorists, to lower fertility. But it did not work out that way. After slight early declines, fertility stalled at about 6.0 births per woman—for about a decade.

By the early 1980s, it became impossible for the average person to ignore signals that the situation was getting rapidly worse. Population growth stayed ahead of gains in wealth so that the per capita shares actually shrank. A historically rich land is now home to 65 million very poor people, over 30 million more than in 1974 and certainly in excess of the longterm carrying capacity. By 1990, the London *Economist* was calling Egypt "the Mediterranean's Bangladesh." Egypt's income from agriculture, while substantial and supplemented by an oil-extractive industry, Suez canal revenues, tourism, and foreign aid, is barely sufficient to maintain all people who claim shares.

This scenario is heralding a now-rapid fertility decline. Egyptian women averaged 4.5 children in 1991. The decline cannot be traced to improving education or improving anything else.

Fertility decline cannot come too soon. The population now almost certainly exceeds the longterm carrying capacity of Egypt's lands and resources. Goods which can be bought with foreign exchange (earned on oil and tourism, primarily) and water are the constraints. Ninety-nine percent of the agricultural base depends on irrigation. Arable land is essentially limited to the Nile delta plus a twelve-mile swath of river valley running the length of the country. Approximately six miles beyond either side of the Nile begins desert—not a gradual beginning, but a stark line of gray-yellow that marks a shift to rock and sand. The desert is broken by *wadis*, where the runoff from occasional rain supports date palms and banana trees, and the still-rarer oases.

Nearer the headwaters of the Nile, Sudanese and Ethiopian populations are also growing fast and it seems possible that, in the not-too-distant future, upstream irrigation in these countries will significantly reduce the water flow into Egypt. (Substitution through processing seawater into freshwater is not a promising alternative because it is energy intensive: Egypt must export its oil to earn hard currency, and its natural gas mostly rises from underwater in the Gulf of Aqaba and is difficult to capture.) Egypt has multiple environmental and resource constraints; water, however, is the most severe.

Because of water, the problem which presses hardest on policymakers is the absolutely limited amount of productive land. As much land as can ever be reclaimed by irrigation (estimated at a maximum 2.8 million additional acres) has already been lost to building. The King Feisal Highway area between Cairo and Giza (the pyramids) was formerly the fruit and vegetable basket for the metropolis but is now solidly built up, mostly in housing. Self-sufficiency in food is tenuous: By the year 2000, Egypt will need to import four times as much wheat as can be produced domestically, and corn, legumes, sugar, rice, oils, and meat in almost the same proportion.

Almost the entire population of Egypt is concentrated in the Nile valley and delta, and along the Suez Canal. Density is growing fastest along the Nile. Indeed, the rapidly increasing number of children restricts hours in school: In Cairo and Luxor, a child attends classes for three hours daily so that three shifts can fit into the school day. Port Said, on the Suez Canal, and other cities with slower population growth operate just two shifts. Other signs of overpopulation are unemployment and under-employment. Both are evident to the tourist, who is approached by all manner of craftsmen and service providers, including cab drivers, *felucca* (boat) captains, guides, restroom attendants who hand out toilet paper, and artisans selling jewelry, needlework, or papyrus drawings. (Artists warn that lower-price competitors substitute banana leaves for the papyrus.) One also discovers that a stall at the bazaar is owned and tended fulltime by a civil engineer, the waiter is a teacher, and one's taxi driver and guide to the pyramids is a college professor.

Work-sharing is the norm because it limits outright unemployment. Bureaucracies proliferate. A search for lost luggage means the passenger's returning personally (with passport) to the airport in order to obtain a claim form from the relevant carrier, instructions from the police, stamps for the form from the post office, approval from the police, another stamp from the post office, and another police approval before searching the baggage room. There are two terminals at the Cairo airport, and searching both means doing the legwork twice. Innovation—such as buying all the stamps that will be needed in a single visit to the post office—creates amazement, but this small efficiency is not illegal. The traveler, fully stunned by the bureaucracy, is now almost surprised.

Both productivity and pay are low, a result of overabundant labor. A teacher gets to teach just one shift. University graduates enjoy a government-backed guarantee of a job—but to honor the commitment, 251,000 new government jobs had to be created in 1988 alone, and one study suggests that the average government employee does thirteen minutes of work daily. The government offers to exchange the job guarantee for a one-time, five-acre land grant; but not even the Nile provides a living with this size parcel and there are few takers.

ECOLOGICAL RELEASE

This context for the rise and fall of fertility in Egypt prepares one for the question: What went wrong? It appears that fertility rose because a resource, opportunity, or technology lifted former economic constraints. *Ecological release* is the term for fortuitous conditions which lift constraints that would otherwise inspire reproductive caution. Examples in this chapter—land redistribution in Turkey, foreign aid and oil revenues in Egypt, and economic liberalization in China—are a small subset of possibilities that can create a perceived surplus, that is, more than people have been accustomed to getting and enough to encourage a preference for large family size.

Cheap land, beans, and double-cropping created a similar condition of ecological release and set the stage for the tripling of population size in medieval Europe. Superior technology introduced into the Americas let settlers take possession of territory and raise as many as ten or eleven children per family. The industrial revolution and raw materials from colonial outposts stimulated seventeenth- and eighteenth-century European population growth (Chapter 14). Trade with Arabs and Europeans and new job opportunities freed Pacific, Asian, and African peoples from the limitations of traditional agriculture, hunting, or fishing and coincided with the start of their population explosions (Chapters 5–9). And upticks in the business cycle set off fertility in the industrial world (Chapters 11–15). Most people seem ready to believe in prosperity. They adjust family-size targets accordingly.

Optimism quite out of proportion to actual prospects often overrides present and past experience. Subsequent events usually prove that forecasts were overly optimistic. But hope is a constant aspect of the human disposition. During periods of favorable change—or even rising expectations—couples appear to adjust family-size targets upward. Thus, contrary to the predictions arising from assumptions about the demographic transition in Europe, various examples suggest that a sense of expanding economic opportunity increases family size. Fertility rises along with actual and anticipated prosperity.

Conversely, unemployment, underemployment, and rising child mortality appear to signal shrinking resources and to promote lower fertility. In Egypt, fertility began to *fall* when grounds for optimism dissipated. Rising infant mortality has coincided with recent fertility declines in the Sudan, East Africa, and Brazil. The historical data of John Knodel and Catherine Rollet-Echalier show that infant mortality remained high while fertility fell in Germany and France. One guesses that, in China, rural resistance to small family size will dissipate as soon as farmers feel the pinch of restrictive migration policies, which force them to keep their unemployed at home.

PUTTING THE DEMOGRAPHIC TRANSITION MODEL TO BED

Reader, take note that even in Europe, the model for *the* demographic transition, a *sequence* of urbanization, modernization, declining infant mortality, and increasing prosperity followed by falling fertility is not real, but imagined. One should look for a continuing stream of new data that document a different sequence. Expect to see that parents want *more* children when they believe that opportunity is expanding. The expected sequence is exactly opposite to what writers on the demographic transition have taught a generation of policymakers to believe.

The next chapters describe further the link between economic opportunity and fertility. The examples will confirm that people want more children when they see (or expect) prosperity; and that they want fewer children when times change for the worse. This connection, which sounds like simple common sense, has to be proved. Indeed, it has to be proved over and over again because it is exactly opposite to pervasive concepts that dominate official thinking.

The following chapter sets the stage by showing that traditional, undisturbed societies have many cultural as well as biological means for keeping fertility low. Populations have remained stable over long periods of time; and *not* because of inordinately high adult mortality, but because cultures have evolved to maintain population size within the carrying capacity of local environments.

4

Cultural Brakes

Within biological limits, children are born or not as the result of particular human actions. Abstinence, mating, contraception, and induced abortion are voluntary behaviors which determine whether a woman will be exposed to pregnancy and, if pregnant, whether she will carry to term.

People in every society know that sexual relations between a man and woman can lead to pregnancy. People in some cultures do believe that it takes repeated acts of intercourse to make a baby. In other cultures, a woman is thought to be impregnated by totemic spirits that reside in sacred places. But everyone also understands that reproduction takes a man and a woman. Magic alone will not do it.

Men, women, and sometimes their families make the decisions affecting pregnancy and birth. A woman may have many more children than *she* wants, but that usually means someone else is in control. Wanting more children is a principal reason that some people have large families while others have small ones or voluntarily forgo childbearing altogether. The idea that family size preference is the most likely determinant of how many children a woman has is not new (see Chapters 5 and 7). The surprise is how much preferences matter. Wanting fewer or more children matters so much that having modern contraception or not seems to make rather little difference.

Perhaps because westerners are used to distinguishing between recreational and procreational sex, and to a pattern in which almost every young person is sexually active, we can hardly envision ways to limit births that do not rely on contraception. Overreliance on modern biological methods results in overlooking cultural and social patterns that affect a threshold factor: exposure to the risk of pregnancy.

This western blind spot can have serious consequences. For example, it encourages the assumption that modernizing will help third-world countries to control their population growth. Traditional beliefs and behaviors may be attacked simply because they are not modern. The possibility that they have had a part in limiting population growth is quite overlooked.

In fact, undisturbed, intact societies usually do well on their own, thank you very much. Without modern contraception, they still manage to keep fertility rates low and population size in balance with available resources. Traditional societies do *not* have natural fertility, that is, all the children that every woman can bear in her natural lifetime. Moni Nag, Kingsley Davis, and other students of culture have found many beliefs, rules, and behaviors which depress fertility. Most of them involve limiting women's exposure to pregnancy, rather than birth control or abortion. A woman who is prevented from being sexually active during most, or even all, of her adult life will not have a large family.

DELAYED CHILDBEARING

Delaying age of first birth, the traditional European pattern, is, in fact, quite common. First, emphasis on virginity before marriage limits young women's chances of becoming pregnant. Then, if marriage is delayed into the late twenties, or if some women never marry, average fertility remains low even if a few women have very large families.

Some African and Muslim societies have particularly harsh ways of enforcing premarital virginity. Some do not flinch at documenting virginity by hanging out bloody sheets from the marriage bed. Gore is at a premium and a chicken may have to make the supreme sacrifice in order to uphold family honor. Other societies, including nomadic Somali clans and some North

Africans, leave little to chance: A girl is infibulated, that is, the labia of the vagina are sewn together when she reaches puberty.

Delaying marriage is another major strategy for limiting fertility. One way to delay marriage is to require property accumulation or a demonstration of economic stability before marriage. Another is to have complex rules about who can marry whom. Rules are effective where populations are small because it is so hard to find an eligible partner.

CHILD SPACING

Even after marriage, exposure to pregnancy can be limited by physiological or behavioral mechanisms. Breastfeeding, for example, delays the return of ovulatory cycles for an average of thirteen months after delivery. The full contraceptive effectiveness of nursing depends on several factors, however. The most important is frequency because suckling depresses the hormones which trigger ovulation. The mother's nutritional status and whether the baby gets supplementary feeding also make a difference. Nursing on demand, and often, is most likely when the baby is carried everywhere in the day and sleeps beside its mother at night—common in polygynous marriages because the husband is not present. Polygyny is often associated with long postpartum sex taboos, also a way to avoid closely bunched pregnancies. In societies that infibulate, a woman may be reinfibulated for a time after each birth. The postpartum sex taboo is often reinforced by beliefs that a malevolent magical influence is triggered by resuming sexual relations too soon or that the mother's milk will be poisoned by another pregnancy, causing the nursling to die.

Both prostitution and polygyny—popularly called *polygamy*—make it easier to observe long postpartum sex taboos. The pressure on women to resume sexual relations after childbirth is less, simply put, if men have more than one wife or sexual partner. Wife-sharing among traditional Eskimo has the same effect.

FEMALE CELIBACY

The mirror image of polygyny is polyandry. Practiced in Tibet, polyandry depresses fertility because many women cannot find a husband when several brothers share one. The paternity of children is attributed sequentially; brothers "pass the arrow." In pre-Communist times, up to 30 percent of Tibetan women remained unmarried and childless because a large proportion of the marriageable men were either in polyandrous unions or dedicated to the celibate Buddhist priesthood.

Analogous to polyandry are two thoroughly western practices, primogeniture (inheritance by the eldest child) and ultimogeniture (inheritance by the youngest). In an agricultural economy, inheriting land is often made a condition of marriage. Where all of a family's land devolves on one heir, as in these two inheritance systems, only one son can easily support a family and he alone is likely to marry.

Other ways of limiting women's exposure to pregnancy are not benign. Divorce or widowhood can end both a woman's marriage and her life, socially or in fact. Rules prohibiting female remarriage are the least of this set. Many subcultures still depersonalize widows even where discrimination against women is officially illegal.

High-caste Hindus in India carried women's marital monogamy to an extreme: *Suttee*, voluntary or not, meant immolation on the husband's funeral pyre. A New Guinea tribe, the Enga, had a similar custom: Within twenty-four hours of becoming a widow, a woman was strangled by her husband's brother. *Suttee* in India was outlawed in the 1920s under British colonial influence. Nevertheless, it persisted in remote areas until at least 1960, and rumblings about it still are heard. A Hindu fundamentalist revival would almost certainly bring back this custom.

The reproductive effect of not letting women remarry varies. If a woman is divorced or widowed very young and cannot remarry, she is unlikely ever to have many children. A young girl married to a very old man might not even reach puberty before being widowed. Anthropologist Mahinder Chaudry (1990) states that during the 1960s the average age of Indian women being widowed was thirty-five, whereas earlier, in the 1930s, women were widowed by age twenty-nine. The six extra years let the 1960s woman have two or three more children than her counterpart would have had thirty years earlier. Thus, the ethos of modernization, which challenges arranged marriage, contributes to population growth; more about this in Chapters 7, 8, and, with attention to ethics, Chapter 12.

WHO WINS

Systems which artificially limit who can marry and reproduce are not particularly fair, but they have not evolved for fairness. Systems evolve as all compete to do the best they can. Men in particular vary in how reproductively successful they are. Some father a lot of children in or out of wedlock or through serial marriages. These men effectively use more than an equal share of women's reproductive effort (and the environment's people-carrying capacity) and leave fewer opportunities to others. Reproduction can be least fair where many women remain childless spinsters and most men are bachelors, as with either ultimogeniture or primogeniture. Polyandry also leaves many women without a mate, but men share procreative opportunities with their brothers.

Polygyny is not particularly unfair to women—a woman might choose to be one of a rich man's several wives, guaranteeing opportunity for her children—but it is among the least fair to men. In a polygynous society, one influential or wealthy man is legitimately able to monopolize a lot of women. A genealogy of a South American Indian society showed that 91 percent of a village's inhabitants traced their descent to one headman who was just three generations removed from the youngest child. That is, nearly everyone was related through one man who was their father, grandfather, or great-grandfather! He was a reproductive success.

Major contribution to childrearing by *both* parents (financially or as caregiver) equalizes somewhat the burden on men and

women. The effect is to narrow the discrepancy in how many
children each wants, making monogamy more likely. Men and
women get the fairest shake in monogamous societies where most
people marry; monogamous, replacement-level fertility by everyone is the only completely fair system that can be imagined. If
every women had about two children, and every man fathered
just this number, no one, genetically speaking, would be getting
ahead of anyone else.

Systems of nearly universal mating but very small family
size—typical of most native-born Americans—have the little-
noted virtue of being fair. They give new meaning to *egalitari-
anism*. A system is supremely egalitarian when exposure to
pregnancy is limited for all by traditional or modern values,
beliefs, and practices held in common by all.

Voluntary behavior which limits women's exposure to pregnancy can have various rationales. People may accept prohibi-
tions on sex during festive and ritual occasions. Planting, harvesting, expeditions for fishing, hunting, and war, and certain
lunar phases are all reasons, in one society or another, to avoid
sex. In the extreme case, where sex is taboo more often than it is
permitted, the likelihood of pregnancy is probably cut by about
two-thirds. Accounts of some traditional societies suggest that
coital frequency averages as little as once every six or seven
weeks. So long as everyone's behavior is governed by the same
norm, reproductive opportunities remain fair.

Whether or not a system encourages fairness, individuals
can be counted upon to act in their own perceived best interest.
Thus, a fisherman avoids sex because he believes this behavior
will improve the catch or, perhaps, make a wave less likely to
swamp his boat. Sexual self-restraint is bolstered by a whole
constellation of beliefs, which are usually part of the male, rather
than the female, culture.

For example, a devout member of the Brahman (Hindu) caste
would ideally sleep *once* with his wife and would on that occasion
father a son. His main incentives are belief that abstinence in life
increases the chances of reaching Nirvana, and fear of losing his
health by succumbing too often to sex. Many Asian and Pacific

cultures contain beliefs that blood and semen are interchangeable body fluids: Both are thought to be finite in quantity and nonrenewable. A man could shrivel up and turn black when his supply is gone, so he should not call on his reserve too often.

Hindu culture is one of those which portray women as lustful and, therefore, threatening;* indeed, such beliefs are spotted across Asia and the Pacific. Nor are western cultures immune to suspicions that sex is dangerous; athletic coaches used to demand that players abstain before a big game. Was frustration supposed to make them mean? Or did this rule hint that sex saps men's strength?

NONPROCREATIONAL SEX

Impediments to sexual intercourse are the principal, but not the only, ways of avoiding reproduction in premodern cultures. Coitus interruptus (withdrawal) is used for birth control in many societies and was known by the time of Augustus Caesar, the first Roman Emperor. Pessaries, plugs placed against the cervix to block sperm from the uterus, are another widely known device. Sometimes, pessaries are used with ointments that supposedly have spermicidal properties. Intrauterine devices have a long history and may have been tried as well. Sixteenth-century Arab drovers used intrauterine plugs on camels because pregnant camels are irritable beasts, suffering extremely from nausea and vomiting. Desert travelers cannot afford unreliable mounts, so stakes for camel contraception are high.

ABORTION

Abortion is known and used by women essentially everywhere. The most common methods are mechanical, including

---

*No psychologist, I. But this looks like *projection*. If men find their own sexual feelings unacceptable, they may attribute them, defensively, to women.

internal probes, blows to the stomach, jumping from heights, and violent exercise. In some societies—including those of American Indian and Pacific peoples—women moved into a separate house on a monthly basis, supposedly for menstruation. Menstrual huts, so-called, are known as a way to protect other members of the society at a time when women are ritually unclean. But retirement for the menstrual period is far from being a burden to women; it is an opportunity for rest and sociability and, if need be, creates an opportunity for discreet abortion. Menstrual huts provided privacy, help from other women, and time to recuperate.

Prescriptions and potions to induce abortion are also common, but not many have proven to be both effective and safe. Most concoctions that would cause elimination of the fetus also poison the mother. Indeed, the British penal code first mentioned abortion in 1803 in connection with the Poison Laws.

Occasionally, a chemical method turns out to be both effective and safe. A lush creeper of the family Asclepiadaceae is known to women in Bangladesh. A twig, inserted through the cervical canal and left protruding into the uterus, brings on cramping and abortion within seventy-two hours. The method was tested by Dr. A. F. M. Burhan-Ud-Din, then with the United Nations, in trials with 108 women who wished to terminate pregnancies ensuing from rape during the 1972 Pakistan-Bangladesh war. Burhan-Ud-Din reported successful abortion in all cases, although the procedure was accompanied by severe abdominal cramps, elevated temperature, and bleeding. Without treatment by ergometrine and broad-spectrum antibiotics, some few women might have died from excessive bleeding.

STERILITY

An overview of traditional abortion practices suggests that they are usually on par with the crude midwifery or quack medicine practiced in any country where abortion remains illegal.

The chances of complicating infections are high, so sterility and mortality are severe risks. Whenever premarital sex is more-or-less allowed (ignored) but premarital pregnancy causes scandal, women get pregnant and then have to hide it. The United States puts women in this double bind except for the relief available through the U.S. Supreme Court decision in *Roe v. Wade* (1973) and some state law.

Nevertheless, abortion as a cause of sterility is less common than physiology, anatomy, and disease. In the United States, sterility affects about 15 percent of couples. Male and female factors are equally likely and may be successfully treated. Usually, diagnosis and prognosis can be completed within one menstrual cycle. An example of a relatively successfully treated male condition is insufficiency of sperm. So long as there is *some* spermatogenesis, semen can often be collected and concentrated for artificial insemination; if these procedures fail, surgical intervention still offers hope. Some problems with ovarian function can be overcome by hormonal stimulation, aspiration of eggs from the ovary, *in vitro* fertilization, and embryo implantation directly into the uterus. Refinements in timing or hormone levels increase the odds of pregnancy, but *in vitro* fertilization methods are expensive, invasive, time-consuming, and successful only about 30 percent of the time, after repeated tries.

In contrast to industrialized countries, sterility rates as high as 50 percent have been reported in third-world countries where sexually transmitted diseases (STDs) are widespread. A public health approach, both prophylactic and clinical, can reduce sterility secondary to STDs in less than a generation. The prevalence of STDs is probably increasing, however, rather than decreasing because prostitution is a major cause of spread. Up to 1 million third-world women and children are sold into slavery by their families, or kidnapped, each year, often for prostitution. Thailand's Foundation for Children estimates that 800,000 children and a further 1.2 million women are engaged in prostitution in that country alone. A respected Thai researcher puts the total at just 200,000 but, reports *The Economist* (Poor, 1991), "Even this figure would mean that 1 in 40 of all women aged 13–29 is engaged in prostitution," and at high risk, therefore, of contracting STDs.

Involuntary prostitution on this scale is without doubt a pathological symptom of overpopulation. Probably it does not belong in a discussion of mechanisms which limit population growth, except that it does take women out of reproductive contexts; overpopulation is real and pathological responses may be unavoidable.

INFANTICIDE

Infanticide is another extreme means of changing reproductive outcomes. No societies rely on it, but in periods of stress or in certain individual circumstances, it is a last resort. Unwed mothers are perhaps the most likely to commit infanticide, both in traditional societies and in the United States. Neglect of prenatal care as well as of the infant is common. Indeed, avoidance of infanticide through neglect was part of the rationale of an early-1970s request for family planning assistance for poor communities in Tennessee, and part of the differentially higher mortality of infant boys can still be traced to neglect. As recently as 1985, the Tennessee Department of Health and Environment reported that young boys die at higher rates than girls from *all* causes, including fire and not being secured in an infant car seat.

Infanticide may be overt but still surreptitious. Bugos and McCarthy (1984) state that although the unwed Ayoreo (South American Indian) woman is not punished, she still tries to keep infanticide secret. Sometimes infanticide is ignored even if illegal. Although classed as murder in Great Britain and Continental Europe, infanticide was relatively common up through the nineteenth century. Dead babies could be found on the garbage heaps of every large European city through the nineteenth century, but no mother was ever convicted of murder. The greater part of official action in Europe was to outlaw taking a baby into an adult's bed: The law was meant to eliminate the excuse "I rolled over and smothered him—by accident."

Infanticide may also be condoned. For example, Early and Peters' ethnography (1990) of the Mucajai Yanomama (South American Indians) reveals that 43.6 percent of all infant mortality is due to deliberate parental behavior. Twinning (among the Australian Aborigines) or a congenital anomaly often triggers infanticide, which may be a parental or paternal right, or even a duty, in some societies.

Nomads who walk and carry all their possessions over vast territories have no alternative to infanticide if the physiological suppression of ovulation induced by breastfeeding fails them. Aborigine mothers in their traditional habitats carried their young on long desert treks, and two at once were too much to handle. The African !Kung of the Kalahari Desert also used infanticide as a backup method for spacing children, but gave it up when they stopped their nomadic migrations and became settled agriculturalists.

Netsilik Eskimo, another people who needed to cope with an unusually harsh environment, practiced infanticide as necessary. The link to poverty (effective overpopulation) is strong: Groups with the lowest sled dog-to-human ratio—meaning that they led a near-marginal existence—had the highest ratio of men to women. More boys than girls are born as a rule, but Eskimo men had high occupational mortality, so more females should survive into adulthood. The more the sex ratio favors men, the stronger the indication of female infanticide.

Female infanticide is the most common type in third-world countries. Sons tend to be valued because their lifelong labor is usually available to their family of birth, and they often have ritual funerary responsibility to parents. But daughters tend to leave home, and marrying them off can ruin—literally ruin—a family in societies where dowries must be large. Some Indian fathers marry off daughters by promising obviously larger dowries than they can ever accumulate. Problems surface after the marriage is consummated and dowry installments come due and are not paid. The bridegroom's family becomes infuriated at being cheated, and the bride (who lives in her father-in-law's house) suffers. Stories crop up repeatedly in the Indian press of young women found in wells or accidentally burned to death. Even in notorious cases, though, the bridegroom and his family have not been convicted of crimes.

The fact is, traditional societies limit reproduction in ways that may be bitter. Women and babies are often victims. Men are luckier. Some religious vocations demand temporary (Buddhist) or lifelong (Roman Catholic) celibacy, but only a fraction of men take the cloth when celibacy is lifelong. Their cost is no more than suppression of sexual drives. Even that can be mitigated, sometimes, by redirecting energy to nonprocreative contexts, including prostitution and homosexuality.

MALE METHODS

With an exception for vasectomy, culturally sanctioned physical impairments of men's ability to procreate are, in fact, rare. Eunuchs formed a class of professional bureaucrats in the Ottoman Empire. Castration so that choir boys did not lose the falsetto singing voice was practiced up to the nineteenth century in Italy. And certain Australian Aborigine tribes practiced subincision. Subincision was part of the rite of passage from puberty to full manhood. A stone knife laid open the underside of the penis, lengthwise, from the base to tip. The urethra was allowed to heal so that an opening remained near the base; henceforth, urine and semen discharged through this orifice. Physiologist S. J. Segal (1972) suggests that such anatomical rearrangement would result in low conception rates because "the semen flow, mainly, is diverted and lost."

Aborigine men explain subincision as (1) making them more like their totem, the kangaroo, which has a bifed penis; and (2) making themselves more attractive to women. Women are said to prefer subincised men because the plateau and ejaculation phases in sex last longer. Each of these explanations is supported by evidence, and the rationales are not mutually exclusive. But the birth control function of subincision may explain why it was rigorously practiced in the desert interior of Australia—where the population-carrying capacity is extremely low—and was merely an option available to men in the rich coastal regions of the continent.

Subincision illustrates the point that behaviors which lead to low fertility are often built into the culture as tastes and conventions. They usually do not require specific decisions about family size but depend on beliefs and rules that are rationalized in ways other than by conscious reproductive goals. Since a successful society (one that lasts) has adjusted over time to the limits and opportunities of a particular environment, the fertility level actually realized is likely to be adaptive to local conditions.

Culture has put, is putting, the brakes on population growth in many settings. Anthropology and history do *not* justify the belief that out-of-control population growth is a necessary human condition. Those who think it is, or believe that modernization is the best corrective, see only a tiny slice of human experience.

5

Where to Look for Balance

The whereabouts of more draconian means of controlling reproduction supports the view that culture is adaptive. As with subincision, religiously practiced in the barren interior of Australia, drastic interferences with people's lives are most common where the margin of subsistence is slim. Where the environment is unforgiving, population growth is quick to threaten survival altogether; not altogether coincidentally, survivors' cultures are characterized by values and customs that militate against growth.

Many peoples have long histories. Few have had the luxury of expansion into new lands and new continents. It is impossible that the population size of these long-lasting societies exceeded the environmental carrying capacity for any long period of time because, if the subsistence base degrades too far, from overuse, populations disperse or die out. Probably, increasing population pressure has often been an inducement to limit family size. People may then embrace whatever means of blocking reproduction that they know or have in their repertoire of possibilities.

Extreme examples of growth beyond the carrying capacity of the environment can be found, both today and in historic populations. With benefit of hindsight, one surmises that certain outcomes are repeated; there is a pattern. Invariably, poorer members of society suffer first, and their poverty appears sometimes to be a consequence of large family size. Emigration and continuing high fertility are one response; but when this option is not available, families modify their culture in ways that depress fertility and halt population growth. The population size at which the system recovers equilibrium depends greatly on how much damage has been done to the environment, that is, whether its carrying capacity was lowered by overexploitation. Illustrations of culture change in response to overpopulation take us first to the Pacific; the Irish and European experiences with overpopulation are described in Chapter 14.

THE ISLAND CRUCIBLE

Islanders may be particularly sensitive to population pressure because limits are brutally manifest. The population cannot easily disperse. Indeed, anthropologist Raymond Firth (1936) links elaborate rules regulating premarital sexuality, marriage, and food exchanges to a history of terrible famine on one small Pacific island, Tikopia. The history of Yap is less well known but possibly more dramatic.

Oral tradition and archaeology suggest that Yapese population pressure climaxed in about 1850, some generations after first contacts with western trading ships. Anthropologist E. E. Hunt and colleagues (1954) use evidence of abandoned dwelling sites to estimate that population peaked at 51,000 persons, or about 1,300 per square mile. Formal records begin in 1899, by which time the population had dropped to 7,808 persons. By 1946, it was down to 2,582, a decline of 2.3 percent per year. Suffering on Yap must have been intense over at least a generation. Oral tradition has it that "Yap was then so crowded that disinherited and destitute men and even their families lived miserably on rafts in the mangrove swamps . . . and that sometimes four hungry men had to make a meal from a single coconut" (Hunt et al., 1954).

Hunt visited the Yapese around 1950 and concluded that contraception, abortion, and restriction of sex within marriage were used to limit family size. All of these methods were probably present in early Yapese culture, but Hunt suggests that they were greatly elaborated in response to nineteenth-century population pressure. Values and beliefs conducive to low fertility were too prominent to be random. For example, the Yapese defined "too much sex" as more than two or three times a month and, writes Hunt, "the usual jibe at a man who is weak or unwilling to work is that he has been copulating 'too much.'" Weakness from sexual excess was caused by loss of vital body fluids. It made one vulnerable to fatal bites from poisonous fish or forms of supernatural vengeance. Hunt questioned informants (presumably male) about sexual frequency and found only four of sixteen who would admit to having had sexual intercourse within the preceding ten to fifteen days. An additional six men reported coitus within the preceding one to eight months.

Yapese women, married or not, were at least as motivated as men to avoid sex and the risk of pregnancy. Ritual age-grading greatly multiplied married women's work in a large family because sex-age groups ate separately and at different times and had to be fed from separate garden plots; their food had to be cooked in separate utensils and transported in separate trips from gardens that lay on top of steep mountain slopes. Women avoided pregnancy by long postpartum sex taboos, reportedly lasting up to seven years. If pregnancy occurred despite both coital taboos and contraception (including bathing with condensed ocean water after coitus and the insertion of grass plugs to obstruct the cervix), secret abortion remained an option. A few days' monthly retirement was available for abortion. Techniques included drinking condensed saltwater and insertion of rolled hibiscus leaves into the cervix. High sterility rates, possibly related to such crude abortions, should surprise no one. Japanese records suggest that gonorrhea also contributed to sterility. All told, between 30 and 35 percent of women surveyed in the 1930s claimed never to have given birth.

Surprisingly, premarital sex was condoned (to the extent of unmarried hostesses serving in the men's clubhouses), but premarital pregnancy was a cause for shame; so unmarried as well as married women may often have resorted to abortion. Moreover, divorce was easy so long as no children had been born, and many women valued this flexibility enough to delay having children until long after they were married.

Hunt *et al.* report that they found no reference to infanticide or female neglect. However, they fail to make some obvious connections. Births registered in the years 1946 to 1951 showed sex ratios ranging from 109 to 160 males per 100 females. Moreover, girls were three times as likely as boys to die in the first year of life.

The Yapese provide an extreme example of a cultural response to population pressure. Perhaps because they had nowhere to go, and so had to cope, the means devised for motivating everyone to avoid childbearing seem both ingenious and harsh. But over a period of one century, they pulled themselves back from the brink of extinction via overpopulation. It is an achievement.

ADAPTING TO POPULATION PRESSURE

Comparisons between societies whose main point of difference is population pressure on resources also show how culture adapts. From Chapter 4 recall a contrast between Eskimo groups with respect to infanticide: It was most prevalent among the Netsilik, who had also the least favorable sled-dog-to-person ratio. And recall that the Australian Aborigines in the barren interior demanded subincision as part of male initiation to manhood, but subincision was optional in lush regions near the coast.

Ecological imperatives may explain another phenomenon: elaborate marriage rules in the Australian outback. Kinship divided a tribe into eight marriage classes, and a woman in one class was restricted to marrying a man from a specific other class or subdivision. That is, only one-eighth of opposite-sex persons were even potential mates. The number of marriage classes dropped from eight to two with nearness to the coast and more rainfall; that is, the ease of finding eligible mates rose along with the carrying capacity of the environment.

Social impediments to marriage recall the *blackwater ecosystem*, which is the extreme of a nutrient-poor region in the

Amazon watershed. Here, anthropologist Emilio F. Moran (1991) found rigidly applied marriage rules, rules enforced through inherited status in a hierarchical structure quite unlike anything seen elsewhere in the Amazon. Inheritance determines not only marital eligibility but also access to fisheries and entitlement to settle in one of the small, very dispersed villages. Outside of this structure, a family cannot survive. Inherited privileges make existence not easy but at least possible. Thus, hierarchy keeps population density low; individuals with least entitlement to resources delay marriage and avoid bringing forth children who cannot be reared.

Two societies in New Guinea, the Enga and the Fore, present another contrast. The Enga (who demanded premarital virginity of both men and women, strangled widows, and made every agricultural, hunting, or warlike event an occasion for abstinence) warred constantly over their insufficient land. Overpopulation was an unrelenting threat, and women and their reproductive capacity were devalued accordingly. Funerary rituals honored men and pigs but not women.

The Fore had the opposite constraint: They were chronically underpopulated and in need of manpower to defend their territory because kuru was endemic. *Kuru* is a fatal neurological disorder transmitted through a virus present in infected organs. Kuru was most prevalent among women and children because preparing relatives for burial, including the ritual tasting of brains, was a woman's responsibility. With replacement continually threatened, the Fore intensely valued women and children, encouraged premarital sex, used fertility rituals to encourage growth in their gardens, performed erotic music at festivals, and expected widows to remarry quickly.

In this vein—traditions that honor women or not, and promote or discourage fertility—reconsider various Asian Indian practices: Do large dowries encourage families to think twice about the costs of childbearing? Does such hesitation not save some families, especially poor families, from trying to raise so many children that most die before maturity? Did *suttee* gain acceptance among the higher castes because of a sudden reversal in fortunes (access to land) rather than, as some say, because fifteenth-century Mogul invaders threatened the chastity of Indian women who had been widowed by the wars? Is polyandry practiced in Tibet (nearly as inhospitable a niche for humans as can be found) because the ecological balance between human numbers and resources has to be fine-tuned?

The answer for polyandry apparently is that limiting the size of each generation yields a more comfortable, prosperous life in the short run and probably enhances reproductive success in the long run. Land is controlled by the family unit, and the brothers appear to gain by concentrating family resources because their children survive much better than children born into monogamous households in the same community. During a famine, far from rare in that setting, the richer, polyandrous households keep many more members alive than do families which hive out to marginal lands on their own. Therefore, a polyandrously married man is likely to leave relatively more of his posterity over the long term.

The Tibetan case shows how, counterintuitively, limiting family size may enhance reproductive success. If offspring have a significantly better start in life, more may survive to eventually outreproduce the reproductively incautious competition. The measure of reproductive success is not the number of children born; it is children of one's own and of one's kin who survive. The technical term is *inclusive fitness*. Posterity means about the same thing.

The wide distribution of beliefs and practices which limit fertility are being recognized because anthropologists have begun to ask how societies strike a sustainable balance with their environment. The occurrence of drastic means of limiting reproduction in very marginal environments and after disastrous episodes of overpopulation shows that people do make the connection between children and added pressure on resources. Scarcity, or fear of scarcity, seems like a major part of the stimulus for reducing demand. Apprehension is expressed, in part, in reproductive self-denial and values and behavior patterns which reduce fertility.

ADAPTATION IN WESTERN EUROPE

Eighteenth- and nineteenth-century scholars were not at a loss in explaining reproductive restraint. Their thinking about the linkages between access to resources and preferred family size was not clouded by the confusion over economic development, poverty, and infant mortality that reigns today. On the contrary, early scholars thought they understood fertility. Ohlin (1961) cites one early analysis of the "curious Tables of the Births and Funerals of the City of Breslaw": "That the growth and Encrease of Mankind is not so much stinted by anything in the nature of the Species, as it is from the cautious difficulty most People make to adventure on the state of marriage, from the prospect of the Trouble and Charge of providing for a family."

Eighteenth- and nineteenth-century travelers to Norway, including Malthus (1803), observed a similar caution in marrying. The average age of marriage was the late twenties but, since taking on the responsibility of a family was tied to having a livelihood, the more affluent generally married younger. Landless farm laborers of either sex delayed marriage until they had saved a small stake. Prudence also recommended that poor men marry older women. Michael Drake (1969) quotes one visitor to Norway who questioned a cottar about the discrepancy in ages between himself and his wife:

> "Tell me Nils, how was it possible that such an active boy as you could go out and take such an old person as a wife? She looks to be a capable person but she is so much older than you."
>
> Nils replies, "I thought that when I took such an old woman the crowd of young ones would not be so great, for it is difficult for one who is in small circumstances to feed so many."

Entries in the parish marriage registers reflected food supply: A particularly short growing season or, in coastal areas of Norway, the nonappearance of herring shoals caused people to delay marriage. Famine was not a rare event, and it was one of the cyclical conditions that influenced marital decisions.

Counterintuitively, prolonged famine from bad growing conditions or disappearance of the herring shoals lowered the age of marriage. Famine kills the young and very old first. Typically, heirs delayed marriage until their inheritance seemed about in hand, so, if one's parents died prematurely, very severe famines might shorten the waiting period for inheritance and marriage. Ohlin's studies (1961) of eighteenth- and nineteenth-century parish registers in France show a similar linkage among death, inheritance, and marriage.

Swedish and Norwegian cultures evolved in response to scarcity in parallel ways. Demographers Bobbi Low and Alice Clarke's study (1992) of nineteenth-century Swedish parish registers confirms that there was caution in undertaking family responsibilities. Poor men married later than richer men and they married women who were in their late twenties, whereas rich men took teenage brides. Young women have most reproductive value because the earlier a woman begins childbearing, the more children she is likely to have.

The pattern linking marriage and childbearing to wealth and inheritance was widespread in preindustrial Europe. By law and custom, marriage was permitted only when a man demonstrated his ability to support a family. Thus, over a period of at least one hundred years, the average age of women's first marriage in Switzerland hovered at nearly twenty-seven years. First births occurred at twenty-eight or twenty-nine years of age. The average encompassed a very wide range: Some women married only near the end of their reproductive life span or not at all; others, fairly young. Except for a period of liberality associated with the Enlightenment, this pattern was typical in preindustrial and most of nineteenth-century Europe. Marriage was prudently undertaken.

Fertility within marriage began to be limited around the mid-nineteenth century in Switzerland, the Netherlands, and Belgium and had become the French fashion somewhat earlier. A decline in marital fertility means that the total fertility rate (TFR) stays low even if more women marry younger. Demographer Etienne Van de Walle (1968) suggests that age of marriage declined slowly, as economic constraints began to lighten, but that continued progress in that direction could have been sustained only by the accompanying pattern of small family size within marriage: "In this view, the decline in . . . marital fertility was a permissive agent without which the nuptiality trends would not have persisted in the long term."

Paul Demeny's study (1968) of Austria-Hungary around 1880 turned up a similar trade-off between the proportion of women married at any given age (or ever) and fertility within marriage. An astoundingly low proportion of women was married in some provinces. The lowest was in Carinthia, where less than 28 percent were married in 1880. By 1910 that proportion had risen to nearly 38 percent. Like Van de Walle, Demeny thinks that declining fertility within marriage permitted the rise in the proportion of women marrying. Demeny adds that many methods of limiting conception had long been known, and only the frequency of using them changed. He suggests that "the decline of fertility would have to be viewed as the result of a merely quantitative change in the frequency of age-old practices that presumably came about as a natural response to environmental pressures."

THE UNIVERSALITY OF CAUTION

Undisturbed societies in all parts of the world show respect for the carrying capacity of their lands. By one means or another, all peoples whose social system survives for any great length of time adjust reproduction and immigration to a sustainable level. The idea that one might be better off with fewer children—or that communities or families must live within their resources—does not wait on modern diaphragms, pills, or condoms.

This insight appears to have been forgotten by those who focus narrowly on just the twentieth-century segment of human history. Social scientists, with the exception of some named here, may have the worst record for distorting history and misreading contemporary trends. On the contrary, Georg Borgstrum, renowned plant physiologist and much-decorated specialist in third-world economies, understands. He is among those who have called attention to the downward pressure on fertility in traditional societies. A 1971 Population Reference Bureau publication quotes Borgstrum explaining that:

> A number of civilizations, including India and Indonesia, "had a clear picture of the limitations of their villages and communities" before foreign intervention disrupted the traditional patterns. Technical aid programs ". . . made them believe that the adoption of certain technical advances were going to free them of this bondage and of dependence on such restrictions."

Most demographers are not so outspoken about why worldwide fertility has risen in modern times. But there is at least a partial consensus that family size preferences explain fertility rates.

MOTIVATION

Demographers can show that (1) modern contraception is not essential to achieving low fertility and (2) women (or families) use contraception both to space children and to limit births. But people limit births when—and only when—they have reached the family size they want.

Paul Demeny (1988) takes the historical approach. He points out that the drop to replacement-level fertility in Austria-Hungary as well as in much of the U.S. urban population by the late nineteenth century cannot be explained by

> people's access to some superior contraceptive technology— "modern methods" were yet to be invented—but was the result of individual motivation to keep fertility low. The experience of Western demographic history resoundingly demonstrated that, compared to micro-level interest in limiting fertility, "really suit-

able technology" was of second-order importance for determining birth rates.

Demeny has little doubt that couples plan family size. He continues: "Lacking such technology, the Mayor of Peipei [in China] still could have been confidently advised to get fertility incentives right and then sit back and watch the birth rate fall."

Not only can small family size be achieved without modern contraception, large families may be commonplace despite it. Charles Westoff (1988) of the Princeton Population Center ruefully concludes that the family-planning concept is widely practiced. He found that the nonuse of available contraception, resulting in very large families, is planned: "By and large, contraceptive behavior—at least in the four developing countries for which data are examined—is not grossly inconsistent with reproductive intention." Women in Brazil, the Dominican Republic, Peru, and Liberia had large families, and nearly 99 percent of them were using contraception in a manner consistent with their completed family-size preference. When spacing children was the issue, the gap between intent to conceive and contraceptive practice approached zero. Not using contraception was almost invariably explained by not being sexually active, being already pregnant or lactating,* or wanting another child. Westoff concludes, "The overwhelming majority of women who want no more children or who want to postpone fertility, at least in the four countries discussed here, are behaving in a manner consistent with that goal."

Westoff's methodology has been criticized. However, data showing that knowledge of modern contraception is very widespread, while family size stays large, support his contention. For example, the Population Reference Bureau reports a 1991 survey in Jordan which indicates that 98 percent of women know

*Trust in lactation can cause error in estimating risk of pregnancy because, in a minority of cases, ovulation resumes two weeks prior to resumption of menstrual cycles.

about either the pill or the intrauterine device (IUD), and most of these also know where to go to get help. But in 1991, Jordanian women still averaged 7.1 children apiece! *Population Reports* from Johns Hopkins University's Population Information Program contain congruent—if less dramatic—findings. The November, 1991, issue shows that at least 80 percent of reproductive-age women knew about oral contraception in ten out of the twenty-five countries surveyed but that, even in the countries where knowledge was highest, as few as 5 percent used this method.

Reviewing the range of introduced family-planning programs, Nathan Keyfitz (1991) agrees with Demeny and Westoff: Completed family size reflects preferences and decisions. Keyfitz writes that "if there is no economic or cultural incentive to population control, then sponsored programs providing contraception will do little." The availability, or not, of modern technology does not preempt choice. Cheap and easy-to-use contraception does not a contracepting couple make. Family planning literally means having the exact number of children one wants. As a euphemism for small family size, it has backfired.

The key question is: What makes people want more children? If policymakers could do more than guess, they might also discover why, at other times, people want fewer children. They could then distinguish, also, between the *motivation* to limit family size and the *technical* means for doing so.

The variety of cultural and mechanical means for limiting fertility, and the circumstances under which they are most unrelentingly practiced, give plenty of answers. Indeed, the matter has been understood all along, but we would rather say it is not so. The data so far point to a conclusion that the reason for reproductive caution is fear of scarcity and of not being able to raise successfully the children one has.

The next chapters examine further the tough questions: Why, in the face of grinding poverty, does high fertility persist? And what will bring about change?

6

Which Incentives?

The culture provides a framework of customs and values. Within it, the number of children a couple wants appears to be the single most important determinant of how many children the couple get. So say ancient and modern scholars alike.

The tougher question is: What makes people want fewer or more children? History and anthropology show that fear of not being able to successfully raise one's children has much to do with reproductive restraint. But humans are not straightforward. We act on hope as much as reality. So, what kind of incentives do the trick?

Roughly, incentives that affect fertility can be divided into two classes: those that alter the ordinary conditions of life, especially economic factors such as would change decisions about lots of things besides family size; and those where rewards and penalties for particular reproductive behaviors, or results, are set as a matter of government policy.

OFFICIAL LARGE-FAMILY-SIZE TARGETS

First, do rewards and penalties for particular reproductive behaviors influence the number of children people have? Briefly, no. Start by noticing that governments do not usually succeed in making people have more children than they want.

For example, Romanians under the Communist regime of Nikolae Ceauşescu were essentially forbidden to try to limit family size. The penalties for using contraception or aborting if one had fewer than five children were severe both for women and any doctor who provided assistance. Nevertheless, contraception, abortion, and (if these failed) child abandonment were widely practiced. The result was that, in 1989, the Romanian crude birthrate was 16 per 1,000 persons. The birthrate in the United States that year, where contraception and abortion were available to married and unmarried women alike, was identical.

Some countries that do *not* have official pronatalist policies have much higher birthrates. For example, the Peruvian government does not require women to reproduce, but there are 29 births per 1,000 persons in the population. Similarly, there are 30 births per 1,000 in Mexico; 31 per 1,000 in the Dominican Republic; and 43 per 1,000 in Nicaragua. These governments are not forcing people to have more children. People have them voluntarily. (Recall from Chapter 5 that Peru was one of the countries where Charles Westoff found virtually no discrepancy between childbearing intentions and contraceptive practice. Women not using contraception had a reason: They were already pregnant or lactating or they wanted another child.)

Government programs to make people have more children failed in ancient Rome just as they did in Romania. Near the end of Augustus Caesar's reign, some members of the ruling class became concerned that they were not reproducing themselves in sufficient numbers. Viewers of the Public Broadcasting System series *I, Claudius* may recall the emperor's castigation of bachelors: Augustus ordered all to marry forthwith! Pronatalist legislation subsequently offered patricians (and eventually all citizens) rewards for having children; offered mothers the honor of wearing distinctive clothing; disbarred unmarried men from holding public office; prevented bachelors from claiming their inheritance; gave family allowances for children; criminalized abortion; and made infanticide a capital offense (it had been a paternal right).

Nevertheless, the citizens of Rome persisted in delaying marriage into their late twenties and practiced coitus interruptus (withdrawal), abortion, and child abandonment. Their fertility rate took on two values: low and lower.

The demographic trend among Roman citizens coincided with steady deterioration in a broad range of political, social, and economic indicators: Family disintegration, high unemployment, and crime were early signs. By A.D. 120, Emperor Hadrian was concerned about Rome's food security; he became interested in tilling marginal lands and is so depicted on an English frieze dating to the Roman occupation. Instability in government, including rapid turnover in emperors (twenty-seven ruled between A.D. 150 and 200), was soon to follow. Food scarcity and frequent public circuses came near the end. Circuses, initially celebrations of skill and valor, evolved into savage distractions for the mob of disaffected immigrants, freedmen, and citizens alike. In those uncertain times—progressively worsening from the period of imperial expansion through economic collapse to invasion by marauders like Attila the Hun several centuries later—large families were an encumbrance that few people wanted. A pronatalist government policy could not overwhelm private inclinations. Many people wished to, and did, avoid family burdens as hard times got harder.

The Emperor Constantine came to power at the start of the fourth century (A.D. 306), and public policy soon began to coincide with private sentiment. Constantine looked out and saw as the people did: an enormous population ("All roads lead to Rome"), a polyglot multicultural society, high unemployment, an indebted government, a decayed infrastructure, and the collapse of agricultural productivity. Reflecting both the public mood and Christian teaching, Constantine rescinded pronatalist legislation.

Recall that Constantine was the first Christian emperor and that early Christians were mainly slaves, freedmen, and artisans. This sector was not criminal or rootless. They were the working and middle class. Such people understood both effort and scarcity. Rewards for their labor had been shrinking as the population (the labor supply) grew. Historian John T. Noonan (1968) points out that "Not surprisingly, a pivotal assumption of the early church was the belief, current among Gnostic and orthodox Christians of the second century, that the world is full: the optimum and maximum number of redeemed exist; the

Messiah has come; there is no need to continue the procreation of the race." Constantine lent official weight to private practice. He proclaimed celibacy to be a holy state and repealed most of the pronatalist laws on marriage promulgated by the Emperors Augustus and Trajan.

For religious persons, celibacy was recommended as the preferred state, marriage was presented as the sole allowable context for sexual intercourse, and sexual continence was advocated even in marriage. The A.D. 306 Council of Elvira imposed perpetual continence on Christian priests. Married priests were permitted to stay married but were forbidden to have sexual relations with their wives. The most extreme position on reproduction was taken by the third- and fourth-century Manichees, who believed, states Noonan, "that the most sinful of deeds is the procreative act: It perpetuates in new human beings the imprisonment of light particles, once parts of the Princes of Light, who should be liberated from the flesh to journey to the Father of Lights."

Thus, over three centuries, the pronatalism of the Roman Empire collapsed. Like that of Romania under Communism, its government was authoritarian. Yet neither government prevailed in a sphere of private action and belief that people reserved to themselves. Both histories show, again, that ordinary people can adjust family size up or down and that they make their own choices. People are not easily induced to have more children than they really want. Governments legislate in vain.

OFFICIAL SMALL-FAMILY-SIZE TARGETS

Rewards and penalties seem no more effective in limiting procreation than in enhancing it. In forty years, there have been few success stories among the dozens of family-planning programs and incentive schemes showered on third-world countries. The more ambitious type of program not only made contraception available but also rewarded contraceptive use and/or one- or two-child families. India, for example, has tried a great variety of incentive and delivery systems. Their highest value may be as a list of what does not work.

One incentive scheme tried in India that looked promising at the time depended upon peer pressure. A village could earn a tractor (or some other capital improvement such as a well) by meeting a percentage criterion of families using contraception. An early 1970s article in *Science* described how it worked, but little about it has been heard since. Maybe enough Indian families used contraception just long enough to get the tractors. If so, it was an expensive way to start people on reversible contraception.

By 1973, India was betting on sterilization. Busloads of volunteers came to highly publicized vasectomy fairs. Men were rewarded in rupees or, sometimes, a transistor radio. Fees for bringing in vasectomy candidates were paid in cash. Unfortunately, the finder's fees were almost too lucrative and may have promoted kidnapping. Moreover, finder's fees produced "low-quality" vasectomies: The payoff was the same for a wizened old man as for a young, married father of healthy children.

Women are the more valued target in birth-control programs because the number of children that can ever be born depends on them. Thus, Indian women who agreed to sterilization received larger rewards than men. But people's independence of mind spiked this strategy, too. The timing of tubal ligations was not what policymakers had in mind. Women came to the clinics only after reaching their desired family size—and their desired family size was often quite large.

Women alone may not have made the decision. Perhaps their husbands or in-laws influenced it. But family size clearly served somebody's perception of his or her own best interest.

John Wyon and J. E. Gordon's project (1971) in Khanna, India, showed up the futility of changing preferences with even the best of family-planning programs. For six years, Wyon and Gordon's group provided a whole village with education, nutritional supplements, public health, and direct medical care. Eventually, everyone knew about contraception, villagers had positive attitudes toward the health-care providers and family planning, and infant mortality had fallen way down. But the fertility rate stayed way up.

Eventually, Wyon and his colleagues figured out why. The Khanna people *liked* large families. Khannaians were delighted that now, with lower infant mortality, they could have the six surviving children they had always wanted.

POLITICS TRUMPS EFFECTIVE POLICY

Wyon and Gordon's conclusions reached high places in the Indian government. Policymakers recognized that it was time to shift gears. As an alternative to rewarding contraceptive use, the administration next tried rewarding results. In 1973, Punjab state enacted laws to restrict government-subsidized housing for families that had further children above two (or above whatever larger number they had already). This was a more serious incentive than a transistor radio—it could drastically alter lifestyle—it concentrated the attention. And the electorate revolted.

Linking the housing subsidy to additional births probably cost Indira Gandhi her reelection as prime minister. Gandhi and the Congress Party lost heavily in the mid-1970s even though the law was rescinded almost as soon as the depth of public displeasure became clear. After this electoral loss, the Congress Party abandoned its most serious attempts at birth control and, subsequently, Gandhi regained her position.

The Indian experience shows that contraceptive availability, even combined with many other health services, is not enough. One-time rewards for contraceptive use and sterilization may change behavior at the margin but do not produce meaningful contraceptive use while family size is still small. Incentives that threaten to change lifestyles would undoubtedly work; and for this reason, in India, they were rejected for being unacceptably coercive.

The lessons are clear. When social and economic conditions promote a family size that differs from official targets, the former win. Government policy is overridden or forced to change. The Roman and Romanian examples show it. So does the Indian example, taking into account that people believed their life prospects were improving and would continue on that path.

In effect, the Indian government advocated small family size but in other ways dispelled individual families' belief in real limits. Electoral campaigns promised much. Political scientist Myron Weiner (1962) describes how the Congress Party learned that continued success at the polls depended on delivery. Subsidized housing, food, education, and government-as-employer-of-last-resort fostered the belief that government could, should, and would provide an adequate standard of living. The culture of entitlements became entrenched; the incentive for reducing family size, close to nil except among a small elite.

The green revolution in the 1970s and international grants-in-aid facilitated the Indian government's posture as provider. When these infusions became insufficient to meet domestic consumption targets, the government took on international debt. By 1980, India had become a debtor nation, and foreign debt quadrupled over the next decade. Debt service reached a (ruinous) 30 percent of government spending by 1991. But at the individual level, expectations of a better future still undercut reasonable responses to actual scarcity.

BEYOND DOMESTIC POLITICS

Sometimes, only circumstances beyond control can force discipline. Credit from international commercial banks has dried up. The International Monetary Fund (IMF) granted India a $1.8 billion loan in January, 1991, but only after exacting government guarantees of fiscal responsibility. Fertility should soon decline in earnest. The downside is that turmoil may increase because reevaluation is painful. Once granted, benefits and consumer subsidies are difficult to take back. Government policy must not look arbitrary or mean.

Benefits that erode gradually may not become a *casus belli*. For example, in the mid-1980s the Egyptian government raised the price of bread in order to reduce somewhat the very large subsidy it could no longer afford. Near-revolt forced recision of the price increase but, more subtly, the intended change was made anyway. The new strategy was to introduce a higher priced, better loaf, then slowly let the quality and size of both loaves slip. Eventually, the higher priced loaf was what the first loaf had been; and the first loaf, its price unchanged, had shrunk to very little.

Absent gradualism, democratic governments have to create some level of public consensus before withdrawing subsidies that encourage large family size. These discussions are difficult but should begin with recognition that market incentives which penalize incremental fertility do work—whereas if subsidies make an extra child relatively costless, the preference for large families persists.

The more totalitarian the government, the more easily subsidies can be withdrawn. The Iranian government was willing to risk internal dissension and has embarked by decree on a daring program to change family-size targets. Children born after 1991 are not eligible for government benefits of any kind if they are the fourth child or higher parity. China has also increased penalties for bearing an unauthorized child. Since 1991, according to the *Wall Street Journal* (China Hopes, 1991), these include "fines of three to 55 times annual pay, pay freezes, and loss of housing and social-service benefits." Internal migration is also limited, so that communities which condone cheating on official family-size targets must live with the longterm results of their excess reproduction. Crowded Chinese cities will no longer try to absorb extra thousands from the hinterland.

Policies enforceable through withholding benefits (a housing subsidy) or privileges (the right to work in a city or a foreign country) have the best chance of influencing family size preference because they affect incentives; on the other hand, rules directed solely at allowable family size do not touch incentives, and some people will succeed in evading the rules through surreptitious within-family adoptions and other stratagems.

ECOLOGICAL RELEASE IN EUROPE, AGAIN

Ironically, governments appear to be most successful in changing fertility when they are not trying, that is, when wanting fewer or more children is an inadvertent response to programs that have other goals. For example, fertility rates in eighteenth- and early nineteenth-century Europe moved up partly in response to legislation that was intended to move people out of poverty into the middle class. The background, briefly, is that birth control in Europe depended, until the late 1800s, upon limiting the proportion of women who married. These limits eased several times; each time, fertility rose. The culturally imposed limits on marrying relaxed in part because prosperity seemed just over the horizon (colonialism and technology had opened new frontiers), and this hope spawned the late eighteenth-century movement known as the Enlightenment. The Enlightenment had a humanitarian message. It taught that poverty is unjust and, also, is correctable.

The philosophy of the Enlightenment was implemented through measures that enlarged the rights of the poor. On the Continent, for example, having a secure livelihood had been an absolute condition for marriage, but Napoleon repealed these laws. Where Napoleonic armies went, financial obstacles to marriage crumbled. Many women who might have remained spinsters now became the wives of poor men who, formerly, would not have been permitted to marry.

In England, spokespersons for the Enlightenment included Percy Bysshe Shelley and his father-in-law, William Godwin. They actively and successfully advocated welfare legislation for the lower class. This poor-relief became known as the *Speenhamland system*. It was first enacted in 1795 in Berkshire and soon spread through southern England. The Speenhamland laws provided for relief based on wages, family size, and the price of bread: The lower the wage, the larger the family, and the dearer the bread, the higher the transfer payment. In effect, relief insulated the poor from the consequences of both poverty and inflation.*

Supporters did not foresee the Speenhamland system's unintended effects. These included making large, illegitimate families economically viable. Furthermore, employers could pay miserly wages for labor because of the mutual knowledge that the difference would be made up by the "poor allotment." And, critics said, the slight differential between lowest wages and the poor allotment eroded incentives to work. Nor was funding the system expected to be such a severe burden as it became. In fact, taxes had to be raised repeatedly as the size of payments and the number qualifying for assistance both increased.

Speenhamland and population growth soon began to polarize the society into rich and poor. The tax burden and inflation pushed down the marginally middle class down until they themselves became needy. At the same time, some employers and investors benefitted because wages fall when rapid population growth creates an abundant supply of labor. Nathan Keyfitz (1991) cites economist Ronald Lee's estimates for preindustrial England which "suggest that a 10 percent increase in population depressed real wages by 22 percent and raised rents by 19 percent."

The longterm effects of the Speenhamland laws were possibly overstated by critics. Whatever the effect of other disorganizing factors, the laws were blamed for all of the increase in England's population size and for the very large number of people who eventually needed public assistance. Politicians

---

*Welfare systems in the United States have some parallel features, but they do not automatically adjust payments to inflation (i.e., index) and do not explicitly make up the difference between actual wages and an income criterion.

pointed out that an extra child brought poor families a fatter welfare payment, and that the bread subsidy insulated them from the inflationary effect of growing demand, that is, a population growing faster than the resources on which it depended.

Reaction set in with enactment of the New Poor Law of 1834. The law repealed the Speenhamland system and was explicitly designed to maximize employment and minimize population growth. Whole families were put into debtors' prison. Another provision established sexually segregated workhouses: Husbands and wives were separated specifically to prevent pregnancy. Meanwhile, legislation on the Continent reimposed financial obstacles to marriage. Swiss cantons made marriage conditional on a man's having not only present employment but also a two-year work history. German city-states demanded proof of employment and of not having been in debtors' prison.

BALANCE RESTORED

European fertility began to fall by the middle of the nineteenth century. It dropped across the board, even in sectors not affected by government intervention in marriage. Traditional standards revived, paralleling legislative restrictions on marriage but much more widespread. These trends plus new ideas about individual responsibility apparently reflected the general concern about limited resources.

Some third-world countries including South Korea, Singapore, and a few Caribbean islands have also succeeded in limiting fertility to replacement level. All have experienced poverty unrelieved by government subsidies on housing or food or a culture of entitlement. Taiwan is an outstanding example of such a transition. The programmatic incentives were right, and so were the conditions of ordinary life that make most of the difference.

Modern contraceptives were introduced in Taiwan in the mid-1960s, precinct by precinct. Education, personalized support, and appeal to the national good were important elements of the program. The family-planning program was complemented by two other conditions. Taiwan had become very crowded, quickly, and women found paid work. Taiwan is not a large island, and in 1949 when the Nationalist Chinese abandoned the mainland to Mao's Communist forces, it must have seemed to implode. Thousands of émigrés moved in on top of three other groups: the native islanders, the descendants of mainlanders from a sixteenth-century exodus, and mainlanders who had fled the 1930s depression and, later, the Japanese occupation.

Crowding, and the suddenness with which it happened, may have been the major incentive for limiting family size. Lots of people living in a few rooms on a smallish island—but accustomed to better—probably did not want to add to the crowd. In addition, but somewhat later, the very cheap labor and industriousness of the Chinese attracted foreign investment. Serendipitously, many of the new jobs were available to women who, with their delicate hands, excelled at electronic parts assembly. Thus, official small-family-size targets coincided with economic and environmental forces that moved preferences in the same direction. By 1977, the Taiwanese fertility rate had fallen to 2.8 births per woman. In 1991, it was 1.7, well below the level where a generation just replaces itself.

Taiwanese population growth will stop eventually and, perhaps, reverse direction. Government policy and strict enforcement hold immigration to near zero. The labor market already has tightened so that wages and the standard of living have risen. Industries in search of cheapest labor go elsewhere. Productivity within Taiwan is rising as industry replaces labor inputs with capital and technology. High-value-added industries prosper. Fertility remains low because the competition for best educations, best jobs, and housing is sharp.

Family planning programs seldom work this well. As Nathan Keyfitz observes, "If there is no economic or cultural incentive to population control, then sponsored programs providing contraceptives will do little."

Development Alone May Spur Population Growth

A 1976 issue of the *International Family Planning Digest* headlined a story "Development Alone May Spur Population Growth." But why? One answer is that development and modernization are promoted as being the path to prosperity. The promise alone sets the stage for rising expectations and, as shown already, rising fertility. However, optimism born of ecological release (recall Chapter 3) may not be the whole answer. New findings from fieldwork in three completely separate parts of the world tell the rest of the story.

The adaptedness of undisturbed cultures should be a tip-off that culture change is likely to upset the balance between population size and the local carrying capacity. The worldview that resources are limited is one feature disrupted by contact with western culture. But it is not the only one. Beyond this, many of the specific beliefs, rules, and behaviors that restrain fertility are systematically devalued as barbaric or simply old-fashioned. Development upsets the balance between population and resources simply by doing away with the traditional values and customs that formerly controlled fertility.

The cases described below show how development, or modernization, causes fertility to rise. Two of the three examples are contemporary. The anthropologist and the epidemiologist who report these findings say that traditional elements which hold down fertility still operate in the societies they describe, but conservative elements are being progressively abandoned with modernization. We begin, however, with historical anthropology.

INUIT ESKIMO

Almost everything, including modernization, is relative. "Modernization" exploded on the eighteenth-century Inuit Eskimo of northern Labrador when their Stone Age society was contacted by Moravian missionaries. The missionaries could be called modern only by contrast with the people whom they set out to change. The missionaries planned to help the Inuit by reforming and converting them to Christianity. Instead, they raised fertility.

Moravian documents from about 1790 report that Inuit mothers averaged over eight children apiece. Adult women are not necessarily mothers. So some women may have been childless. That would lower the average. Nevertheless, other manuscript data suggest that the overall fertility rate was 7.3, a large number of children by any standard.

Anthropologist David Scheffel (1988) thinks that the precontact rate was less than half this high. Indirect evidence comes from the Aborigine Greenlanders, who were culturally almost identical to the Inuit; this people reportedly had just "three or four" children. And an 1820 document states that "the natives, after being told 'of the fecundity of Europeans, . . . compare them contemptuously to their dogs.'"

Study of the original Moravian accounts of the Inuit, written in German, convinced Scheffel that Inuit fertility also rose after a period of indoctrination by missionary teachings. The evidence is spotty, but it all points one way. First, early missionaries wrote that "aboriginal Labrador Inuit women displayed a lower fertility than their converted counterparts." Women in the traditional, precontact culture seem to have begun childbearing late and spaced children more than three years apart. Moravian records show that intervals between births averaged thirty-nine months among the oldest group of women (those whose childbearing was least influenced by contact), whereas younger cohorts spaced children just twenty-nine months apart. Scheffel infers from scandalized missionaries' reports that a very long postpartum sex taboo (bolstered by polygyny, wife exchange, and male masturbation) accounted for the long intervals between births.

Accounts of both Inuit and Greenlanders appear to hint at coitus interruptus. The following, which Scheffel has translated from the original German, dates from 1786:

> Our workers among the heathen have to be on their guard against a concealed continuation of superstitious and unclean ideas in the matter of marriage which derive from the pagan traditions of our brethren and sisters. One of these is the idea held by the Greenlanders that a woman should be ashamed to bear a child within the first year of marriage; equally, that they don't like having more than one child within three years, although they live as wife and husband frequently enough during that time. Such a way of thinking must be eliminated entirely. . . . Otherwise, it is to be feared that sins related to masturbation will occur, which are a horror to our Lord.

No date appears on the following text:

> We know moreover that the unbelievers have several bad habits. When they have sick people they let . . . [indecipherable] to heal them by witchcraft. When they have caught a seal, they sprinkle it with water. When they have caught a whale, they build a festival house and sin day and night. They abstain from intercourse and many more things like that.

Scheffel suggests that the missionaries promised the Inuit economic security in order to induce them to move to the mission and that, indirectly, this encouraged the Inuit to change their family-size targets:

> The arrival of the Moravian missionaries confronted the natives with a set of values which encouraged unrestricted population

growth, monogamy, sedentism, and an exaggerated faith in divine providence. Although the Moravian modernization program was implemented gradually—an example of this approach was the concession to polygynous unions closed prior to conversion—a conscious effort was made from the beginning of missionary work to create the impression that all problems of aboriginal life would dissipate upon settlement in the Christian enclave. In the words of Cranz, 1820, which are equally applicable to Labrador, "if any temporal advantage must be confessed to have an influence in inducing heathen Greenlanders to join the believers, it is the prevalence of honesty and good order in our congregations, where every one is secure of his property . . . friendless widows are relieved, none are obliged to marry against their inclination, no wife is turned away, or husband permitted to marry more than one wife, and where all fatherless orphans are maintained and educated."

Not surprisingly, temptations of the good life were irresistible, and traditional practices and incentives that limited fertility eroded. A population explosion, Inuit-scale, ensued.

Unfortunately, the missionaries could not deliver on promises of economic security. Hardship was widespread by about 1830. Ill health related to sedentism and a changing diet—starch replacing protein—added to Inuit troubles. The Inuit now had a resurgence, evidently, of their ancient goal of limiting family size. Even without polygyny, couples returned briefly to observing long intervals between births. But deprived of the supporting lifestyle, a healthy balance eluded them. In Scheffel's words, and then quoting a missionary:

The Hebron death register contains nine cases of infant deaths caused by suffocation between 1858 and 1905. The missionaries attributed such mishaps to the children being crushed by their sleeping mothers, but the possibility of infanticide cannot be ruled out. . . . The suspicion of concealed infanticide is reinforced by numerous reports describing the apathy of weakened mothers when confronted by the high mortality of their children. [And, from a 1918 Moravian account]: "Year by year it is becoming more difficult for the Eskimo mothers to rear their babies, and it has become quite a common saying now, when a child is born, 'The child will probably die.'"

And that is the story of how modernization helped the Inuit.

SHIPIBO

A similar tale of culture loss and gyrations of fertility and mortality rates can be told for tribes of the Peruvian and Brazilian Amazon. Some tribes became extinct in the centuries after contact with western civilization. The survivors, however, are experiencing very rapid population growth even while their jungle habitat is wiped out by roads and deforestation.

The Peruvian Shipibo and the Brazilian Bororo, Xavante, and Yanomama, like many other Brazilian tribes, traditionally practiced abortion, infanticide, and sororal polygyny (a man marrying sisters). As many as 50 percent of all marriages were polygynous in traditional Yanomama villages, but it is much less common in more acculturated groups. In the 1970s, only about 10 percent of reproductive-age Shipibo women were in polygynous marriages, and the practice was declining.

Epidemiologist Warren Hern (1991) makes a strong case that polygyny is one of the key mechanisms for limiting fertility in traditional cultures. He found that Shipibo women in polygynous unions have longer intervals between births—4.5 months longer—than monogamously married women. The Yanomama, indeed, average forty months between births, at least partly because of widespread polygyny. The length of birth intervals affects fertility. Polygynously married women that Hern studied averaged one to two fewer births than their monogamous counterparts. Hern sees "an almost straight line negative relationship" between village fertility rates and the proportion of polygynous birth intervals. The greater the fraction of women whose childbearing occurs in a polygynous context, the lower the fertility rate.

Postpartum sex taboos and breastfeeding are both likely to last longer in polygynous marriages. Breastfeeding itself delays the return of ovulatory menstrual cycles, adding to the effect of limiting women's exposure to pregnancy. Emphasis on the taboo may also increase abortion and infanticide, because children conceived in illicit sexual activity are not wanted. Female infanticide is probably most common. Surveys show about 104 male for every 100 female Shipibo—whereas a more balanced ratio is expected if there is no discrimination by gender.

All these practices are abandoned as South American Indians become a part of communities that are more attuned to western values. Shipibo fertility has soared, rivaling the Hutterites, edging close to ten live births per woman in some villages. Hern estimates that villages are growing at about 4 percent annually,* which suggests that populations are doubling every seventeen years. The increase seems entirely due to changes which come about as the Shipibo and other Indians' jungle homes become the fringe, and then are absorbed by modern settlements.

Bereft of traditional folkways, Shipibo women take desperate measures to avoid closely spaced pregnancies. Some use a caustic substance for contraceptive purposes which, says Hern, contributes to their very high mortality from cervical cancer. One fairly concludes that Shipibo women would be receptive to modern contraception. Whether the family power structure and/or their husbands' approval would allow it to be used, if available, is a separate question, one which can only be answered by research.

First steps into a more modern world have not brought much good to the Shipibo. Modernity intruded on them. It did not seduce them. The development process itself probably fueled

---

*Anthropologist Robert L. Munroe (n.d.) reports a similar rate of population growth: "The people of Margoli [in East Africa] are so far above their estimated aboriginal density . . . that their putative long-term rate of population increase is, so far as I am aware, unprecedented. Their twenty-fold increase in numbers would have required an annual population growth rate above 4% sustained over a period of 66 years (1896–1962)."

fertility. Hern concludes, "From this and other studies, I think one should expect higher fertility in tribal societies making the transition from traditional to peasant to urban societies, and it appears unlikely that the native Amazonians will be able to escape this process."

INDIA

Traditional practices could be discarded without raising fertility if modern contraception were swiftly accepted as a substitute. However, customs that depress fertility are often lost faster than modern contraception becomes available or is accepted. Countries in flux, such as India, let us catch a glimpse of the process. Anthropologist Mahinder Chaudry (1990) expects that, in India, the transition from a partially traditional society to one where couples take responsibility for small family size will take twenty years. In the meantime, Chaudry expects the progressive loss of indigenous cultures to enhance fertility more than the spread of contraceptive use depresses it.

The behaviors being lost are often not consistent with western values, which is a principal reason they have been attacked and are disappearing. Nevertheless, those mechanisms were effective. Before contact, they probably were fully effective in keeping population size about constant, except for invasions. Kingsley Davis (1951) suggests that traditional ways probably accounted for a significantly lower fertility, even as late as World War II, compared to what developed later.

Perhaps independence from Great Britain, accomplished in 1947, triggered the surge in fertility because it promoted exuberant faith in the future. Moreover, people who had clung to traditional practices as a nationalistic statement might have become inclined to abandon them. Despite the jumps in fertility rate, the six to eight children that was average for continuously married Indian women by 1950 was still at least 20 percent below the biologically natural level. So fertility remained below the

Hutterite rate, below today's Shipibo rate, and below the 9.9 children per woman found in a 1941 census of rural Quebec.

Today, the decline in Indian fertility seems stalled at just below four children per woman, although deteriorating economic conditions could prod it further down. It is not good news that Chaudry expects new contraceptive acceptance to have a weaker effect on fertility than the offsetting effect of abandoning traditional practices.

ETHICS IN CALAMITOUS SETTINGS

Ambivalence about liberalization or conservatism is nearly unavoidable. Many of the traditional Indian ways disregard basic human rights. Rapid contraceptive acceptance is the best solution, but will it happen in time? Should one root for conservative elements or for culture change?

Whatever the preference of outsiders, India will find its own way. And some things go on. Discrimination against widows even unto murder, abuse and murder of brides, female neglect and infanticide, abortion, and the caste system (which preordains who will go without when there is not enough) go on. Although illegal, abuse persists because it is supported, or at least tolerated, by secular and religious authority. No one has ever been convicted for being a party to causing a woman to catch fire in the kitchen or fall down a well. The scheduled classes (*harijan*, or untouchables) have made progress on civil rights, but many avenues remain closed to them, and official efforts to advance their access to opportunity at the expense of the middle class do not get far. Tolerance has a short fuse when most people's standard of living is falling. In 1991, a program to reserve a larger share of government jobs for *harijan* was rescinded because of violent student protest in the universities.

In every caste, females are the most frequent victims of both crime and neglect. Bajpai (1991) reports, "In Punjabi families where there is already a girl, the mortality rate for the next daughter is as high as 53 percent." Similarly "in one community in Rajasthan State, the sex ratio [is] one of the lowest [sic] in the world at approximately 550 women per 1000 men." Nationwide the sex ratio is slowly becoming more extreme, revealing more and more discrimination against women and female children. Bose (1991) finds that in just the decade from 1981 to 1991, a ratio of 934 females per 1,000 males changed to 929 per 1,000. Restating these data for comparison with Ansley Coale's numbers in the next paragraph: A ratio of 107 males to 100 females rose in one decade to nearly 108 males per 100 females.

Demographer Ansley Coale (1991) of Princeton University calculates that India would have 102 males for every 100 females if the sexes were treated equally. Comparison with the actual ratio suggests that nearly 6 percent of India's women are missing! Comparing expected and actual sex ratios, demographers calculate that 60 million females are missing in Asia alone. Worldwide, the number may top 100 million. Other countries with fewer females than expected are Afghanistan (despite military losses in their long war with the USSR and their civil war), Bangladesh, Bhutan, Nepal, Pakistan, Papua New Guinea, China, Egypt, and Turkey.

In-laws in a household, which in most societies means women, are the first deprived and after them, their daughters. Bairagi's observations (1986) in Bangladesh during a famine show an increased disparity in the treatment of boys and girls: Boys remained better off in terms of both mortality and weight for age, and the greater a family's wealth, the more pronounced the male advantage.

Overpopulation is hard on women, possibly an adaptation related to women's being the limiting factor for future births. As westerners, we are offended. Nevertheless, an ethical question that begs a hearing is whether inhumanity to woman, man, and child is defensible if it prevents famine, suffering, and a probable increase in the premature mortality of a very much larger number of future persons? And, even if not defensible within the western value system, can one ethically disturb an indigenous culture that maintains balance by resort to such mechanisms? What if a country cannot otherwise avoid a cataclysmic imbalance of population and resources?

If one accepts either a utilitarian principle, or the principle of nonintervention in other cultures, or that humans are uniquely entrusted with management of the transition into the ecozoic era (a utopian, environmentally responsible future proposed by Thomas Berry, a priest whose ministry is to the Earth), can one oppose indigenous population control mechanisms, even those sometimes called coercive?

The matter is not academic. Chinese culture legitimizes intense social pressure to act for the good of the country rather than in the service of individual goals. When such pressure is exerted to compel one- or two-child family size (or for some other social good), ought outsiders protest? Again, should outsiders provide any stimulus for further modernization in the third world, given that loss of traditional cultures due to modernization often raises fertility? Can any country survive rising (or the present level of) fertility in coming decades?

India and China together account for over 2 billion of Earth's more than 5.5 billion people, so the environmental consequences of growth are not trivial. Nor is the suffering of their future multitudes trivial, suffering that will be beyond the power of human agency to allay. Clearly, the preferred solution in all countries is voluntary substitution of modern contraception for less desirable alternatives. But in many regions, low levels of contraceptive acceptance continue to frustrate family-planning specialists.

CONTRACEPTIVE ACCEPTANCE

In 1991, the U.S. Agency for International Development (USAID) suspended free condom distribution in Egypt after learning that pharmacies had sold several million as balloons. The graft itself is deplorable. But assume that the storekeepers made the most profit they could: What does it mean that condoms' highest value to consumers is use as balloons? A decade earlier, John Wyon's group learned that lavishly laying on resources did not induce people in Khanna, India, to limit family size. Health care, knowledge, and access to the technology of modern contraception are not the whole answer, or probably even the larger part of it. Recall Paul Demeny's (1988) certainty that technology is of "second order importance for determining birth rates," whereas individual motivation is primary.

Contraception may be no more than one more facile answer to developing countries' dilemma over population growth. In theory, it replaces traditional practices that depress fertility. The transition appears far from being so simple, however.

The switch to fertility control through contraception may not be made because of information lag. Alternately, forest and peasant peoples acquire rising expectations because modernity is often introduced with a message that the new ways will make lives easier and better. The message undercuts former incentives to live within the bounds of a known environment. Small family size, even if once valued, becomes irrelevant. Even in countries where extensive efforts are underway to spread the use of modern contraception, the abandonment of traditional practices appears to offset, even overwhelm, the effects of new technology. Hern and Chaudry assert that in South America and India ground can still be lost. Those who would modernize and develop may work at cross-purposes with their own goals, tampering with traditional culture to the peril of humanity.

The conclusion, that modernization initially raises the fertility rate, is a discouragement. *No one will hazard to guess how long the unwanted effect on fertility will last*. Presumably, it lasts for some time after the most traditional elements of society abandon their ancient practices and assumptions. Since modernization promises affluence, the first exposed generation has little incentive to adopt modern contraception. As Charles Westoff and others can show, contraception is accepted only after family size is large—larger than might formerly have been desired. The most prolonged adjustment problem is likely to be just what Georg Borgstrum said: Traditional communities fully understood the limits of their environment; but the introduction of new crops, technologies, and job opportunities destroyed their vision of limits. Modernization brought rising expectations. This will be a long-lasting destabilizing factor.

RECOUPING LOSSES OR MORE BAD STRATEGY?

The spiral of population growth and poverty is headed toward disaster. Development has brought matters to this pass! So how can a thoughtful person advocate more culture change? More development? "Hair of the dog" is recommended after a binge. Is this the rationale?

More development is the prescription by which Mexico is advised to get its population growth—and emigration pressure— under control. The 1990 report of the Commission for the Study of International Migration and Cooperative Economic Development (the Asencio Commission) states, "Economic development and the availability of new and better jobs at home (i.e., in the [migrant] sending countries) is the only way to diminish migratory pressures over the long term."

The time frame for this process is of utmost importance but here, the commission's report is not reassuring: "Development, if sustained, can eventually reduce immigration pressures, but it may take several generations. . . . In the interim, it can be expected to exacerbate emigration pressures." The Center for Immigration Studies (1990), a nonprofit think tank in Washington, D.C., concludes that the report's short-run projection is that "The economic development process itself will actually stimulate more migration to the U.S. by raising the expectations and enhancing peoples' ability to migrate. The Commission therefore acknowledges that economic growth in sending countries is likely to further increase migration to the U.S., both legal and illegal, in the near term."

The Asencio Commission Report does not anticipate that the fertility rate will also rise. Nevertheless, this unwanted effect is likely to occur as still-isolated and traditional elements of Mexican society come into the mainstream. Abandonment of traditional assumptions and practices makes babies. Thus, Dianna Solis's prediction (1991) that imports of cheaper corn into Mexico will displace peasant families, driving them into urban settings in Mexico and across the border into the United States, is alarming on several counts. Sudden moves out of a peasant economy shatter the image of limited good which, in many people's accumulated cultural experience, is a constraint of Ricardian* proportions; that is, it is the limit on quantity of arable land. Wrench people out of *known* environments, and how long is it before they understand the constraints of the new—or even understand that, in the new setting, constraints operate at all? The risk is that urban poverty will be perceived as a distributional problem unrelated to environmental limits or population pressure on resources.

Mexico has 90 million people, and the population doubling time is thirty years. Job growth will never pull ahead of ever larger waves of young adults seeking jobs. A rise in fertility, or even a steady state, makes a happy outcome still more improbable. Therefore, one cannot see how the proposed development for Mexico will relieve poverty and pressure for immigration into the United States even in the long run.

HUMILITY

Sadly, one concludes that there are no easy answers, no painless remedies. Those who want to help should note: Modernization may be the enemy of longterm well-being and sustainability, because loss of the traditional culture often leads to higher fertility and rapid population growth.

*David Ricardo, 1772–1823, English political economist. See Chapter 8.

An anthropologist avoids labeling cultures as good or bad but never intends to say that any culture will do. A culture develops in a particular place, against the backdrop of a particular environment, and in response to historical events. Culture belongs to a people with a common history. It defines them, gives unity, and creates consensus that underpins formal and informal codes of behavior, justice, and government.

An unfortunate idea now loose in the United States is that any culture can have equal relevance for anyone. That is a strange belief, one that could hardly be farther from the truth. Nevertheless, this idea that cultures can be switched, mixed, and matched makes Americans both too careless in protecting their own heritage and too ready to impose western culture on others. Next we see the great damage done as more aspects of culture change promote population growth.

o

8

Culture: Make or Break

The amalgam of shared assumptions, values, beliefs, codes of conduct, and technology make up a community's culture. Culture is a set of ideas which have been described as a *cognitive map*. Understanding other people's roles, values, assumptions, and expectations, a person is able to get along effectively, without too many miscommunications, in his or her own society.

Children learn their culture in the course of growing up. Usually what one learns as a child is a reliable guide to adult behavior because common assumptions, codes, and morals facilitate communication and also match the possibilities and constraints of the environment. Thus, in a stable system, culture is time-tested; when behavior is guided by culture, it usually benefits both individuals and their families. Ideas work in settings where they develop because, there, they are the result of trial and error. They survive, in fact, because the people who hold those ideas have prospered enough to pass them on.

This process of transmission almost always occurs in the context of competition with neighbors and with the bearers of different cultures, because few human families or communities remain isolated. If others have ideas and patterns of behavior that enable them to raise *more* children to maturity, *their* culture is likely to become the dominant one. More surviving children is nature's way of sorting for whatever works best in competition with other possibilities.

BEST STRATEGIES

Social and physical environments change, so strategies which work best also change. Sociobiologist Edward O. Wilson (1975) describes best strategies under opposite conditions of population density. When individuals are part of a very small group (an outpost of pioneers, for instance), cooperation is usually the strategy which maximizes each individual's chances: One for all and all for one. The many become one. *E pluribus unum.* But when population size rises relative to available resources, the optimizing strategy changes: Individuals are more likely to succeed (leave posterity) if they redefine boundaries; close kin become the more relevant cooperating category.

Humans differ from other species primarily because political organization makes cooperation advantageous within larger and larger groupings. Nevertheless, density affects cooperation. Unity is easier when there is plenty for all, whereas polarization into rich and poor within communities and nations accompanies overpopulation. Turnbull (1972) and Laughlin (1974) describe how polarization occurs and cooperation flags, as resources become more and more scarce. In even the simplest societies under stress, adults in their prime separate themselves socially from other sectors, isolating the dependent old and very young.

Fortunately, whole societies and communities are seldom *in extremis.* Cultures evolve that work, usually in the long term, for many people. Stability oils the wheels, whereas problems develop if too many of society's members are detached from the common moorings of their time-tested ways. Change as well as density increases the difficulty of remaining culturally united. Rapid culture change is dysfunctional on several counts. One problem is with feedback: The pace of change can prevent consequences from being felt and appreciated while there still is time to turn back. A second problem is that, typically, just one set of beliefs shifts.

CULTURE CHANGE

A culture never changes all at once. For example, words and technology are likely to change faster than values and assumptions about reality. Stress can occur when the replacement ideas are borrowed rather than internally generated, because they may not mesh well with other components. The seamlessness of the culture is lost. Without balance, the society may gyrate off course. If foreign ideas and motivations are adopted piecemeal, they create fault lines and threaten the borrowing society's adaptive mechanisms.

Thus, societies that borrow foreign concepts do so at some risk. The new elements may not fit anything else. Without the checks and balances which exist in the home-grown setting, new ideas may have unforeseen consequences, like a species turned loose in an environment where it has no natural predators. Think of rabbits in Australia and gypsy moths in the United States.

Elements that formerly kept population size in balance with resources may be among the casualties of borrowed culture. Chapter 2 describes how Arabian technology unleashed a population explosion in medieval Europe. Chapter 14 tells how a South American import devastated Ireland. Good ideas and technology in one setting may be disruptive in others *even if all they do is dispel the local image of scarcity*. Nobody talks about this effect even though it is exactly the way in which western culture harms the third world today.

Neither western ideas, nor anybody else's ideas, are intrinsically bad. It is just that particular values and assumptions evolve in tandem with all other realities of a particular culture and society. Ideas are part of a fabric in which other threads do matter. As a *whole*, the pattern works.

WESTERN IDEAS ABROAD

Just how has western culture brought havoc in its wake? What western concepts have been cut loose from their cultural moorings to run wild abroad?

One candidate for destabilizing the third world is the western industrial and scientific assumption of renewable abundance and unlimited resources. In the western mind, scarcity is an aberration correctable by the appropriate application of capital, technology, and labor. The response to scarcity is to apply more of these factors of production. Neoclassical economics, which has dominated theory for over a century, assumes away all *natural* limits on the size of an economy: In this view, manmade capital is a perfect substitute for natural capital (i.e., for fertile soil, pure water, clean air, and stable climate), so the wealth available for human use can grow indefinitely.

Western assumptions about wealth can be traced more-or-less directly to Graeco-Christian-Judaic thought and the later Protestant Reformation of northern Europe. The Calvinist doctrine of predestination (one is saved or damned according to God's will) was paired with "Thou shalt be known by thy works." Wealth was the earthly sign of God's favor. Work and saving became virtues in themselves; habits of austerity tempered consumption. Manmade capital accumulated, a foundation for the future. Within this tradition, seventeenth-century philosopher Francis Bacon spread the faith that science would bring prosperity, health, and security to all, an idea that transformed scarcity from an absolute phenomenon to one remediable by human effort.

Trade, colonization, and the industrial revolution further promoted the view that the total quantity of resources fluctuates and can be modified by human ingenuity. During the twentieth century, the industrial revolution seemed about to fulfill not only Bacon's promise of renewable abundance, but also its humanitarian corollary, that no sector of the society or world should be allowed to remain in want. These aspirations burst from the west onto traditional cultures worldwide.

RENEWABLE ABUNDANCE VERSUS LIMITED GOOD

The idea that prosperity can be realized through technology challenges the very premise of most societies. The more common worldview is that resources are finite, and that scarcity is the ultimate condition of existence: The pie's size today is its size tomorrow. When technology is slow to change, as it has been over centuries of human experience, no other assumption is tenable. No other belief lets one's family and posterity survive.

Belief in absolute scarcity is seen in the view that good luck for one family implies bad luck for another, a zero-sum game. It underlies the widespread assumption (in Indian, Ceylonese, Yapese, and some African and American Indian societies) that the quantity of blood and semen is finite and nonreplenishable. The assumption of *limited good* was the underpinning of institutions and practices which, over long periods of human history, kept population numbers stable and in balance with the carrying capacity of the environment. Viewing scarcity as an absolute leads to accepting limits on demand as an unremitting fact of life.

It was this assumption of absolute limits which was both directly and indirectly assaulted by the neoclassical economics of modern western culture. The damage done by the "renewable abundance" idea was proportional to how much the traditional culture depended on the "absolute scarcity" idea as the rationale for limiting demand.

Let it be said that Europe did not escape unscathed. Classical economics as developed by David Ricardo never assumed that manmade capital could substitute perfectly for natural capital. Ricardo treated land as the ultimate constraint and thus assumed that scarcity is an unremitting fact. *Neo*classical economics, on the contrary, took its vision from the raw materials pouring into Europe from colonies around the globe. Real abundance made it easy to assume perfect substitutability of manmade for natural capital, so that abundance seemed renewable. To the neoclassical economist, a shortage of natural capital is inconceivable, or at least inconsequential, so confidence in prosperity growing on itself stimulated optimism and the philosophy of the Enlightenment. Fertility rose and European populations grew apace (as, all too soon, did poverty). The checks on fertility restored later (individual responsibility and the imperative of saving) took time to revive, evolve relevance to new social systems, and spread through mainstream culture.

SAVING

Two ideas limit demand in western cultures. One is the notion of nuclear family responsibility; the second is that one must save, purposefully, in order to create wealth. It is understood that the accumulation of capital requires savings. Saving amounts to a postponement of consumption. It depends upon the discipline of delayed gratification, a lesson taught whenever children do not get the treats they see and want. Denial of children and, with maturity, self-denial in the context of abundance is the western way.

In theory, saving is a temporary reduction of demand which should lead to greater wealth. But it often happens that self-denial and saving are addictive. The culture values saving for its own sake. Many Americans are wealthy but consume little. They invest pennies for a rainy day, pennies to support a golden age of retirement, and the having gives greater pleasure than consuming ever could. Their savings fuel economic growth.

The concept of accumulating capital through saving in order to put it, like land, to work is not unique to western societies. China, Korea, and Japan offer clear examples of the same mindset. Investment in children's education is a form of capital accumulation. So are pooled savings, where bits of capital accumulate until one family member can be set up in business; then the process repeats to benefit another family member.

But in most countries that are in trouble today, "letting capital work" is a foreign idea. There, people find it hard to accept the discipline of saving at the same time as being told that they will soon be better off. And without the concept of saving for investment, how can it be sensible to forgo present consumption if resources are unlimited and renewable?

In this light, the third world's use of international aid to finance consumption is not surprising. Saving for capital investment—the engine of nineteenth- and twentieth-century industrial success—is in many cultures an unknown concept because wealth creation is itself a foreign idea. Western thought overturned a traditional notion of absolute limits and scarcity as a fact of life; but the mechanism, savings, by which one gets from poor to rich, never completely penetrated. This example shows how ideas do not travel well because, often, they travel alone. The pieces of the patterns do not mesh. A foreign strain runs wild.

LOCUS OF RESPONSIBILITY

The definition of *family* is another obstacle to transferring western ideas to other settings. Social anthropologists have made the largest contribution to understanding that *family* has many meanings. The western concept centers on a man and a woman and their children. This is the nuclear family. Each generation begins over as children mate and become parents in their own families. Responsibility for raising and providing for children rests primarily within each of these nuclear family units. A man does not marry if he cannot provide, which is a major constraint on population growth because marriage rates usually affect fertility. Moreover, children born out of wedlock are not as likely as others to live to maturity.

The responsibility of the nuclear family for itself stimulates self-definition in terms of vocation, accomplishment, and recognition. It also reinforces self-denial and saving because each person prepares for responsible adulthood by becoming self-reliant. The corollary is that demands upon goods must be limited. Saving is both a prudent approach to financial security and a means of accumulating capital, the basis for achievement and further upward mobility of oneself or the nuclear family one founds.

Achievement goals frequently underlie desires for small family size and fertility control in the mature industrial nations. In the United States, the most commonly cited reasons for contraceptive use are that child spacing (1) reduces the financial strain on the family, (2) makes it possible to provide children with a good education, and (3) allows parents to do better by children than was done for them. This upwardly mobile orientation keeps open some options in parents' lives, while providing children with opportunities for further advancement. Thus, individualistic achievement and planning for the future motivate a conservative approach to personal resources, even within the context of wealth. In essence, these ideas become functional equivalents for the assumption of absolute scarcity.

In contrast, many nonwestern families are extensions over time of all relatives traceable through the man's or the woman's line (one lineage or the other). The language for categories of relatives both reflects and reinforces this collective mindset. When kinship is traced through the lineage system, the term for *father* is applied to all of the father's full brothers and often, as well, to all half brothers and male cousins of the same generation traced through *male* kin. The logic extends to the word for *mother*: The biological mother, this woman's full sisters and half sisters of the same mother, and all female cousins traced through *female* kin are known by a single term. A person literally has dozens of brothers and sisters, sons and daughters. An ethic of collective responsibility holds these lineages together. Far more than in western families, collateral relatives in each family line are bound to take care of kin, especially children.

INTERNATIONAL AID

With neither an ethic of individual or nuclear family responsibility nor a goal of capital accumulation, the idea that resources are unlimited becomes pernicious. Longterm dependency relationships with the international aid community have arisen because only the western belief in unlimited resources has penetrated worldwide. No amount of aid can be enough because it will ultimately support consumption, including high fertility, instead of appropriate investment. Indeed, most kinds of aid probably do harm by reinforcing the destabilizing belief in unlimited resources.

The greatest damage done by the rhetoric of aid, development, and prosperity could be that it undermines incentives for family planning. Africa, which has received more per capita in foreign aid than any other continent, has the highest fertility rate in the world: about six children per woman. It was not always so. In the 1950s, fertility in Africa averaged about one-half child less per woman than in South America. What changed? Could it be that Africans got three times as much aid per capita? Admittedly, Africa has among the highest illiteracy and mortality rates in the world. But improving these conditions might not reduce fertility; illiteracy and mortality rates were both declining even as fertility rose! Anthropologist Penn Handwerker (1991) says that, in Africa, educating women barely changes completed family size; at best, it delays the first birth for a few extra years while girls remain in school.

Aid encourages a cargo-cult mentality. This attitude is named, tellingly, for the enduring faith of some New Guineans that Curtis-Wright C-46s will fly in, as in World War II, and open their bellies to disgorge jeeps. The cargo-cult mentality is manifest in assuming migrants' *rights* to move into richer countries and in displays like the June, 1992, United Nations Conference on Environment and Development (UNCED). This Rio de Janeiro conference exposed environmentalists to the wrath of third-world representatives demanding both technology transfers and financial support. Some representatives to UNCED from industrialized countries were cowed by the demands. Others, captive to the demographic transition model, appeared to believe sincerely that every step toward development in the third world brings one closer to stopping the runaway freight train of population growth. One hopes that these misguided beliefs soon run their course. The policies of large-scale international aid, migration, and development dispel the traditional image of limited good and lead to ecological catastrophe.

THE FACILITATOR

Dependence on others did not develop in a vacuum. It required some country or countries willing to give. Since World War II, the impetus for international transfers in the form of grants, low-interest loans, debt-forgiveness, and openness to immigration has come from the United States. This generosity, almost unique in world history, can only be explained by a culture that was quintessentially American.

In *People of Plenty* (1954), historian David Potter provides insights into what was different about America. Potter proposes that, despite the Great Depression, Americans barely conceived of a zero-sum game; most Americans were willing to believe that more for one need not mean less for others. He writes, "Occasionally, one encounters the statement that Americans believe in leveling up rather than in leveling down. . . . It is by this stratagem of . . . drawing on nature's surplus and on technology's tricks, that America has often dealt with her problems of social reform." Americans saw—and may still see—an expandable pie.

Potter offers the example of Franklin Delano Roosevelt's New Deal. He argues that Roosevelt never saw it as taking from the well-off to give to the poor. Rather, Roosevelt considered it a reorganization of production and credit so that everyone would prosper. Thus,

> Franklin Roosevelt, too, was an apostle of abundance and, accordingly, of the view that the one-third who were unfortunate could be cared for without detriment to existing interests. . . . At the nadir of the Depression . . . Roosevelt unhesitatingly assumed that the country could afford to pay capitalism's ransom and to buy reform, too. One of his most irritating and most successful

qualities was his habit of assuming that benefits could be granted without costs being felt—an assumption rooted in his faith in the potentialities of the American economy.

Optimism flowed from the frontier experience, cheap energy sources, and the American genius for organization. Opportunity and reward for work were the dominant American experiences until the closing of the frontier. All factors together made wealth appear inexhaustible.

The frontier is said to have closed in 1890, one hundred years ago. That would be a long time for belief in prosperity and renewable abundance to persist without reinforcement. Events that let Americans proceed, secure in their faith that technology, science, and organizational skills would make each generation better off than the one before include, preeminently, the discovery of abundant oil and its uses in the late nineteenth century. Increases in the per capita use of energy have paced every recent advance in the standard of living. Without oil, would the automotive or aviation industries have developed? Would one have the pesticides and fertilizers that so expand agricultural production? Could one otherwise conceive of large-scale irrigation? Besides oil, accidents of history have handed the United States a unique competitive advantage over other industrial powers. Twice in the twentieth century the United States survived world military conflagrations without waging war on its own soil. Fortune smiled. No wonder Americans believed they could create prosperity limitlessly and forever and at the same time distribute largesse to the world.

Presidents of the United States, indeed most politicians, still give compulsory testimonials before the altar of blossoming prosperity. A very few dare suggest a zero-sum game. Nevertheless, ordinary Americans sense limits and begin to resent aid that goes abroad and immigrants who enter. The mood is that Americans need to concentrate on those who already call the United States their home. More for one may mean, all told, that less remains for another.

Ironically, the completely closed view of the ecosystem which characterizes traditional societies is emerging in America today. Americans sense that their brushes with scarcity are not solely aberrations of the business cycle. The strained capacity of the environment to neutralize pollution, set against the limited quantity of natural resources, cannot be indefinitely denied. The economy runs on raw materials and generates toxic as well as useful outputs; at both ends, the economic process exhausts nature.

The public, and the few politicians who accept the principle of absolute limits, may be on the cutting edge of culture change. So long as the change is home-grown, it will probably be good for America. Our about-face, properly and sensitively communicated abroad, can only help others to rediscover for themselves the constraints on which responsible choices depend.

III

THE BIG PICTURE
Politics, Incentives, and Strategies

9

One-World
A Global Folly

"Personal responsibility is
the brick and mortar of power."
SHELBY STEELE
Washington Quarterly, Summer, 1990

Just as there is a global economy—international trade, aid, and investment—there is a global environment. All of mankind lives on a single planet. The phrase "one world" recognizes that simple fact. "One world" properly refers to features of Earth's environment that, by their nature, transcend national borders.

The ozone hole, the carbon dioxide and methane buildup (linked to greenhouse climate change), acid rain, radioactive clouds, tropospheric ozone, and the depletion of natural capital (such as stocks of oceangoing fish) degrade Earth's environment. All of humanity contributes to the mess. All of humanity is likely to suffer. Kenneth Boulding (1976) put it apocalyptically: "There are catastrophes from which there is recovery, especially small catastrophes. What worries me is the irrevocable catastrophe. That is why I am worried about the globalization of the world. If you have only one system, then if anything goes wrong, everything goes wrong."

ONE WORLD VERSUS ONE-WORLD

Nevertheless (and fortunately, Boulding might have added), there are many ways in which the environment is not global. Some places are better or worse off than others. Features which are purely local include soil, air, and water quality; crowding; traffic congestion; social services; and public safety. The phrase "one-world" with a hyphen is used to obscure these important differences between neighborhoods and nations. This usage politicizes the term. It transforms occasionally global environmental conditions into a political manifesto. One-world was the catchword at UNCED. One-world, some say, *ought* to be the basis for foreign policy.

Maybe "one-world" is a popular phrase *because* it obscures differences, letting it be used to pressure industrialized countries to help. It can be a code for advocating international aid, forgiveness of third-world loans by private banks, and open borders between nations. "One-world" is a political statement when it invokes community—the "international community."

The transitions from global, environmental activism to a recipe for foreign policy are slippery and sometimes circular. Rich countries are invariably reminded that they mindlessly pollute—which is too true albeit less true than it was—and are told simultaneously to support industrialization in the third world. Rich countries are often tried and found guilty of being better off as well as of making the global environmental stew.

GUILT

Ironically, all strive to mimic the industrialized countries' standard of living. The third world struggles to reach a higher average level of consumption, which is to say pollution generation, and those of their citizens who can afford it are as consumption-oriented as any. Migration is one strategy for adopting a richer country's level of per capita consumption. The greenhouse gases produced to support the lifestyle of an average American are thirty times as great as those generated by the average Bangladeshi, but the difference vanishes if that Bangladeshi immigrates to the United States. The moral high ground is far from clear when those who deplore waste want to partake of it.

Another consideration: The environmental record in third-world countries is dismal; per unit of product, they generate much more pollution than anyone else. Moreover, the large population base means that every increase in the third-world standard of living drops an enormous added burden on the environment. Small increments in their per capita use of resources and polluting emissions multiply into an enormous total.

But these embarrassing points are seldom made. Indeed, Albert Gore's *Earth in the Balance* calls on the United States to assist in industrializing the third world. Support for worldwide industrial development is the industrialized powers' almost reflexive response to the charges of greed leveled against them. Expiation may be noble—or so destructive of the Earth that it is anything but.

Finally, feeling guilty about being richer than someone or some other country just conceivably makes sense within a moral community—a religious order, for example. But the world is not a moral community. One country (and even the United Nations) does not intervene in the internal affairs of another, except by consent or force. Realistically, nations answer to no higher law.

The world, not a moral community, is not even a garden-variety community; not as you and I know it or as Webster's (1975) defines it:

COMMUNITY a: State. Commonwealth. b: the people with common interests living in a particular area. c: an interacting population of various kinds of individuals (as species) in a common location. d: a group of people with a common characteristic or interest in living together within a larger society.

These definitions have little applicability to global politics. Even the European Community (EC) struggles with a unified structure that treats each member-nation equitably—while citizens of each country feel cheated and strive equally to retain the separateness of language, currency, and custom.

ONE-WORLD BEARS ON INCENTIVES

Community, by evoking a special relationship, lays claim to charity. So within one-world, help would be a right of poor nations and a duty of richer ones. The international community, a community brought into existence by the one-world catchword, is thus made to feel obligated to sustain the needy wherever they may be. One-world ideology creates (is intended to create) ambiguity over boundaries, so it tends to undercut the legitimacy of national ownership. Present rights to resources, not to mention their future and potential benefits, come into question if the so-called community of nations is obligated to help the world's poor. Real or not, this call on duty has often succeeded in mobilizing support for substantial wealth transfers and redistribution among nations.

One-world ideology thus bears on incentives. Citizens in countries being coerced to give see no end to want and feel threatened by a commons (see Chapter 10). Why save, why postpone consumption, why conserve, if the benefit goes to strangers? Countries that expect to get suffer because of the implicit message that they cannot help themselves. Is there a quicker way to erode self-confidence? Dependence on others is not a happy adult condition: Failure can be blamed on someone else; energy that could go into work or planning is dissipated in resentment when things go wrong, or in resentment simply at being dependent. Poor countries that count on foreign aid risk losing their resolve to become self-reliant. When dependence undermines self-confidence and stymies both foresight and planning, how can the future get better?

ONE-WORLD BLURS LIMITS

A further serious problem with western-inspired, internationally sponsored help is that it feeds cornucopian fantasies. The apparent willingness to give without return reinforces the belief that the givers have unlimited resources. In most cultures, such aid would otherwise be inconceivable.

The idea of a pure gift—a gift without expectation of return—is exceedingly rare. The usual pattern is reciprocal giving, or exchange. Between strangers, exchanges are immediate and of equal value: barter or sale. Among friends, the return for a gift may be delayed; value is not equalized over every trade although, in the long run, gifts and hospitality are expected to come out even. Reciprocity is expected. A person with normal self-esteem, feeling short-changed over a series of trades, looks for a different friend. Only kin do not always expect a close return of value. Kin help each other without hurting their own posterity (the total of their direct and collateral descendants) because, to the degree that they share genes, individuals are biologically interchangeable.

Christianity has spread the ideal of an unreciprocated gift beyond the circle of kinship; nevertheless, it remains essentially foreign to many local belief systems. Exchange, always favoring kin, still is the dominant ideology—as well as practice. The more distantly one's trading partners are seen, the more one tries to get the better of the bargain. Taking without giving back counts as a coup. Christian nations are often misunderstood because they have made giving an ideal of their foreign policy. When international bodies proclaim an intention to give—expecting nothing back—it means one of three things in most parts of the world: (1) the givers are fools; (2) they are very devious and plan to entrap recipients in a web of obligations; or (3) they have so much wealth that they have stopped counting. But for the salutary developments that western banks are demanding repayment of their loans, and international agencies are attaching political as well as economic conditions to their *new* loans, the third world would still be settled on one of these interpretations.

The most dangerous conclusion that any country can draw is that wealth is abundant and renewable. Nevertheless, that unfounded view is widespread and is encouraged by the international rhetoric of aid. Promises overwhelm the reality that Earth is finite, that resources are limited, and that population growth is outrunning every possibility of providing sustenance to all.

The scale of the global effort to help the third world (and the deception it fosters) can hardly be overstated. Harper's Index (March, 1989) reports that forty countries rely on foreign aid for at least a quarter of their national budgets. Aid is a tidy sum when single-government grants, credits and loan guarantees, International Monetary Fund (IMF) and World Bank lending, and private bank lending—which become *de facto* aid through deferral of principal repayments and interest—are totted up. Easy borrowing from private banks ended only when Mexico defaulted on its debt in the summer of 1982. By then, Latin America alone had received $500 billion. The May, 1989, issue of *The World Monitor* (Mathews, 1989) recalls annual giving in the early 1980s: "donations from foreign countries averaged about $20 per person in Africa . . . $7 per person in Latin America and $5 per person in Asia."

Direct U.S. government aid alone amounted to about $10 billion in 1987: Over $3 billion went to Israel, $2.5 billion to Egypt, $500 million to El Salvador, $700 million to assorted other countries in Central America, $400 million to the Philippines, and most of the balance to Asia and Africa. Outright U.S. aid climbed to $14 billion in 1990, and much more is masked within unlikely-sounding programs in the Departments of State, Defense, Commerce, Health and Human Services, and Education. Including its contributions to the World Bank and IMF, the United States dispersed $92 billion to developing countries in 1988 (Harper's Index, Dec. 1989).

Such transfers of wealth cannot but perpetuate trust in one-world rhetoric—a belief that the community of nations can be relied upon to help, just like family. A sense of security grows along with the felt entitlement to share in the world's resources on the basis of need. Behind it all is the fantasy of abundance. Efforts to plan for one's own future do not thrive in this climate. Neither do private birth control decisions nor national policies promoting population control advance in the purposive mode essential for avoiding the looming tragedy.

THE FRUITS OF SELF-RELIANCE

Leaders in China, a country of 1.2 billion people, have seen the characters on the wall. They regard their population as dangerously large and hope to stop growth. Their reported longterm target is to decrease population to less than half of the present size. Gradual reduction through no immigration and below-replacement-level fertility is the goal. Birth control, education, and social pressure are the means. China should be honored if its goal is reached—and even for trying. Coercive inducements to limit families to one child each may, in hindsight, look compassionate. Within China, it already is widely accepted that the one- or two-child family is a patriotic duty.

China's way looks better and better as other strategies fail. Its emphasis on limiting demand seems sounder than anything else being tried—the only rational strategy. It is home-grown, straight from China's own recent history of famine. Communist China never sat at the table of international aid. Self-imposed isolation, beginning before 1949 and reinforced under Mao Tse-Tung, meant that self-reliance became a core tenet of national policy. Indeed, news of a serious famine which ran from 1958 through much of the 1960s barely penetrated China's borders to reach the western world. Certainly no international assistance was asked or offered. One-world thinking did not blur China's perception of reality.

Mao's subsequent policy shows that he acquired a crystal-clear grasp of the finitude of resources and the need to limit demand. Reduction of population pressure became a central part of the longterm solution. Before the famine, official Chinese policy was aggressively pronatalist: More children meant a greater nation. By famine's end, the policy had reversed. The one-child-per-family goal was in place by 1970.

Local party cadres organized family-planning education programs and contraceptive distribution. Birth control was presented as a patriotic duty which would contribute to China's long-run prosperity. Schoolchildren were indoctrinated with the goal of a common good and the one-child family as fundamental to that end. "Barefoot doctors" were trained to insert IUDs and check monthly that they remained in place. Rough-and-ready abortions were performed with a tube and mason jar: Heat creates a vacuum in the jar and suction does the rest. Scientists developed a cheap and effective version of the contraceptive pill: wafer-thin perforated paper, like sheets of postage stamps, soaked in a solution of estrogen and progesterone. One stamp a day, taken by mouth, suppresses ovulation and has increasingly let contraception substitute for abortion and infanticide.

Exposure to pregnancy became another matter of official concern: Premarital sex was forbidden, and the minimum marriage age was set at twenty-one for women and twenty-five for men. One birth was permitted after marriage, but the timing and even possibility of a second rested on approval by the local Communist cadre.

The high priority put on self-reliance undoubtedly guided China's response to famine. Where other countries in dire straits have become accustomed to call for help, China moved to take responsibility for its own future. Its population policy, a response to scarcity, would probably have been muted—perhaps absent entirely—in the presence of help from outside.

Habits of self-reliance may lately have been breached: The Chinese leadership reacted to floods in the summer of 1991 with requests for international aid. Almost fortunately for them, one may think, other facts in the international equation militated against their receiving any large response. The international reluctance to assist, after Tiananmen Square, probably benefits China in the long run. Its resolve to limit demands on the national carrying capacity is less likely to weaken.

Myanmar (Burma) is another country that makes self-reliance a tenet of national policy. The trade-off for doing without international aid is "isolation and lack of a full-fledged national family planning program" (Population Reference Bureau, 1991). Nevertheless, without benefit of technical assistance or funds for deploying modern contraception, fertility has dropped. In 1983, women averaged 5.2 children. In 1990, the fertility rate was below 4.0, a significant decline. The Population Reference Bureau comments that professional demographers are bemused: How the Myanmarians did it "is unclear." But it is not unclear. Limits to resources were widely apparent, and no cargo-cult mentality clouded thinking. Never in fact or fantasy did one-world illusions of being bailed out of their predicament enter into calculation.

Assumptions and values give form to behavior. When ideas are unrealistic, the behavior they promote is likely to be unrealistic and maladaptive, too. A sense of security based on expectation of international largesse neutralizes local signals of scarcity that should be warnings to reduce demand. Countries' beliefs that others have the capacity and will to take care of them over the long haul put them at added risk. A greatly underestimated danger is that such trust will undermine incentives for third-world countries to help themselves. A way to reduce demand is to have fewer children. Population control, by modern or traditional means, is the irreducible bottom line by which third-world countries can respond to environmental limits. Indeed, they can save themselves in no other way.

DENIAL AND UNCERTAINTY

Population growth threatens billions of present and future lives. It is *the* global question; so serious, indeed, that one wants to pretend otherwise (denial is a well-known but self-defeating psychological mechanism). But part of the difficulty in grasping the dimensions of the problem lies in the quality of information. No one knows, for sure, how fast world population is growing. Demographers think that world population will soon be growing by 100 million a year, equivalent to a steady annual 1.7 percent rate of natural increase. A formula shows that, with this rate of increase, numbers will double every forty-one years. The number 70 in the equation is a constant in a well-known mathematical equation. Divide it by a percentage (the rate of population growth, or the interest on your money) in order to get the doubling time:

$$\frac{70}{1.7} = 41.2$$

Systems analyst Stuart Umpleby *et al.* (1988) state, however, that a network of mathematicians and physicists have calculated that the estimate of a steady 1.7 percent growth rate is too low. They observe that the doubling time for world population has steadily decreased and that the trend line still seems on track for ever shorter intervals. It took seventy years, from 1880 to 1950, to go from 1.25 billion to nearly 2.5 billion people; but just thirty-seven years, from 1950 to 1987, to double again. A mathematical equation based on the increase in human numbers through the year 1960* predicts that the next doubling time (starting from 1987) will be twenty-three years, not the forty-one years projected by demographers.

Disagreements over the constancy of growth rates in recent decades may arise from a difference in method. Mathematicians stick with the estimate of the total world population made *closest* to the date that is being estimated; then a comparison of totals at two dates shows up all of the numerical increase. See in Table 1, however, that *demographers adjust the numbers well after the year being estimated is passed*. Demographers then compute the growth rate using the revised base. If the revision of the base was

*See Von Foerster *et al.*, 1960.

Table 1. Estimates of Human Population in Billions as a Function of Time (United Nations, 1951, 1966, 1982, 1985, 1986, 1989)[a]

Year in question	Year of estimate						Doomsday equation
	1951	1963	1973	1982	1984	1988	
1950	2.406[b]	2.517	2.501	2.504	2.516	2.515	2.432
1955		2.731	2.722	2.746	2.751	2.751	2.599
1960	2.731	2.988	2.986	3.014	3.019	3.019	2.792
1965		3.281	3.288	3.324	3.334	3.336	3.015
1970		3.592	3.610	3.683	3.693	3.698	3.277
1975		3.944	3.968	4.076	4.076	4.080	3.650
1980	3.277	4.330	4.374	4.453	4.450	4.450	3.969
1985		4.746	4.816	4.842	4.837	4.854	4.438
1990		5.188	5.280	5.248	5.246	5.292	5.033
1995		5.648	5.763	5.679	5.678	5.766	5.814
2000		6.130	6.254	6.127	6.122	6.251	6.884

[a] *Source*: Stuart Umpleby, "The Scientific Revolution in Demography," *Population and Environment* 11(3):159–174, 1990.
[b] The underlined numbers are the estimates made closest to the date in question.

upward, part of the "growth" being calculated gets excluded from the computation: It got lost in the revision.

Umpleby (1990) observes that "Estimates of human population continue to rise after the fact. . . . This peculiar post hoc rise in population estimates may shed light on an inconsistency in the interpretation of population data. Since the mid-1960s demographers have been saying that world population growth rates are declining." On the contrary, states Umpleby (1991), "natural scientists . . . observe that for the past 30 years human population data have exceeded a curve based on an assumption of increasing growth rates."

Recall that numbers plotted on a logarithmic scale fall in a straight line if the total is multiplied each year by a constant number (such as the 1.7 percent annual growth rate estimated by demographers). But the line curves upward if the rate of growth is itself rising. Figure 4, which plots world population growth

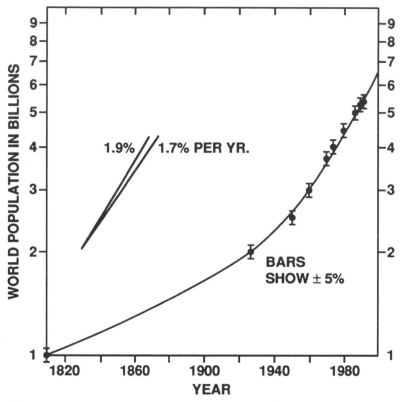

Figure 4. World population on semilog scale, A.D. 1820 to 1980. *Source*: Albert A. Bartlett, Department of Physics, University of Colorado.

against time on a semilog scale, shows that the line was still curving up and away from a straight-line incline until about 1965– 1970. Umpleby and a number of other mathematicians and physicists would say that not only the base (population size) but also the rate of growth may be rising still; and that (the frequent) upward revisions of demographic numbers will, in due course, show it.

Umpleby's confidence is based on the congruence between two curves: the mathematically computed predictions for every year since 1960 and the upward-revised demographic estimates. Figure 5 shows the curve predicted by what has come to be known as the *Doomsday Equation* along with the demographic estimates of growth. The curves run close together right up to the date when the graph was drawn because the demographic estimates have been revised many times. Points have tended to rise not only after the fact, but also as the date in question approached.

The Doomsday Equation developed by Heinz von Foerster *et al.* (1960) modeled population growth using pre-1960 data. Since then it has been more accurate in prediction than any

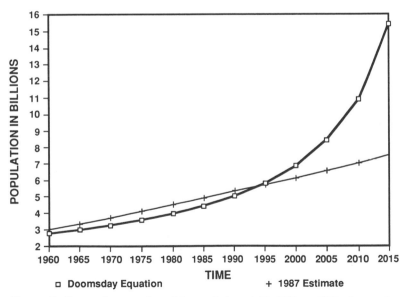

Figure 5. Two estimates of world population, A.D. 1960 to 2015. *Source*: S. Umpleby (1988), "Will the Optimists Please Stand Up?" *Population and Environment* 10(2).

demographic method. The annual totals predicted by Von Foerster *et al.* appear as the right-hand column of Table 1 (p. 123). His equation is

$$\text{Population size} = \frac{1.79 * 10^{11}}{(2026.87 - \text{time})^{0.99}}$$

For any given year since 1960, Von Foerster *et al.*'s equation predicts a larger total world population than expected by the United Nations, the Population Reference Bureau, or any other demographic research group. As each year has passed, the actual numbers have surpassed all predictions, including that of Von Foerster and his colleagues. But since their formula yields the highest numbers, they have been closer to the mark. It is not encouraging, therefore, that Von Foerster *et al.*'s model of accelerating growth shows world population approaching unimaginable numbers by the year 2026, foretelling a region of instability about fifteen years before that. *Region of instability* is a mathematical term meaning that the curve will begin to behave unpredictably.

So much for the way numbers are used. Other analysts challenge even the way that raw numbers are collected. For example, epidemiologist Warren M. Hern (personal communication) observed census taking in Brazil and estimated that over half of the population in some areas was not counted. The census takers approached their job by the hilltop method: Start at the higher elevations of a city and work downhill. Some distance down the hillside the job is considered done—finished. Hern quotes the census taker as saying that the rest of the people "don't count." Those at the bottom, who live densely packed into hovels and catch the sewage from upper slopes, are not in fact counted.

Such challenges to official data are interesting and alarming and may be on target, but let us stick with the more conventional estimate of a 1.7 percent rate of growth per year. Even at that rate, the total doubles every forty-one years. The average growth rate for the world does not tell the story for most third-world countries, where growth is much more rapid. The world average is held down by lower rates in China (1.4 percent), the United States (1.1 percent), and most of Europe.

But why attend to the facts? Helping *feels* good to many westerners and "one-world" sounds great. Third-world spokespersons sound reasonable and do not personify their people's poverty. So why rethink policy? The answer is that one needs to really help. Little time remains. Delay only increases suffering. One-world ideology, which implies that resources will be shared, is one of the villains in the persistently high fertility of the third world. A great irony—and one of the saddest—is that promises of aid, and the aid itself, endanger the very countries that receive the most. Good intentions cannot excuse dealing the final blow to the preservation of livable environments in the world's poorest countries. Summing up, the global population threat may be worse than we think, and some impulses to help may do more harm than good. Those are bitter pills.

Potlatching Twentieth-Century Style

Give first. Ask questions later.

Spanning more than three decades, NATO and the Communist bloc vied for the hearts and minds of the third world. Aid and technical transfers gained support at the highest levels of government partly because they were seen as adjunct strategies in the Cold War. The goal was winning loyalty from foreign governments. Whether the assorted dictators, military chiefs, and bureaucrats who accepted aid on behalf of their country were capable of delivering loyalty mattered less than preventing some region from publicly lining up behind the opposing faction. Another goal was, yes, to help. Assorted technocrats and do-gooders furthered their own careers and also hoped to significantly improve the health and well-being of large numbers of people.

The world may never again see so much competition to give. But still, it is not an unknown phenomenon. It can be put into a broad evolutionary perspective. Humans and many animal species give when something is wanted in return.

MUTUAL RECIPROCITY

One of most common forms of giving is mutual reciprocity, or *reciprocal altruism*. It usually, but not necessarily, involves individuals of the same species. This kind of exchange is advantageous to both parties when participants in the exchange (1) have ways of recognizing each other; (2) expect repeated encounters over the long run; (3) can give services or goods that are relatively costless to themselves but have greater value to the other; and (4) have confidence (or ways of monitoring) that the other does not cheat on the implicit deal.

Human exchanges are legion. Sometimes, especially in small, stable communities, they are simply kin helping kin. Often, however, no kinship is involved. Here, too, exchanges tend to occur in stable communities, because these are the settings where the four conditions for mutually favorable terms are most likely to exist. Exchanges count as simple neighborliness.

Animal exchanges also occur. Chimpanzees, for example, call loudly if they are the first to discover a tree with newly ripening fruit. This action involves not only sharing, but also risk. The chimpanzee calls attention to itself; all in the forest, including predators, know his or her whereabouts. Risk is involved whenever animals in a colony (of birds, monkeys, and many other genera) give an alarm call to warn of predators. Signaling sometimes delays the individual's getaway and he or she is singled out. Among primates, males may even go out to meet the danger. Young adult male baboons put themselves between the breeding females of a troop and a leopard, for instance, and have been seen to fight to the death.

The question always arises: Why do individuals sacrifice themselves? Sometimes the answer is that they don't: The risk is small enough so that, on average, they expect a net gain. For example, the individual gains if a predator learns not to bother stalking its particular troop or herd because everyone gets a warning and usually gets away. In many settings, however, individuals seem to help others at real cost to themselves. In these instances, observers try to sort out if they are watching true mutual reciprocity or simply kin helping kin. Evolution—natural selection—favors kin helping kin because the result is that duplicates of one's own genes, some of which probably encode the helping behavior, are passed to succeeding generations.

True mutual reciprocity occurs when partners to an exchange are not related. Therefore, their benefit comes from giving up something relatively costless in order to get something that they could not do well for themselves. U.S. foreign aid supposedly had this quality so long as we believed that wealth could be limitless and renewable. What we gave, therefore, was relatively costless to ourselves and thought to be of very great value to others; what we hoped to receive back were allies in the Cold War.

Some would stretch definitions of kinship, of course, to argue that all humans are related. Technically, then, foreign aid would be kin helping kin instead of mutual reciprocity. Rather than labor the point, let us acknowledge that examples of true mutual reciprocity are found in the animal kingdom. One recognizes this kind of exchange when individuals who are parties to a relationship cannot possibly be kin.

Sociobiologist Robert Trivers (1971) delightfully describes the interchange between "cleaner fish," who live in individual territories among coral reefs, and much larger fish such as grouper which come regularly, repeatedly stopping at the same station, to be serviced. Other observations show that groupers suffer from dermatitis-like diseases if they are not cleaned, and the cleaner fish get a meal from parasites found on their customers. Both gain. The fish being cleaned could, however, gain still more: When the cleaner swims into the big fish's mouth, it is a ready meal. But the fish being cleaned does not take the opportunity; even if alarmed into making a sudden exit, it shakes its head, opens its jaws, and the cleaner swims out. Giving warning costs the grouper a split second, but the cleaner fish will be around to work next time a service stop is needed. Here is an example of repeated exchanges over time where small costs to each party have high value to the other.

Humans clearly exchange goods and services time and time again. The more distantly the parties to an exchange are related, the more likely they are to expect the trade to be mutually rewarding—and the more closely they watch each other for signs of cheating on the deal. Trivers suggests that the subtleties of exchange are among the principal pressures leading to the evolution of the large human brain. Indeed, humans are different from other animals in special ways that involve giving. People feel good, often, just because of doing a good deed, and they *say* that is sufficient reward. (Nevertheless, few go on doing good without recognition, and those few get known as saintly.) Humans also accept intangibles like prestige in exchange for real goods and services.

INFLATION

Prestige and political loyalty were the stakes in the twentieth-century international giving war; and it is not the first time that this typically human competition has shifted into an inflationary spiral. The Kwakiutl Indians of Vancouver Island developed the *potlatch* until it became an extravaganza of gift-giving, ostentatious display, and waste. The potlatch became so wasteful by the 1920s that it was outlawed by the Canadian government.

Potlatch is an Indian name given to days of feasting and entertainment. High chiefs competed with each other by potlatching each other's community. The host made presentations of valuable commodities to each guest according to his rank. Not to be outdone, the guests threw their own potlatch as soon thereafter as sufficient goods could be accumulated, enough to shame the original givers by the much more lavish return. Even in the early days, the host would exaggerate the extent of his power and wealth by destroying or casting into the sea the most valued of Kwakiutl prestige goods: an incised, beaten shield of copper. The last potlatch of the 1920s was a bash that included destruction of property as well as gifts of motorboats and refrigerators, all to prove the host's largeness of spirit.

Fur blankets were among the most valued staple goods presented in the traditional potlatch. These took a long time to make, with the result that stakes were kept at a fairly steady level. Inflation hit, however, when the nineteenth-century expansion of the Hudson's Bay Company started the trade in wool Pendleton blankets. *Trading* furs and pelts for blankets was more efficient than using them to *make* blankets. Blankets began to accumulate very fast indeed so that, as currency, their value was debased. Lots and lots of wool blankets began to make the potlatch rounds.

The escalating sums spent on international aid can be seen as a similar kind of inflation. Never in history had two such powerful and rich nations as the United States and the Soviet Union opposed each other for world hegemony and tried, under the nuclear threat, to do it peaceably. Bidding for the loyalty of the third world took precedence, arguably, over careful study of what would actually be helpful.

Fortunately for the United States, the USSR outbid us on one aid project, the Aswân High Dam, where the repercussions may yet affect more people than ever before have been harmed by being helped. The Aswân High Dam is big-time. But it is common for foreign programs and ideas introduced into another country to *not* help. And they sometimes harm. Here are four examples of international economic assistance that have done damage although the intention was beneficent: new water holes and wells for stock in the African Sahel; agricultural development projects in the fertile but arid and semiarid southern lands of Somalia; the Aswân High Dam in Upper Egypt; and the green revolution.

WELL-WATER FOR THE SAHEL

First, the well-digging projects: In the late 1950s, agricultural economists studied the stock-raising African peoples of the Sahel. The distance between water holes appeared to be the limiting factor in increasing the size of herds. If access to water could be improved, experts reasoned, so could the number of animals maintained on the land, and the standard of living would rise. Accordingly, international assistance was provided for digging many more wells, so that cattle could utilize more of the grassland areas.

Several miscalculations contributed to the subsequent debacle. In the first place, no thought was given to the danger of triggering a "tragedy of the commons." The grasslands are unfenced; they are used as a commons, but the cattle grazing them are family-owned. No provision was made for regulating the number of animals that could be added to each family's herd.

Second, it should have been noticed before the well-digging program started that grasslands within a several-kilometer radius of water were overgrazed and trampled to dust. So long as this destruction was confined to the surrounds of naturally occurring water, enough grassland remained in good condition to keep the area in a climate-balance: The relative coolness of vegetation encouraged precipitation from rain clouds, and more grass grew. But the addition of many more water sources, which denuded much more land, changed the balance.

Third, the herds increased as expected and more, but so did the number of people dependent on herding. A population explosion happened! Men accelerated their marriage plans because the main hindrance, the expense of the brideprice, became inconsequential. Brideprice is paid in livestock—so many cows, so many goats—and the much greater number of animals brought down the effective price, that is, the price in constant animals. Until inflation caught up, the availability of animals meant, simply, that it was much easier to get together a brideprice. New families mean more babies. The fertility rate rose, not surprisingly, because population growth in response to new-found prosperity is the commonest of events.

Soon, moreover, the basis for prosperity began to vanish. Wells dotted regularly over the landscape resulted in trampled areas beginning to overlap. Progressively more grassland became dust. The heat that now rose uninterruptedly from the plains could not trigger rain, so the region's climate changed as well.

The result is well documented. Livestock and people starved together. Where a small population had lived in balance with nature, now almost no man nor beast survives. The carrying capacity of the land was exceeded, and nature struck back. The spreading desert and famine in the Sahel are history.

EMPTY IS NOT UNUSED

In a second example, irrigation projects in southern Somalia effectively dispossessed nomadic animal herders in order to settle formerly landless farmers. The development experts who looked at the semiarid and arid lands south of Mogadishu, Somalia, saw empty country. Mostly engineers, they foresaw no obstacle to irrigating the land for agricultural development and, apparently, were warned of none. Investigation by any competent anthropologist would have dispelled their naïveté. The land was usually empty, but *not unused*. Nomadic herders counted on it as part of the annual, transhumant grazing cycle for their animals. When farmers were settled on the most easily irrigated, naturally lushest pastures, the nomads lost out.

The loss of access to part of their grazing territory meant that the herders had to intensify their use of the lands to which they could still go. These grasslands soon became overgrazed and began to deteriorate irreversibly. Destruction of the ecosystem, which formerly was in balance, is well advanced. The Somali nomads' decent, traditional lifestyle is devastated.

Development specialist Jon Unruh (1990) describes the resistance of farmers who are in possession but are now being encouraged to share land use with nomads. Crop residues substitute more-or-less readily for grassland fodder, but their availability is limited. Settlers, especially the small subsistence farmers, own livestock; these animals compete seriously with the nomads' herds in dry years—just when the need is greatest for all because graze in other areas is scarce also.

Looking at the big picture, one has to admit that the western technical-assistance experts played God: They dropped great blessings on one set of agriculturalists at the cost of impoverishing others. Possibly the experts were unwitting pawns of long-standing Somali clan competition. That is, the reins of government were held by the settlers' clansmen, and displacement of the nomads was a conscious goal. If nomads are recovering seasonal access to land, it may be because the clans' political fortunes have reversed.

Experts also reason that more people can be supported by irrigation than by nomadic herding; maybe the utilitarian principle of greatest good for the greatest number should prevail! But this rationale for dispossessing nomads begs the matter of sustainability. The windfall probably promoted a rise in fertility rates among the settlers (just as happened in the Sahel, Turkey, Cuba, and medieval Europe; also see Chapter 14), so that the carrying capacity surplus was soon gone. Longterm effects may be feared for a second reason: Irrigation is an unsustainable technology. When it depends on underground aquifers, the water will be depleted if use exceeds the recharge rate; even when river water is available, as it was from the Tigris and Euphrates Rivers in ancient Mesopotamia's Fertile Crescent, soil salinization eventually renders irrigated land infertile. All told, in Somalia, an unstable system replaced an ecologically stable one.

LAUNCH PAD FOR INDUSTRIAL TAKEOFF

A third example, the Aswân High Dam, promised much. The dam provides hydroelectric power which was to bring Egypt to the threshold of industrial takeoff. However, the energy is now fully allocated, and Egypt has fallen further into poverty. The dam's unforeseen negative consequences are still developing; but some are clear already.

The flooding upstream of Aswân took a portion of Egypt's all-too-scarce arable land. That much was anticipated. *But* the ebb and flow of the Nile, before the dam, had fertilized the river delta and spilled out nutrients into the sea. Without this enrichment, the fisheries of the southeast Mediterranean have significantly declined. A former reliable food source is endangered. Loss of the Nile's annual floods means that nature's way of fertilizing and restoring riverine lands is also gone. Now, artificial fertilizer and irrigation are both needed, so farming is much more dependent on petrochemicals, and progressive salinization will ultimately result in abandonment of much farmland. In the meantime, the still water in irrigation ditches breeds snails, which are the vector for bilharzia (schistosomiasis), a debilitating disease that has become endemic in all of Egypt's agricultural regions.

Next, silt used to reach the delta and restore land lost to the Mediterranean; now the delta, home to 10 million people, is subsiding. Unusually large quantities of silt—because of deforestation and erosion in Ethiopia and Sudan—are accumulating *behind* the dam. This silting threatens the dam's primary benefit, hydroelectric power. The rush of upstream water from seasonal rains will someday bring a deluge that returns the Nile to its former downstream floodplain. The people who have moved right up to the banks will lose their homes if not their lives.

Finally, the prosperity expected from the dam was probably a factor in stalling early successes in birth control. Egypt cannot begin to overcome its many problems while the preference for large families persists. Population growth means that Egypt cannot foreseeably save, borrow, or be given enough to make the investments which would produce meaningful jobs. And jobs for women—which are particularly important in connection with fertility because women's employment imposes an opportunity cost on childrearing—are unlikely to become a priority in a male-dominated society so long as men are underemployed.

HYBRID GRAINS

The green revolution is a different sort of case. World food supplies could never have kept pace with population growth (which they did up to 1984) without it. Plant physiologist Norman Borlaug deserves his Nobel Prize. He knew as well as any, however, that his research breakthroughs were only buying time. The third world had gained a decade or so to reverse its population growth humanely, before the fat was in the fire again.

Balancing even this limited benefit are costs: The new varieties of grain grow only with ample water and fertilizer applications, so manufactured fertilizers and irrigation are often essential. Both of these use up nonrenewable petrochemical resources. Also, land is salinized by irrigation, and much of it is ruined already. Acre upon acre is being pulled out of production in Pakistan, for example. In addition, the new methods selectively benefit large landholders because of their cost for pesticides, fertilizer, and dependable water. Thus, many small farmers and agricultural laborers have been displaced to urban slums, hardly an improvement in their lives. The food crop, moreover, is often destined for export. Even if available to the local population, it is often less nutritious as a single staple than was the mix of the traditional subsistence diet. Environmentalists David Durham and James Fandrem (1988) point out that "The new varieties have themselves contributed to poverty and malnutrition in third world populations through changing labor and landholding patterns." Further, they warn that "The crop monoculture associated with new varieties is not without risk."

A MIXED RECORD

Wells, irrigation, a dam, and the green revolution have not brought unalloyed good. Indeed, the minuses probably outweigh the pluses. Altogether, they make a bad record for international aid. Nations gave out of a combination of competitive self-interest and desire to do good; but no one making policy or in the scientific community expected to be doing harm. The poor results were as unforeseen as they are horrifying to environmentalists and humanitarians alike.

Even food aid given without thought to global realpolitik has its critics. Ethicist Joseph Fletcher (1991) and biologist Garrett Hardin (1968) concur that, when populations exceed the carrying capacity of their lands, famine aid may exacerbate longterm shortages by keeping the starving alive long enough to add to overpopulation by their reproduction. Fletcher tempers Hardin's conclusions by urging

> as an ethical guideline that relief be withheld in only two kinds of famine situations: (1) when the probable consequences of sharing would actually endanger the survival of the giver, and (2) when the probable consequences of sharing would increase rather than decrease the recipients' misery; . . . This second principle forbids giving food when it can be foreseen that the recipients will thereby live on to reproductive years and thus increase the number of starving people, plus the predictable diseases that go with starvation, because their country has already exceeded its carrying capacity.

Fletcher asserts that it is incumbent upon the giver to know the numbers, so that the consequences of aid can be estimated realistically.

UNSTABLE ALLIANCES

Whether or not aid is wise over the long run, it tends to be sought by national leaders, in part because it entrenches those who already control the power structure. The prestige of bureaucrats or dictators rises with the amount of largesse that becomes theirs to dispense. As domestic political situations become more unstable, the demands for aid increase. Faced by rapidly growing populations, governments that want political stability try to keep the lid on by dedicating revenue to ever more consumption goods and social services. But that strategy has a short horizon because the number in need always grows.

Third-world nations may also believe that their demands on international bodies are enforceable. Requests for aid are often framed by an unspoken threat that problems will be exported if help in containing them at home is not forthcoming. Lindsey Grant (1991), formerly Deputy Assistant Secretary of State for

Environment and Population Affairs, calls attention to an explicit message: "The President of Mexico [Salinas] has been telling American audiences that, if there is no free trade agreement, we will be swamped by illegal immigration." Grant continues, "This is very close to blackmail. We do not need to accede to the threat."

Indeed, this kind of relationship is both unsustainable and dishonorable and, while the industrial world lets it go on, gives incorrect signals about the worldwide stock of natural capital and the industrial countries' ability to generate wealth. It casts poverty as a distributional problem (rich countries will always have enough to share if they choose to do it) rather than a problem of absolutely limited resources. The results are sadly counterproductive: Poor countries are encouraged to live beyond their means in the belief that they will be bailed out, and third-world couples go on thinking that large families are affordable.

Industrialized countries cannot pretend to act responsibly and walk away from disaster. But next moves must be carefully thought out because most kinds of aid do not actually help and, in any case, needs may already exceed resources. Chapters 12 and 13 address a selected few of the resource considerations that will limit aid; juxtaposed with the enormous scale of basic needs, no coalition of nations will conceivably be in the position of coming to the rescue. Experts think that, by the year 2000, 64 out of 117 third-world countries will have become dependent on donated food, and the majority of these 64 countries will be unable to support as many as half of their projected numbers. Three billion people will lack adequate fuel wood or other energy sources. Water demand, spurred by population growth, will exceed rainfall in most of Africa, the Middle East, north Asia, and parts of Mexico, Chile, and Argentina. And, warns environmentalist Cynthia Green (1991), "The growing volume of untreated human wastes and toxic substances could render as much as one-fourth of the world's water supply unsafe for human consumption."

So what can one do next?

11

Helping While Not Harming

Modernization and development have a history of overwhelming accepted ideas about limits to resources and propriety. The psychology of prosperity encourages people to break with older values and customs, especially those that restrict personal choice. Without the old ways as a guide, many people enter into sexual relationships that formerly would have been unavailable to them. Too many become parents too soon.

Prosperity also changes family size preferences. Concern about being able to successfully rear children normally counteracts the motive to reproduce at near-maximum capacity, but it is allayed when couples expect to become better off. This motivational effect does not depend on intervening culture, such as rules about who may marry, and when. The belief that more children are affordable follows closely on the availability of government subsidies and the rhetoric of international aid. Comprehensive health and social programs, or food and housing subsidies, dispel the assumption that wealth is finite. The dilemma is that, while helping and often offering contraceptive services, aid programs may undermine the motivation to plan for small family size. Our goal must be to help while not harming.

Perceived opportunities to emigrate may be just as corrosive as large-scale aid. Emigration appeals to many of the most energetic people of a society—exactly those people who would be most likely to promote constructive reform at home. One quick way to stop dissent is to expel the troublemaker, the way the ancient Greeks dealt with social critics. Socrates was urged to leave Athens peaceably, but he made a political statement instead by drinking the hemlock. By dint of ostracism, the USSR got rid of dissenters too prominent to kill or jail: Solzhenitsyn was not given the option to die for his country. Communist leaders in Poland would have been smart to make one shipyard electrician get out: What would the former Eastern Bloc be today if Lech Walesa had not got the ball rolling?

Driving out the tree-shakers does make for soothing politics. At the same time, emigration creates a safety valve for excess population. The understanding that some people will remove themselves lifts pressure that would otherwise encourage everyone to confront the limited nature of resources. Recall the stubbornly high fertility of precisely those nineteenth-century Welsh and English as well as contemporary eastern Caribbean villages where emigration was (is) a tradition (Chapter 3).

These adverse effects of emigration and development narrow considerably the options for helping third-world countries to help themselves. A constructive posture begins with review of what already is being done and what works. A few principles emerge, and these can be briefly summarized.

Avoid projects that depend on subsidies. These create long-term dependencies; they may harm. Projects that help are *small-scale, home-grown,* and *give women opportunities to work for pay or profit.* The strategies that have promise include

- Supporting family-planning assistance programs.
- Supporting microloans.
- Supporting job creation for women.
- Using limited immigration visas as an incentive.
- Making the United States an example of the sustainable society.

THE RATIONALE FOR FAMILY PLANNING

True, Charles Westoff showed that for four third-world countries, the overwhelming reason for not using contraception was that people wanted another child (see Chapter 5). Information and access to contraceptive supplies were not the problem. *Motivation* is the critical component of effective birth control. The number of children a couple wants is the best predictor of how many a couple gets. Nevertheless, much can be said for having contraception available, just in case people decide, at last, to use it. Humanitarian reasons are foremost.

Some of the richest people in the world are nationals of third-world countries, but most children born in the third world are born into poverty. Many die prematurely. They can expect a life of servitude, suffering, hunger, and disease. In 1992, Sri Lankan authorities exposed a baby-selling ring. Families, mothers as well as fathers, sell their daughters into prostitution (the Asian-Pacific euphemism is *sex worker*). Bangladeshi girls eight to ten years old are sold at auction. Thailand is known as the largest brothel in the world: Girls are forced into prostitution and even chained to beds. Japan, where legal immigration is rare, carries on a surreptitious trade in young Filipino women: Girls are promised jobs in the entertainment industry and find themselves locked into "monkey cages" for the use of clients.

Voluntary prostitution by poverty-stricken people occurs under conditions almost as bad. Both boys and girls trade sex for food or money in the Philippines. Half of 7 million prostitutes in France are from the third world, mostly South America; pimps smuggle them in, arrange a location, and collect weekly fees. Prostitutes contract and spread disease. Male prostitution in Haiti may be the contact by which AIDS entered the United States. In Asia, AIDS spreads through heterosexual prostitution, particularly along drug routes of the Golden Triangle: Thailand, Burma, and southern China. Few of today's young in the third world can expect anything better than disease, drudgery, exploitation, and early death. Avoiding births is kindlier by far than what already is happening.

Moreover, if people decide to limit family size and do not have access to modern contraception, they use traditional means. Crude abortions, infanticide, abuse of women, and general curtailment of freedoms mushroom as conditions deteriorate and the motivation to control births rises. How much better to *be there* with the contraceptive. How much better if Shipibo women had access to Depo-Provera,* replacing pathetic methods like smearing caustic ointments on the cervix!

Environmental concerns add to the humanitarian imperative. Family-planning dollars are environmentally cost-effective because, even though third-world citizens do not consume or pollute very much per capita, the total environmental impact of so many people is awesome. Whether industrial or agricultural, the sheer scale of human activities is at issue. The poor (even conservationists) pollute and consume. Thus, every birth avoided, anywhere, helps the global environment.

The United States funds international family-planning assistance programs, although such assistance is available only to countries that exclude abortion from the officially sanctioned methods of birth control. Our Mexico City policy—to not use U.S. funds for programs that do abortions—distracts attention from our real contributions. The United States provided more than $250 million of family-planning assistance in the fiscal 1991 Foreign Operations Appropriation bill. This amount is several times greater than that contributed by any other country. Japan contributed less than $60 million to international family-planning assistance efforts in 1991.

Nevertheless, under a formula developed by the Amsterdam Forum, the United States should have given $570 million. The Forum calls for every country to direct 4 percent of its total foreign aid to family planning. The United States is out of compliance because it gives too little to family planning, or too much of all other aid. By halving the latter, the United States would look better on family planning—and could afford much more of it. Setting aside the Amsterdam Forum, it is true that we might do more. And so might others.

*Depo-Provera is a long-lasting, injectable contraceptive.

MICROLOANS: WIN-WIN INVESTMENTS

Microloans are a second strategy for helping people overseas and south of our border. Microloans do not promote belief in vast resources, support vast projects that ignore women, or direct money into the pockets of a few power brokers. Microloans are unlike large-scale government aid, which may no sooner be received than it is diverted to a politician's bank account in Geneva. The rich in third-world countries know that their money is safer elsewhere.

Enter nongovernmental organizations (NGOs) and microloans. These channels are much more likely to meet the needs of women, by helping them to become economically independent. Moreover, funding a self-help project does not give misleading signals about worldwide abundance. Assistance is on a modest scale, a scale people can understand, and a scale where their contributions of sweat equity are significant to the success of the project. Such help is seemly; it does not overwhelm or demean recipients.

A microloan is made directly to an entrepreneur for a simple business venture: a vegetable stand, for instance, a chicken farm, or a backyard clay-figurine workshop. Microloans are funded both privately and by the U.S. Agency for International Development (USAID). In 1991, the USAID microenterprise budget, which includes microlending, was $114 million. The loans are administered by nongovernmental organizations. Examples are Trickle Up (in New York City), Accion International (in Cambridge, Massachusetts), and CARE (in New York City). From London, the Harold Macmillan Trust supports local entrepreneurial efforts to write, print, and sell textbooks: Experienced textbook writers volunteer for stints as advisors; the result is books a third-world country can call its own.

The typical microloan funded in the United States is about $100. The repayment rate approaches 100 percent, which is testimony to how much poor people appreciate credit on fair terms. The secrets of success are that loans bypass the middle-

man, are made by development specialists who work closely
with the local entrepreneur, and do not overwhelm borrowers
with debt. Loans are tailor-made to people and projects. The
modest, mom-and-pop enterprises that develop this way are
necessarily hands-on and owner-operated. Congress, impressed
with the success of microloans, now wants to mandate minimum
loan amounts. If a little is good, more would be better, the
reasoning goes. Bowers (1991) reports that USAID is wisely
resisting.

ECONOMIC OPPORTUNITY FOR WOMEN

The virtues of small loans, made directly to entrepreneurs
and administered by NGOs, lead to the third strategy: creating
jobs for women. Women are about as likely as men to apply for
microloans. In some African tribes, women are the traditional
traders. Yoruba women (in Nigeria) space children (even providing their husband with an extra wife in order to limit their own
exposure to pregnancy). Their choice, rather than childbearing,
is to continue market activities that may take them away from
their village.

Planning for large-scale international aid usually, but un-
wisely, ignores women. Foreigners assume that men can identify
needs and opportunities for the community when, in fact, it is
women who do most of the work and have firsthand knowledge.
The typical development project also directs jobs toward men.
Especially in Africa, this is misguided strategy. It does not build
on traditional roles even where those can be useful. The typical
economist negotiating with third-world government officials
knows little about the local culture and its sex roles. But economic
development that does not explicitly address women's participa-
tion in the labor force ignores a critical element. Worse, it
reinforces the idea that childbearing is a woman's primary
function.

All of this results in women becoming still more economically and socially dependent on men. As women lose influence, they become wholly unable to assert their family-size preferences. Their choice would often be to have fewer children. When male preferences prevail, fertility remains high because men in third-world countries bear much the lesser cost of childrearing, and many dislike both the idea and the mechanics of contraception. So contraception is not used.

Anthropologist W. Penn Handwerker and many others, in research going back twenty years, have shown that fertility declines when women get job opportunities. Handwerker (1991) shows that even uneducated women reduce fertility below replacement level when they become financially independent of boyfriends and husbands. On several Caribbean islands, menial hotel jobs became the harbingers of change.

The relationship between women's work and fertility holds true in many settings. When textile manufacture (employing women) in nineteenth-century Europe evolved from a cottage to a factory setting, fertility rates fell sharply. In recent Taiwanese and Korean experience, women went to work and fertility rates plummeted. Where Caribbean women found work in the tourist industry during the 1980s, the fertility rate fell below replacement level. In the 1960s and 1970s, American and European women went to work in very large numbers and fertility also fell. The connection is clear and the rationale is compelling: Fertility falls when women, or others who control them, can profit from women's work outside the agricultural sector or home. Childcare acquires an opportunity cost if the time spent raising children subtracts from the time available to earn money. When the family standard of living depends partly on women's earnings, husbands also have an incentive to limit family size. Moreover, a woman with independent income does not have to marry young or barter sex or childbearing for support.

Save the Children Fund is a leader in creating economic opportunity for women. In Bangladesh, it has addressed women's needs with projects that are small scale and build on local efforts. Savings cooperatives help women invest in simple technology such as mechanically operated sewing machines. Sometimes sewing results in financial independence, sometimes not. Men also see the advantage of putting women to work. Reportedly, one Muslim man has married the four allowable wives and has got them all sewing commercially. Exploitative? Probably, yes. But for Bangladesh and, arguably, the women themselves, that is better than pregnancy.

Even transfer payments that make women financially independent may have a bearing on fertility: Some women who became infertile allegedly as a result of the Bhopal gas disaster in India suffered abuse at their husband's hands because of infertility. But, reports Renu Kapoor (1992), the abuse ceased and power relations reversed when the women were awarded small disability stipends. The lesson may be that small sums could be paid for *continuing* use of some highly effective contraceptive such as Norplant implants. Past experience shows, however, that the program should be made available only to women whose family size is still very small. Otherwise it is open to abuse by those who see it as child support and are actually enabled to raise their family-size target.

Unfortunately, employment for women is not at the top of most planners' agenda despite the many studies which show its effect on fertility. It is irrational—but not mysterious—that development projects have failed to target women. Money sticks to the fingers that touch it first. Large sums, especially government-to-government transfers, seldom bypass men. Women are last in line and, too often, last in the minds of their countrymen.

More problematic is the belief that educating women, *per se*, lowers fertility. In some parts of Africa, even highly educated women who are unemployed or marginally employed continue to bear many children. Handwerker (1991) shows that they get resources only through men, and that their best economic strategy is to have serial sexual relationships, strengthening ties to as many men as possible through bearing their children. It might be better to defer education and use the money to create jobs. Simple tasks (repetitively assembling electronic parts, operating a sewing machine, working as a chambermaid) do not depend on literacy but are associated with declining fertility.

Studies linking women's education to declining fertility are largely correlational, and one learns to distrust those. Faith in education may be part of the unfounded myth that modernization, development, lower infant mortality, and a general level of rising prosperity cause lower fertility. But it is seen repeatedly that declining fertility accompanies economic gain only when one's own effort and savings are demonstrably necessary to eventual success.

A BOOTSTRAP BANK

The three principles that do work (small-scale enterprises, self-help, and involving women) are nowhere better shown than in Baisaisa, Egypt. Baisaisa developed into a prosperous village through the dedicated efforts of Dr. Salah Arafa, chair of the Science Department at the American University in Cairo.

The Baisaisa bank is a bootstrap operation. It started with a few families pooling savings to form a cooperative: One family borrowed the pooled funds to buy a knitting machine and designated an unmarried daughter to learn the skill and produce knitwear for sale. Initial proceeds from sales were returned to the cooperative, with interest, to pay off the loan. Now a second family that had put in capital could borrow. Another knitting machine was purchased. Other villagers became interested and, in order to get in line for the privilege of borrowing, put up their equity to join the cooperative. More families were able to draw on the cooperative's capital. Villagers now had a reason to save, the principle of capital accumulation was established, and young women had a way to earn money. The village began to thrive from manufacturing sales. Best of all, women wanted to delay marriage—or, if married, to limit childbearing.

How did Dr. Arafa do it?

It was slow going. Dr. Arafa picked a poor village where he

had connections, north of Cairo, similar to the village where he grew up, for his experiment. On Friday afternoons, he sat in the local meeting house and talked. He talked about hopelessness: no way to help oneself or get a toehold, too many babies, daughters' labor nearly worthless (better they marry young and leave home), and the grinding poverty.

It took Dr. Arafa, not an economist, a year of weekly visits. But he and the villagers invented a bank. The villagers and Dr. Arafa figured out equity contributions to raise capital, the right to borrow being contingent on an equity contribution. They set out interest charges, repayment schedules, and interest-bearing savings accounts so that families not immediately able to raise the equity for joining could work toward eventual membership in the cooperative.

Baisaisa is bootstrap. So are grassroots efforts said to be taking hold in other parts of Africa after decades of mutually disenchanting international aid and government policies have failed.

The pitfalls of foreign aid and interference with market mechanisms are legion. Nevertheless, ways of helping can be discovered.

THE BEST AND WORST OF FOREIGN AID

The lessons of microloans and opportunities for women are *not* that foreign aid has no role. The lesson is that modesty, frugality and personalized help with local entrepreneurial activity are crucial. International aid goes astray by trying to implement large-scale programs which involve bureaucrats, are insensitive to local and ongoing economic activities, and damage or deplete natural resources. The single most destructive aspect of foreign aid may be that it dispels the former cultural balance based on understanding limits. Large-scale foreign aid reinforces unrealistic expectations and belief in abundance.

Couples raise their family-size target when they think prosperity is on the horizon. Although children are rewarding in many ways, they are costly to raise. Children can be a type of consumption good, and when people get a windfall, they want more of them. The result for a nation is population growth. Africa, the recipient of large-scale foreign aid and investment through the late 1970s, now has the highest population growth rate in that continent's history, 3.2 percent per year. Fertility rose in the decades after World War II as though in response to international aid and economic activity.

The actual amount of foreign aid to third-world countries, both bilateral or funded through international agencies such as the World Bank and the International Monetary Fund (IMF), is steadily diminishing. Nevertheless, the rhetoric of foreign aid goes on. Calls on private banks to forgive debt and make new loans are examples. How often have we heard it said that the only impediment to "growth and development" is the foreign debt of a country? But do growth and development help? Or do they, on the contrary, create illusions which are obstacles to a constructive response?

MANAGED IMMIGRATION

A fourth strategy for helping is to use limited U.S. immigration visas as an incentive for reducing fertility abroad. This is a totally new concept and would work this way. Instead of giving preference to "family reunification," which presently accounts for over 90 percent of legal immigration to the United States, one could emphasize the fertility rate of the country of origin (not a consideration under present law, or even a thought).

Immigration visas might be used as an incentive to lower fertility to replacement level in whole countries, in order to earn the right for some of their nationals to immigrate to the United States. This incentive would have broad appeal because many countries remain vastly overpopulated and resource-short for years after attaining replacement-level fertility. That is, they continue to suffer even though their citizens are making every effort to act responsibly.

Countries whose nationals would have preference for visas under this system (but the list would grow) now include: Antigua-Barbuda, Australia, Barbados, Canada, Cuba, Martinique, the Netherlands Antilles, Japan, Hong Kong, Mauritius, Macao, Singapore, South Korea, Taiwan, all Europe (except Albania), and New Zealand. Countries that might soon get on the list are Cyprus, Israel, Réunion, Thailand, China, and Uruguay.

Countries now using the United States as a safety valve for excess population but not making satisfactory strides toward reducing fertility would find their visas eliminated. This list includes all of Central America and the Caribbean (except those countries listed above), India, Mexico, the Philippines, Cambodia, and Vietnam.

Why not? The alternative is to continue acting as a safety valve for excess population from countries whose main product is people—and whose fertility may be staying high because of reliance on emigration.

The United States can help by refusing to send false signals. The message of redistribution makes good politics, but has disastrous effects over the long run. Belief in renewable wealth and inexhaustible nature will doom first the countries where the weight of population already is heaviest. Large-scale aid gives a false signal about resources. So do the relatively open borders fostered by current immigration policy. These may hurt, rather than help, the very countries for which, geographically and historically, the United States holds the greatest attachment and concern.

MODELING THE SUSTAINABLE SOCIETY

On the positive side, the United States can become a good example. We will not be very credible in preaching environmental responsibility until we redirect our own lifestyles and policies.

The United States must stabilize its population size and reduce consumption. Our present population growth of 58,000 persons per week promotes neither a better quality of life for Americans nor a positive image as world leader. Our goal must be the sustainability of our system over the long run.

The United States must intend to be self-reliant—which we are assuming that the balance-of-trade deficit is righted and all debt to international creditors gets repaid. For the future, Americans should try to determine what is the carrying capacity of the United States. The *product* of population size and resource use per capita has to adjust to a level that is sustainable over the long term. If we fail to bring national needs into balance with nature through forethought and self-restraint, nature will make the cut for us. Should this Armageddon come to pass, we will have lost the capacity to help ourselves, much less others.

Conservation, Incentives, and Ethics

Conservation depends upon getting the incentives right. This is not a new idea. Plato and the Bible both have it. It follows from modern economic theory. Yet the idea that self-interest motivates people to conserve, or abuse, resources gives rise to a great deal of heated controversy. Some ethical systems teach that self-interest is not a legitimate motive, presenting it instead as mean or dishonorable. "Altruism," acting *against* one's own interest in order to benefit another, is held out as the ideal for ethical conduct. Exhortations to be altruistic discount human nature, that is, other players in the game are all too ready to take without giving back fair value. The argument about ethical conduct and human nature continues on many levels, and at least some of these bear on the environmentalist's incentive to conserve.

THE UNREGULATED COMMONS

In a now-famous paper published in 1968, biologist Garrett Hardin explains why a scarce resource is inevitably used up when those who use it most intensively and fastest get the most benefit. Hardin's paper is entitled "The Tragedy of the Commons." It shows how, in an unregulated commons, the advice to "use it or lose it" takes on a new and decidedly unfunny meaning.

A "commons" is a resource treated as though it belongs to all. When anyone can claim a resource simply on the grounds that he needs to use it, you have a commons.

The system may work so long as demand is low. A tragedy of the commons is in the making if demand rises to a level where a resource is being damaged from overuse. Seeing that the resource is being used up, some people are likely to increase their take; those who stand back, lose out. Soon, those who were inclined to conserve the resource stop being players. These types have been outcompeted. The scenario applies equally to use of an unregulated commons for grazing livestock (Hardin's hypothetical example) or other, even industrial, settings. In exploiting a geothermal field, a fishery, or a forest where supply is limited and access to the resource is unrestricted, he does best who takes out the most, fastest.

The condition foretold as the tragedy of the commons is unfolding on Palawan Island, the Philippines, which contains the country's largest remaining expanse of unbroken forest. Losses here account for the Philippines being number one in the world for rapidity of losing forest cover. Anthropologist James Eder (1990) concludes that population growth is the underlying cause of the disaster. The indigenous tribal community is both growing from within and lacking in political power to resist migrants from other overpopulated areas of the Philippines.

Countrywide population growth, holding at 2.4 to 2.8 percent a year (a doubling time of about twenty-seven years), is the underlying factor in overexploitation of the forest, but the slash-and-burn agriculture of the tribal people is taking the blame. In fact, immigration into Palawan Island is pushing tribal Filipinos out of more and more of their forest land. With a smaller area to use, they are forced to shorten the fallow part of the agricultural cycle, that is, the years in which forest plots are left to regenerate. Whereas a cultivator used to revisit a plot about every fifteen years, use it for two or three years, then leave it to reforest, the fallow period now is less than five years. Moreover, tribal Filipinos see the forest disappear to commercial logging and know that their use-rights in trees are no more secure than their forest plots. The best remaining strategy is to join in the plunder. Thus, they have added logging to their traditional cultivation of shifting garden sites.

This kind of impact from logging and slash-and-burn (swidden) cultivation, driven by population growth, is increasing worldwide and with ever more serious consequences for long-term productivity. The number of swidden agriculturalists grows by 4 to 12 percent annually, both because of their own high fertility (recall the Shipibo in the Peruvian Amazon) and because migrants move in from other, more crowded places. Loss of biological diversity accompanies the increase in the human population. As forests disappear, species loss accelerates. Today, plants and animals are disappearing at the rate of 4,000 to 6,000 species a year.

Fisheries in international waters are another example of a commons that is hard to regulate and subject to overexploitation. Dwindling fish stocks and difficulty in allocating shares lead to rapid use of the resource and give impetus to ever-more-sophisticated technology. Radar tracks schools of fish, and drift nets (used by the Japanese through 1991 despite outcry over the slaughter of whales, seabirds, and dolphins) effect a near-total harvest. Fisheries easily become an unregulated commons, even in domestic waters. New England fisheries, for example, face no foreign competition within the twelve-mile coastal limit. But with no regulation on the size of the fishing fleet, the sophistication of technology, or poundage landed, stocks of some species have been reduced to levels from which recovery may not be possible.

USE-RIGHTS AND REGULATED COMMONS

Traditions of tenure can be diverse, but foresters Louise Fortmann and John Bruce (1988) find that the expectation of enjoying a longterm benefit is a feature of all successful forest management. Their research on several continents shows a diversity of workable traditions for tenure in trees, but a commons is least likely of all to promote conservation. Private ownership of land on which trees grow, or a system which gives secure ownership of trees to the person who plants them, are two arrangements that encourage conservation.

Those commons that work have a long-established tradition of use-rights within a well-defined community of users. People who do not belong to that community do not get access to the resource. A variation found in the Senegal River Basin depends on giving outsiders use-rights so long as graze and crops are plentiful but expelling them in seasons or whole years of scarcity. In fact, destruction of the English commons did not occur as readily as Hardin imagined it because use was regulated: Only members of a given village had access, or use-rights, to particular lands. In the same spirit, Tibetan nomads (technically, transhumants) who visit mountain pastures only during summer months have fixed destinations. Tradition governs which family's animals use what pasture. Use-rights, explain Goldstein and Beall (1990), are clear.

POPULATION GROWTH AND THE COMMONS

Even a regulated commons breaks down if a community is growing rapidly from within. Growth of human and cattle population in the Sahel is one example. English landowners barely forestalled overexploitation of the land ensuing from population growth in the eighteenth and nineteenth centuries. The Enclosure Acts barred villagers from using the commons as had been their privilege, and destruction of the agricultural base was avoided.

No conservation traditions governing use of pasture, forest products, or other resources survive pressure from growing populations where all have a legitimate claim. The gradual movement toward more intensive and ultimately destructive use resembles the shortening of fallow periods in shifting-agriculture economies beset by overpopulation. A technology can be benign under conditions of low population density but will devastate an environment when use intensifies. Slash-and-burn (swidden) agriculture is a sustainable system so long as garden plots have fifteen or twenty years to recover from bouts of cultivation. But plots become weed-ridden, exhausted, and hardly worth the effort of cultivation when population growth forces more frequent utilization.

THE MODERN COMMONS AND CONSERVATION

Private ownership is one mechanism that avoids the tragedy of the commons. Regulated public ownership, such as with parks, is another so long as squatting is never tolerated and public management is trusted. But whenever the allocation and rights to future benefits become insecure, the individually "best" strategy is rapid consumption. For example, U.S. loggers stepped up the pace of cutting the Northwest's old-growth timber in expectation that the spotted owl habitat would be protected. Significantly, this abuse of a very slowly renewing resource occurred on public land where individual use-rights are inherently insecure. U.S. logging companies which harvest and replant their own timber resource—on privately held land—have a greater incentive to conserve, and they often do. Efforts to regulate (a way of commonizing) a privately managed resource should be judicious or they undermine confidence in owners' rights to future use.

Sometimes politics creates a commons unnecessarily. In the twentieth century, the system of political philosophy identified with the Soviet Union made the pure commons an ideal. Its ethos lingers on. The possibility of a commons looms over every claim that it is equitable for persons to have access to resources on the basis of need. The gist of it is the communist ideal, "*From* each according to his abilities and *to* each according to his needs."

In the west, philosopher John Rawls (1971) dressed up this message as the ethic of "distributive justice." The idea is that the distribution of wealth is truly fair only if each of us would be contented to draw lots for our share and abide by the result. This ethos would ensure equity, Rawls believes, because no one would want a skewed distribution of wealth if he ran the risk of drawing a low-end portion. A distributive-justice type of ethic clearly implies taking from some and giving to others. The number of political yea-sayers to distributive justice is striking since, in practice, this creates a commons—and the destructiveness of an unregulated commons, especially in the context of growing numbers who need, is now known.

DISINCENTIVES TO CONSERVATION

A belief that it is fair to redistribute wealth according to need undercuts the basis of ownership. But without assured rights to the *future* use of a resource, what happens to the incentive to save? Saving takes discipline and self-denial and means postponing consumption. Saving starts out with a big handicap, because enjoyment which might be had today is put off until tomorrow. Add in insecurity over rights to future benefits, and the incentive to save is overwhelmed. Now what happens to conservation, since saving is at its heart? Both saving and conservation depend on expectations that future enjoyment will compensate for present self-denial. Uncertainty undercuts conservation, whereas conveying a resource with as much certainty as social institutions can muster encourages it.

The commons and the redistribution ethic not only undercut incentives to conserve but, in a vastly overpopulated world, may be impracticable. Even division of the Earth's resources into absolutely equal shares—a theoretical possibility—would not provide a decent livelihood for everyone today, and still less tomorrow as population growth continues.

In fact, division into more equal shares has been tried on a national scale. In the third world, where the privileged few often hold vast (almost feudal) estates, some governments have made redistribution of wealth a priority. In 1977, the Peruvian military government of Gen. Velasco decided to control the price of milk so that the poor could have milk. The prices of inputs into the milk production process were not controlled, however, so it became uneconomic to produce milk; the producer lost money on every drop. Consumers were initially pleased with the low price but were less pleased as milk became scarce. Near Lima, one of the largest dairies was able to survive only by selling much of its production on the black market, where demand was strong and, of course, the price uncontrolled.

Milk became still scarcer in Lima with implementation of another redistributive plan, Gen. Velasco's program for *propriedad social*. Ownership of the dairies was turned over to the collectivity of workers, while former owners were compensated with (worthless) bonds that could be used only for investment in government enterprises. Workers proved no more able than previous owners to operate a dairy under price controls. They broke even only by pricing their own labor at zero. They could pay themselves, however, by decapitalizing the operation. And they did. Equipment, machinery, bulls, and cows, all were sold or eaten. And since ownership was held in common, rapid consumption became the way for individuals to maximize their benefit from the proceeds.

The consumption binge lasted about nine months. The dairy no longer is a dairy. Little milk is for sale in Lima. A small cheese factory, built nearby at about this time with USAID funds, never has produced cheese; its milk supply never materialized because the market-driven price incentives which would have stimulated production were quashed. The net of Gen. Velasco's gambit was that Lima's poor could afford milk for the month or so that milk was available, many people lost jobs, no one was employed in the cheese factory, and no one has domestic cheese.

Variants of this experiment (different commodities, other places) have been tried many times. Land redistribution has also been tried. The large number of landless peasants means that redistribution results in very small individual plots. Small holdings get smaller when inheritance further subdivides land. (An extension of the redistribution idea is that all children should get equal shares.) The smaller and smaller units reach a point where subsistence needs overwhelm all possibility of protecting longterm environmental carrying capacity. The threat of famine is a quite sufficient inducement for planting every last hectare in food crops, which sooner or later results in cultivation of marginal lands. Hillsides, poor soils such as often support rain forest, or drought-prone land come under the plow. Land blows away, washes away, or becomes rock-hard. Cynthia Green (1991) with Johns Hopkins' Population Information Program puts it this way: "As resources become scarcer, efforts to obtain them entail higher costs and greater environmental damage."

A CONSERVATION ETHIC

These few examples suggest that equity issues need to be reexamined in terms of the global goal of conservation. A conservation ethic may require a renewed acceptance of uneven distribution. Not only human nature—people are usually motivated by self-interest so a scarce resource held in common is soon destroyed—but poverty itself forces this rethinking. Nations, institutions, families, and individuals can afford to conserve only if they are not compelled to consume their wealth, including natural capital, as a last-ditch survival strategy. A degree of distributional equity is probably a luxury available only to relatively rich nations with stable populations.

Urging redistribution on policymakers in poor countries is almost certainly inappropriate. Hard thinking and difficult decisions seem in order because, where there is overpopulation, those who are destitute will consume, before they die, the future potential productivity of any part of the environment to which they have access. Witness the Sahel, Ethiopia, the Sudan, Haiti, the Philippines, Vietnam, Nepal, and Bangladesh.

A tragic testament to today's destitution and overpopulation is that those who can afford to conserve may be in the minority. But wealth does not guarantee conservation. Control over some critical minimum of resources as well as secure rights to benefit from them in the future are necessary conditions for conservation, but alone they may not be sufficient. Destruction of resources results not only from unregulated use of whatever is held in common, but also from owners of resources gaining more by using them up quickly. V. S. Naipaul (1989), a widely read commentator on the third world, states that the element of society most upsetting to him is "cynicism." He explains cynicism as "Fouling one's own nest at home and feathering another abroad. The cynicism bred perhaps by this availability of emigration abroad, which is very demoralizing. People are able to create a mess at home, build dreadful skyscrapers in cities like Bombay, yet buy nice apartments for themselves in foreign countries that are better organized."

The mobility of monetized capital makes it difficult to envision a sufficient incentive, or workable enforcement mechanism, to tie wealthy individuals to land or any particular natural resource so that they have a stake in conserving its longterm productivity. Yet this must eventually be part of a solution. Whereas conspicuous consumption has been a sign of wealth, conservation would ideally be tomorrow's status symbol.

The well-off are no different from others except that they do have a choice. Like anyone else, they are generally motivated to protect the Earth's natural resources just insofar as it is in their interest to do so. The very rich have global mobility, and increasingly neither people (nor corporations) appear to have the loyalty to country that economists such as David Ricardo and John Maynard Keynes took for granted. "This is my own, my native land" is a sentiment too little heard. Citizens of the world are patriots of nowhere. In the first quarter of 1989, for example, nationals of the third world's fifteen largest debtor nations were holding $350 billion in foreign banks, up from less than $100 billion in 1980. This is money that passed briefly through a third-world country either as loans or aid from international sources or as export earnings. Too often the exports represent depletion of nonrenewable natural capital.

Some of the wealthy may not feel bound by a national identity (although one wonders increasingly where there is left to go). But most workers, with fewer resources, are stuck with the hand their country deals them. Few Americans, indeed, contemplate leaving their country.

On the other hand, some industries and multinational corporations seem to espouse globalism at the expense of loyalty to any nation. The export of high-value-added jobs and especially the import of cheap labor to compete with one's own show a disregard of country (see Chapters 15–17). They amount to letting the few ruin one niche and then move on to another. That it happens means that the incentive system and ethics have gone awry. And for this, government bears some responsibility.

Economists John Culbertson (1989) and Herman E. Daly of the World Bank writing with ethicist John B. Cobb, Jr. (Cobb and Daly, 1990) tackle the problem. These authors agree that the possibility of perpetual economic growth, the neoclassical myth, is the underlying problem. They see a zero-sum game as being a good approximation of reality. Thus, both free trade and a liberal immigration policy betray the interests of wage-earners in countries with a relatively higher standard of living. The one may result in exporting jobs, and the other brings surplus labor to the United States. Cobb and Daly (1990) write that both free trade and a liberal immigration policy run the risk of undermining "the national community that embraces both labor and capital." Such policies also undercut the conservation ethic, which depends upon confidence that one can benefit tomorrow from what one saves today.

PUBLIC MANAGEMENT OF RESOURCES

The national interest is also betrayed through negligence in pursuit of environmental goals. Too often, government proves itself an unreliable caretaker. In the recent past, the Brazilian government regarded international efforts to protect the rain forest as intrusive. Worse, tax policy rewarded those who exploited the trees. Most virgin-forest logs from the Amazon are exported to Japan, and the government gave tax credits to encourage earning foreign exchange. So Brazilian nationals and foreigners jointly lumbered off the rain forest, sold the denuded land, and deposited untaxed profits in offshore banks. This treatment of forest lands as "resources to be exploited and as space for its fast-growing population" was ostensibly a public response to populist demand, writes Cohen (1989). Conservation came in second. Brazil, arguably, came in third.

Economist Richard Stroup (1991) concludes that

> Most tropical forests currently being clearcut do not have private owners deciding whether to preserve or to harvest. Most are on government lands. Frequently they are being harvested through government-subsidized projects or by citizens operating under government regulations that permit ownership only by those who clearcut and "improve" the land. There is some evidence that sustained-yield management would in fact be financially preferable in the absence of subsidies and government homesteading rules to speed the clearcutting.

U.S. Government policies also support unwise exploitation of natural capital. For example, sale of cheap (below-market-price) crop insurance encourages planting grain in the fragile, drought-prone prairie grasslands of Oklahoma and other dry states. When the crop fails, the U.S. taxpayer pays for it. The farmer's gamble on rain is, for him, nearly costless and risk-free. Meanwhile, the soil erodes and some farmers tap underground water (the Ogalalla aquifer) for irrigation.

Similarly, water subsidies throughout the west encourage agriculture in areas that are naturally desert. Some estimates suggest that the price charged Southern California farmers for water does not cover the cost of operations, much less amortization of the capital invested in dams, aqueducts, and so on. Given the price incentives, flood irrigation (which wastes water) will continue until salinization threatens to deprive farmers of their use of land altogether!

Stroup suggests that government control of productive enterprises and natural resources almost inevitably leads to waste. Stewardship is problematic because bureaucrats are not managing the resource for their own future benefit, so they are likely to be swayed by incentives that have little to do with longterm productivity. Carlson and Bernstam (1991) describe the Soviet economy as an extreme case of bureaucrats putting personal goals above best management of resources. The longterm carrying capacity in the USSR was significantly sacrificed, and without corresponding benefit to those governed.

THE NECESSARY CONDITION FOR CONSERVATION

Most arrangements for control of resources (the owners' collective, the bureaucrat manager, the internationally oriented corporate owner, and the jet-setting owner) lack one thing: linkage of individual longterm benefit to a particular piece of land, resource, community, or nation. Lacking this connectedness in place and time, control is not conducive to conservation. The rare patriot remains attached to land and country despite all else. Policy should nurture loyalty—not bank on it.

Waste and degradation of natural resources become normal practice when the private, local incentive to conserve the carrying capacity disappears. If everyone owns or uses a resource, who is going to conserve it? The consumption and loss of natural capital is inevitable when ownership is ambiguous. The key appears to be accountability to one's own future and that of one's children within a secure niche. Without control, without secure rights to longterm benefits, or with the possibility of moving on, conservation is a sometime thing.

When the condition of irrevocable linkage to country and

rights to land are not in place—and in the global economy they increasingly are not—ways to promote connectedness and conservation are not obvious. Their essential element, nonetheless, is a climate in which citizens can trust that their own and their children's rights to future use of assets remain secure. Thus, all efforts fail if domestic population growth continues. Within this framework, national resources may be protected through either regulation or market incentives including taxation and user fees.

CONSERVATION THROUGH REGULATION

After decades of regulation, certain flaws in this method of control have become apparent. Private or public entities often comply with regulation, usually at great cost, without getting the desired result. For example, mandated requirements for automobile fuel efficiency meet widespread resistance and, when implemented, have little to show. Only new cars meet the higher efficiency standards, but because their cost is higher or performance lower, consumers often delay buying them. The fleet turns over slowly, so polluting, less efficient vehicles stay on the road.

But if taxes on gasoline are raised, market incentives go right to work. Some people save by driving less; others shop for the most efficient car and are more (rather than less) likely to trade in older models. And when car manufacturers see what the consumer buys, efficiency comes on fast.

CONSERVATION THROUGH MARKET INCENTIVES

Across the board, market incentives are more promising than regulations because they focus on results rather than on procedure. For example, exploitation of virgin forests can be discouraged by taxing each old-growth log that is cut; call it a severance tax. The entrepreneur who harvested only trees he (or a former owner) had planted could avoid the tax. Taxes may also be scheduled to promote the desired result: For example, no tax charged for logging a hardwood that was planted to replace a hardwood or less desirable species; some tax on pine that had replaced hardwood; more tax on logging virgin pine; and the most tax on logging virgin hardwood. (Computers could aid in developing a "genealogy of trees," that is, what follows what in the forest.) Conservation is encouraged by taxing—and never subsidizing—activities that deplete nonrenewable natural capital.

Similarly, taxes on emissions that pollute air and water encourage both prevention and cleaning up at the emission source. Alternately, the government can define a tolerable level of pollution and sell rights to pollute up to this limit; a given industry or factory makes an economic decision on whether to buy pollution rights or invest in cleaner technology. These market solutions were incorporated into the 1990 Clean Air Act.

NO COSTLESS SOLUTION

Regardless of the means used to encourage conservation and discourage pollution, business justifiably fears that the added costs reduce their competitiveness in the global economy. With unmanaged trade, capital investment and jobs do flow to countries that accept environmental degradation, just as they flow to countries with low labor costs. Witness Korea, Thailand, and Mexico.

The answer cannot be to lower one's own standards for environmental quality, no more than to undercut American workers' wages with cheap immigrant labor or to accept unlimited goods from countries that produce at any human cost. As an industrialized country, the United States can compete through innovation, automation, and employment of a skilled labor force, plus protection of its markets against other industrialized countries that resort to unfair trade practices. Bilateral trade agreements should aim for equal trade in the sum of high-value-added goods. In short, fair trade plus higher productivity.

America the beautiful is a clean and bountiful America, for tomorrow and tomorrow and tomorrow. The American way is to let incentives work. Even where the global economy loosens ties to community and place, the right incentives, structured through national governments, can be found. Citizens, labor and business alike, will protect and conserve land, resources, and environmental quality where they have secure rights to the future benefits that flow from their effort and frugality.

13

Limiting Factors

Plenty of *almost* everything most of the time does not sustain a biological system over the long run. Living populations are limited by whatever essential factor is in shortest supply under the least favorable conditions. Having sufficient fresh, clean water in most years is not enough. One season of drought can disperse a population that depends on this supply.

A single bad season does not usually break down human societies, however, because man devises backup systems. Expedients such as drilling for groundwater, aqueducts to transport water from distant places, reservoirs, or water processing let human populations survive even under desert conditions. Ultimately, though, limits show up in the substitute systems.

WATER

Take Southern California. Much of California is a natural desert, and drought is not an unexpected event. Fresh water is a candidate for being the limiting resource. Indeed, after several years of drought, agricultural users of water line up against urban users to fight over a diminishing supply. Meanwhile, further curtailment of supply gets more probable. The water table is dropping, and more demands are made on river water. Users downstream from Los Angeles hold water rights, and as population grows—in Arizona perhaps—these claims may be exercised.

Aquifers bring water to Los Angeles from 400 miles away.

The long-distance transport of water requires large capital invest-ments as well as the forbearance (codified in water law) of upstream users. A new problem upstream is that the delta smelt may go extinct, and environmentalists assert *its* rights to water.

The delta smelt live in the estuaries formed by the Sacra-mento and San Joaquin Rivers north of San Francisco. The estuaries provide a large share of Southern California's water; drawdown from the rivers is so great that seawater now runs ten miles up the San Joaquin. Possibly the changed water flow, maybe pesticides, but more likely the increased salinity from backed-up seawater have taken a toll. In twenty years, the population of the delta smelt plunged an estimated 90 percent—a loss from which they may be unable to recover. (A rule of thumb for another fish, guppies, is that the population dwindles to extinction on its own once it has been reduced by 60 percent from normal density.) Environmentalists are alarmed not only for the smelt but for other life in the ecosystem. They say that the smelt is an *indicator species*; if it is in trouble, other populations are threatened, too. Indeed, another species is almost gone: The Chinook salmon, which once ran up the Sacramento 150,000 strong, numbered just 230 individuals in the winter, 1991, count.

EXTINCTIONS

The human species rolls on. The more of us, the worse for most others. Extinction is getting serious. Norman Myers (1991) writes in *Science* that ecologists are not crying wolf: Just eighteen imminently threatened areas contain 20 percent of the world's plant species (about 50,000) and each of these is accompanied by twenty to fifty animal species. Myers warns, "So in just these eighteen hot spot areas, we face the prospect of an extinction spasm to surpass anything that has occurred since the late Cretaceous crash." He refers to the last curtain call for dino-saurs, about 65 million years ago. The comparison is stark.

Species extinction hits close to home. Florida has liquidated 50 percent of its native forest, which continues to disappear at a rate of 1 percent per year. Only 20 percent of the original hardwoods are left in the Mississippi Valley, and replacement by uniform stands of (less valuable) pine continues. Forests nationwide are fragmented, thus not useful for animals needing to maintain genetic diversity and access to seasonal feeding grounds. Whereas we have plenty of "wildlife," specifically animals that can live in proximity to humans, the United States has lost its vast, former diversity of fauna.

The smelt extinction represents a larger question, one which may contain the urgency of a constraint. How far do backup systems compensate for nature? How many, or what percentage, of species can we humans eliminate before the threatened species is us? Who wants to find out? Some Californians seem readier than others.

BACK-UP SYSTEMS

Southern California might reduce its draw on the San Joaquin and Sacramento Rivers, but do not bank on it. Even with that water, they are water-short. Expensive alternate sources are under consideration. One option for Los Angeles is desalinization of seawater, and Saudi Arabian experts in the process have been brought in as consultants. However, the process is energy-intensive. Southern California does not have nearly as much cheap natural gas as Saudi Arabia, while its water needs are far greater. Desalination would take six times as much energy as pumping the same amount of fresh water through the California Aqueduct. If oil were used as the energy source, it would take 81 million barrels of oil per year to meet the anticipated annual needs (2.7 million acre-feet of water) of the Metropolitan Water District of Southern California. At $40 a barrel, the price of oil during the 1991 Gulf War, the annual cost of the 81 million barrels would be $3.2 billion. And Metropolitan Water District officials point out that "Metropolitan's entire 1990–1991 annual operating budget is $628 million" (Hallwachs, 1991).

Desalinization plants would have to be sited on the coastline, so land acquisition is another cost. Add to this the infrastructure (massive pipeline) and one is talking real money. Moreover, depending upon what energy source is used for desalinization, the release of volatile organic compounds (VOCs) into the atmosphere would increase, with consequences for smog (tropospheric ozone) as well as global warming. Solar collectors, harnessing tides, geothermal differentials, and winds will not produce enough energy with foreseeable technology.

Technological optimists have suffered a recent setback in the prospect for geothermal energy. In 1985, expectations for the Geysers, a field of steaming fumaroles one hundred fifteen miles north of San Francisco, ran high. The Pacific Gas and Electric Utility Company foresaw steady expansion ("No definite estimate of ultimate capacity is possible," they said) and no need to restrict access (Kerr, 1991). Six years later, $3.5 billion had been invested in plant, but steam delivery was dropping by 11 percent a year. The field is running dry. The heat still is trapped in underground rocks, but so many users have tapped into the steam that the groundwater and pressure are nearly gone. Richard Kerr calls this debacle "the geothermal tragedy of the commons" and quotes a frustrated executive of the Calpine Corp. of Santa Rosa: " 'Put simply, there are too many straws in the teapot.' "

The Geysers debacle is all of that. In California, one apparently needs water to release energy, but a principal use of energy is to get water. Will salt or wastewater infusions into the Geysers be a solution? Is nuclear power the only answer? Will California go nuclear so that the state can augment the water supply, accommodate more people, and increase the scale of industry?

So, what is the limiting factor in a desert? Water? Energy? Air quality? Hazardous waste? None of the above? One thing is certain. *We can't do just one thing.* Systems are linked and technological solutions often have unforeseen side effects. Since natural systems have evolved in balance over time, most disturbances (i.e., side effects) have a negative impact.

WATER POLITICS

California may have to make do with its present water sources or, maybe, with less. Large populations may not survive in Southern California—not in the long run. The final struggle for water could be violent; in the meantime, water will simply be rationed—either by becoming high-priced or by bureaucratic per capita allotment. Political decisions will be made about whether to subsidize water use by the poor.

For the time being, most urban users appear to be allied. They are portrayed as pitted against farming interests to see who gets what and for what price. A 3 percent reduction in agricultural water use, advocates say, would be equivalent to a 25 percent reduction in urban use. The urban argument—made by developers—is that agriculture wastes irrigation water and that fruit, vegetable, rice, and livestock growers have been subsidized for too long by water that is priced below its true cost. Misallocation is compounded because some crops qualify for price supports.

Farming interests point out that they have begun to conserve water and that massive changeovers to drip irrigation are underway. They also note that low-cost water is the basis for low-cost food—which urbanites buy. What will happen if California growers are forced out of business?

California produce is shipped all over the United States, which raises another stirring question: How much interest have the other forty-nine states in what happens to California's farms? Can a consumer in Denver—also water-short—afford to be a bystander while Southern California cities grow and exert ever-more-effective political demands for larger shares of water? Or what about the taxpayer in Chicago who may find that he or she is contributing to federal subsidies of desalinization plants for Los Angeles? Stand back, folks. This is about to get interesting. And bear in mind that water is only one resource—one type of natural capital—that is a potential limiting factor on population size.

ARABLE LAND

A shortage of water is hard to distinguish from a longage* of people. It focuses our attention on the big question: Just what is the longterm carrying capacity of the United States? Western states' water fights are bringing a number of sobering issues to light. For example, the Imperial Valley north of San Diego is suffering from soil salinization. The salt residue brought on by irrigation is making soils less productive. So some agricultural areas will be phased out even if growers make their water claims stick.

Lands which are losing their fertility or are lost to agriculture altogether can be found throughout the United States. Over 300,000 acres of irrigated land have been abandoned in Arizona because the groundwater table has been pumped below the level where recovery is cost-effective. Water which took thousands of years to accumulate is being "mined" wholesale from the Ogallala aquifer; in parts of Oklahoma, the groundwater table falls by ten feet a year. Nebraska's Central Platte Natural Resources District also warns of an end to irrigation agriculture. Groundwater levels are dropping in 72 percent of the state's wells, and only a series of wet years can prevent loss of irrigation in parts of Nebraska.

In the United States as a whole, irrigation problems, erosion, and urbanization together account for the loss of 3 million acres of agricultural land each year. Often the best agricultural soils are lost to urban development. Towns are established because of their

Longage is a useful term. It was coined by Garrett Hardin, (Emeritus) Professor of Biology at the University of California, Santa Barbara.

attractiveness to settlers, usually agriculturalists of some kind. When towns become cities and then sprawl into suburbs, the finest feature of the site, fertile soil, is buried under pavement. Columbus, Ohio, is a sad example. Corn fields that still surrounded Ohio State University and residential Bexley in 1945 are sown now to concrete; the city's corn products sprout from taco bars.

Topsoil loss from farms still in production poses another threat. Iowa has lost 50 percent of its topsoil from wind and water erosion in the one-hundred-fifty years that it has been intensively cultivated. Five tons of topsoil loss a year is about average on an acre of good, flat land under plow agriculture. Hilly land is more vulnerable. Flooding in the spring of 1990 cost parts of Ohio thirty tons of topsoil per acre. The principle that the best land is the first lost to urbanization means that agriculture on less-productive acreage intensifies over time. Eventually, cultivation shifts to marginal, more vulnerable lands, such as hillsides.

Food security for the United States is not in question today, but Cargill, Inc., a leading U.S. commodity trader, warned in the fall of 1991 that world grain inventories were at their lowest levels since the mid-1970s. With low reserves, crop failure in a major producing country can trigger a global food crisis. So slim a margin may explain consumer acceptance of subsidies of agricultural output even though they raise present food cost. In 1990, government price supports accounted for 44 percent of the value of total farm output in rich countries, up 17 percent from a year earlier. Japan's producer subsidy equivalent (PSE) was 68 percent, compared to 48 percent in the European Community and 30 percent in the United States.

ENERGY

Fuel is another candidate for being the limiting factor for the carrying capacity of the world. Quantity of supply is difficult to separate from pollution constraints because use of today's major fuel sources imposes a heavy burden on the environment. Fossil-fuel burning releases carbon dioxide, and nuclear power may be worse. Both the United States and China have enormous coal reserves. It is difficult to imagine that they will not be used, especially by China, unless clean and cost-competitive energy can be quickly developed.

Operation of nuclear-fission plants carries the constant risk of accidental release of radioactivity into the surrounding countryside; and disposal of nuclear waste, the by-product of generating energy, is an unsolved problem. Not-in-my-backyard is the well-nigh universal response. Money may not be enough to buy off citizen objections to nuclear waste dumps near their town or water supply. Pressure is building to sacrifice Nevada.

France has long experience with nuclear power. For several decades, 75 percent of its energy needs have been met by fission. Now, plants are aging. Concern about accidents is growing, and nuclear-waste dumping is an environmental issue just beginning to raise public concern. France is a country to watch as the United States considers its energy future.

Nuclear plants, like coal burning for electricity generation, have to overcome the inefficiency of transporting energy to the point of use. Energy is wasted as distance between generation and destination points increases. Moreover, power lines crossing residential communities are expensive to install, unsightly, and may be a danger to health. Magnetic fields surround these high-voltage wires; studies to determine health risks, particularly risks to children, are inconclusive.

Supply of the raw material for nuclear fission is not a probable limiting factor; nor is coal scarce. But the supply of petroleum, oil, is. Jan C. Lundberg (1989), former publisher of the *Lundberg Oil Letter*, writes, " 'Party's over. That's enough folks.' But how come the guests keep on revelling? . . . Sometimes the lights have to go out before people pay attention." (See Chapter 18 for analyses by John Gever *et al.* and industry spokesmen.)

EXCEEDING THE CARRYING CAPACITY

Insults to carrying capacity such as are occurring in the United States are magnified in the third world. Land hunger of growing populations drives cultivation of dry land on steep mountainsides, deforestation of rain-forest areas that soon turn rock-hard (laterite) and support nothing, and overgrazing of grasslands that deteriorate into desert. Land that had supported a stable (if low) level of population then supports almost no one. Lester R. Brown (1990) writes that "The environmental degradation of the planet is starting to show up at harvest time. . . . The 1989 estimated harvest (1.67 billion tons) was up only 1 percent from 1984, which means that the grain output per person is down nearly 7 percent."

Growth in the food supply has slowed, while births are outnumbering deaths by a greater and greater margin. In some parts of the world, food production itself is already dropping. No new green revolution is in sight, although efforts continue. The International Rice Research Institute (based in the Philippines) is endeavoring to raise funds for a network of Asian laboratories. The immediate objective is breeding high-yield, disease-resistant rice strains with which to pump up the 1990 total crop of 520 million metric tons by about 10 million metric tons per year. The estimated cost: $5.5 million over five years. In the heyday of USAID, the sum might have seemed inconsequential. Today, the international community guards its dwindling wealth.

THE ENVIRONMENTAL SINK

Worldwide industrialization proceeds, to the detriment of both air and water quality. Chemical stress is reducing the productivity of those forests that escape being burned down or chopped down. German and Polish forests are collections of ghostly pylons, trees dead and dying from acid rain. Pollution abatement was neglected in the Communist bloc and is simply not affordable in third-world countries. Any available source of energy including wood or dirty coal is made to do. Industrial scrubbers for limiting air pollution might as well be unknown. Chemicals poison air and water. "Dead lakes and dying forests have become a natural accompaniment of industrialization," writes Lester Brown.

The carbon dioxide (CO_2) and chlorofluorocarbon (CFC) effects of industrial activity are more subtle, but equally insidious. Inefficient industrial processes and forest burning together appear to make the third world equal to the developed world in contributions to CO_2 and CFC concentrations in the atmosphere. A unit of production in India creates far more pollution than the same production in the industrialized world. The "tigers" of the Far East—Korea, Singapore, and Taiwan—are among the most polluting producers anywhere.

Even very modest increases in per capita consumption of fossil fuels in the third world will overwhelm very large per capita reductions in industrialized countries. Such is the impact of population size. Cynthia Green (1991) forecasts that

> Due to population growth, developing countries will account for 60 percent of the new municipal and industrial waste generated between 1985 and 2025. If [third-world] incomes as well as population grow, developing countries could contribute 83 percent of the new waste generated during this period. By the year 2025, developing countries could generate more than half of the world's wastes.

Chemist Gad Fischer (1992) concludes that a 40 percent per capita reduction of CO_2 emissions in industrialized regions will be offset many times if third-world countries increase their per capita use just marginally, that is, to a level still leaving them at less than half of industrialized country rates.

CO_2 is not the only greenhouse gas. Methane, produced by decomposing organic matter, is second in importance. Although released in less quantity than CO_2, methane is more hazardous to the atmosphere per unit. Third-world peoples are already the largest producers of methane. Rice-growing in artificially created swamps has the single largest impact on its accumulation. Another major contributor is stock raising. Durning and Brough (1991) write that India and China are the titans: "India is browsed by 107 million goats, 196 million head of cattle, and 74 million water buffalo." In comparison, the U.S. cattle herd (dairy and beef) numbers about 130 million head. Goats, horses, and hogs are much less represented. We are tops in chickens.

These comparisons show that much of the present third-world contribution to greenhouse gases is a by-product of agriculture. Their industrial enterprise is small (albeit growing). Industrialization is a nearly universal political objective, however, and is seen as the answer to widespread underemployment. Ironically, the most desired and prestigious industries are often the heavy goods, capital-intensive manufacturing enterprises that pollute inordinately when technology is unsophisticated, and which employ relatively few men and virtually no women per dollar of investment.

FOREIGN POLICY ISSUES

Industrialized countries asked for assistance confront an array of possibilities. One choice concerns trying to affect, or not, the pace of worldwide industrial development. Should one help the third world industrialize? Hope they cannot do it? Help them do it cleanly? (Who will pay and is containment possible?) Give them goods? (Who pays and will it solve the problem?) Take their people? (How many and won't their high fertility replace any number that could be taken into Europe or the United States? And isn't people's main reason for immigrating a desire to raise their standard of living, that is, shift to the richer country's rates of fossil fuel use and pollution?) The ethics of supporting—or taking a neutral stance on—industrialization in third-world countries is daunting. What should be the response, knowing that an extra unit of production in India or Mexico puts more pollution into the atmosphere than equivalent production in mature industrialized nations?

Explosive population growth means that every human activity puts critical pressure on the environment. Moreover, more people must take any opportunity to survive that comes to hand. More and more are pushed to marginal niches where their efforts to extract a living are disproportionately destructive to the environment. Conservation and pollution control are luxuries that give way to the short-run survival of the individual. But overuse of life-support systems must exact its price in the end. The scale of human activities is eroding environmental carrying capacity so that fewer persons than before will find subsistence.

IV

AMERICA
Past and Future

Kissing the Blarney Stone and Other Tales

Economic growth is not a Johnny-come-lately. And its effect on fertility seems the same across countries and time. At every point where serious economic opportunity beckons, family-size preferences expand. Newly perceived opportunity frees individuals to make decisions which raise fertility.

Optimism, however, is usually short-lived. Cycles of economic expansion, population growth which overshoots resources, population crash, and the emergence of fertility-limiting behaviors appear throughout human history. In worst-case scenarios, the environment is damaged by overuse so that the carrying capacity actually shrinks.

IRELAND'S BABY BOOM AND BUST

Two centuries of Irish history illustrate the full cycle. Irish experience with the potato shows how opportunity lets fertility and family size rise and, then, how reversing fortunes make fertility fall. The potato, introduced from the new world around 1740, started Ireland on a demographic rollercoaster. A mostly rural population of 3.2 million people in 1754 more than doubled by 1845, to 8.2 million, before crashing to nearly its original level in long years of low fertility, famine, high child mortality, and emigration, in that order. For many Americans, this story is family history.

A sense that the boom times were over dawned even before the great famine arrived. Marriage patterns had begun changing back to the traditional way some decades before the actual crisis. But the momentum of population growth—propelled by a huge baby-boom generation—made tragedy inevitable. The momentum of growth had broken entirely by 1880 when the population stabilized at 4 million. There it stayed until after World War II. The story in detail is this.

The Irish had a stable and diversified agricultural economy before introduction of the potato. Population was stationary because nobody married without a secure livelihood, and not many people fooled around outside of marriage. Waiting for marriage until a man could make a living usually meant waiting to inherit the farm. Premaritally pregnant women were disgraced and might be disowned. That meant out—maybe not quite a death sentence, but it was the risk one took. Both community and religious norms supported parental authority over children's social life and marriage.

Farming was the principal—and almost the most prestigious— occupation available. The youngest son (rule of ultimogeniture) inherited the family farm. Since only one son expected to inherit land, only one among any number of brothers expected to marry. Very much to the point, most women did not find a husband and so remained childless. The extended family included unmarried aunts and whichever uncles did not join the army or depart one way or another.

Even men and women who married often did so late in life. Generations were long because a man delayed marriage until near to parents' deaths and coming into his inheritance. If many marriages are late and a goodly portion of the population never marries at all, wishes for a large family seldom materialize. Even if many children are the ideal and some families are very large, average fertility stays low so long as few young people have the chance to start a family.

In Ireland, potato culture after 1740 vastly increased the

productivity of land. One effect was to change the perspective on how many people an area could support. If a farm could be subdivided into pieces that each produced a living, more sons could marry. Soon, inheritance and marriage rules relaxed. More people married, and at younger ages. Now, large-family-size ideals made a difference.

Population growth also got a boost from better nutrition. A well-fed population has good resistance to infectious disease, which changes mortality rates because infections are the major killers in premodern societies. However, the health benefits did not last long. The rural population soon expanded beyond the number that could be absorbed locally, and many people migrated to cities. Even though public health measures were introduced at about this time, the cities became sinkholes of filth and disease. Thus, improved health was not a longterm factor in Ireland's population growth. Earlier and nearly universal marriage was!

Potato-driven prosperity affected fertility by undercutting religion as well as by directly encouraging earlier marriage. When young people sensed their freedom from the traditional, very limited opportunity structure, church teachings came to seem irrelevant. Abstinence, obedience, respect were the message. But who was listening?

Theologian John Noonan's (1968) study of old letters and manuscripts shows that the fortunes of the Roman Catholic Church went down as economic opportunity went up. Defeat by the English in 1690 at the Battle of the Boyne had taken a toll on the Roman Catholic Church, but the religious life remained vital even when forced underground. On the contrary, *prosperity* dealt Catholicism a nearly final blow. Clergy lost the support of their parishioners. Bishops became unprotected fugitives from the English law. By mid-century, no Roman Catholic seminary remained in Ireland. Noonan writes:

> In the mid-eighteenth century, the outlawed bishops lived the lives of itinerants staying in "places of refuge"; the parishes were irregularly supplied; the religious orders were criminal; Catholic education consisted in the uncertain efforts of "hedge schools."

Indeed, so long as secular opportunities seemed abundant, religious vocations and influence remained at a low ebb. The Church was regarded as irrelevant if not intrusive. Prosperity played havoc with religion.

As people turned away from Catholicism and became more materialistic, church influence on sexuality and, inevitably, reproduction nearly disappeared. Control—observe sexual abstinence outside of marriage, marry only if a livelihood is secure, and obey church and parental authority—was the Church's constant message, but the audience had vanished.

The period of optimism and opportunity lasted no longer than fifty years. Even as grandchildren multiplied, the new practice of subdividing family farms was pushed beyond sensible limits. Farm units reached about minimum size for providing livelihoods at the same time that marginal lands, including peat bogs, had to be brought under cultivation. Hardship mounted as the population grew.

A generation grew up to face the distinct possibility that they could be worse off than their parents. Economic security was once more in jeopardy. With virtually no opportunity outside the family, the young had to pay attention, again, to authority.

Not quite coincidentally, the fortunes of the Church reversed as well. The Catholic Relief Act was enacted in 1782, priests became respected figures, the famed St. Patrick's College at Maynooth was founded, and young people flocked to take vows.

With traditions reviving, indefinitely postponed marriage began to control fertility as it had done before introduction of the potato. By 1845, the start of the nine-year famine, fewer than 30 percent of twenty-one to thirty-year-old women were married. Late marriage again prevented many women from ever starting families, although the large number of women of child-bearing age (Ireland's baby-boom cohort) meant that population growth had yet to run its course.

Replacement-level fertility set in before 1845 but came too late to ward off the nine-year crisis. The population crashed—through famine that killed the old and young, and emigration of young adults—then stabilized between 1860 and 1880. A sense of limits returned to Ireland.

The potato—so small a vegetable—had given the country a wild ride. And the people who had had the fun did not pay the price. It seems unfair. Limits, inequity, no free lunch—these parts of the human condition are forgotten in half a generation and relearned in a half century of pain.

IRELAND'S SECOND ROUND

The Irish seem no different than others struck by sudden prosperity, and opportunity tripped Ireland's population roller-coaster again, around 1960. The emerald isle gained popularity as a vacation spot when the economies of other European countries revived from World War II. Tourists coveted Waterford crystal, fishermen's knit sweaters, and fine woolens. The Germans bought land. So actively was Irish real estate traded that legislation was enacted to limit foreign land-ownership. Again, more people married. Fertility rose. Children grew. The inevitable happened: By the 1980s, Ireland had a 25 percent unemployment rate. Again, fertility fell; today, it hovers at replacement level.

EUROPE: 1600–1914

Ireland was not, is not, an isolated case. Earlier than Ireland, other parts of Europe including France, Great Britain, and Scandinavia also experienced population growth. Colonialism, trade, and the industrial revolution did it. Jobs and prosperity occasioned by the new crops and industrial technologies inspired optimism, culture change, and new marriage patterns. Fertility increased, and for two or three centuries the population grew at an annual rate of 0.5 percent.*

*Population doubles in 140 years at a 0.5 percent per annum rate of growth. The U.S. rate is 1.1 percent per year. The doubling time is 64 years ($70 \div 1.1 = 63.6$).

Fertility was highest in the countryside. One strategy to keep production in step with the larger human population was to increase the number of farm animals. The bigger herds, however, put pressure on grazing lands that had been used in Scandinavia and England for centuries as a commons. Landowners and communities saw the commons being overgrazed and tried to implement a variety of conservation measures. In England, the Enclosure Acts eliminated the commons.

Much maligned at the time and the cause of great additional suffering, the Enclosure Acts were not mindlessly selfish. Rather, they represented an effort to prevent further abuse of the land. Pastures had been pushed beyond their carrying capacity; without protection, their productivity might have been permanently diminished. The length of time needed to restore productivity to degraded land depends on many factors. One is the extent of damage. Another is climate. In the Arctic tundra, it takes twenty years for lichens (an important caribou food source) to recover. Eroded mountain slopes may never spontaneously recover. Scottish hillsides are covered today with gorse and heather, where once there were forests.

LABOR SURPLUS

While land is still viable, total agricultural yields can be raised somewhat by applying labor. However, there comes a point where workers consume more than they add. The point of vanishingly small net returns from agricultural labor was reached in most parts of Europe somewhere between 1750 and 1850. The transition occurred while most people still expected that industrial growth could be, for them personally, a path to prosperity.

Indeed, cottage industry associated with textiles employed part of the excess labor. But people with the least capital—land, education, or tools—migrated into cities to join an army of underemployed. The rapid growth of urban labor depressed wages and fed sweatshop employment practices.

Thus, the overcrowded countryside pushed out excess labor and industrializing cities pulled it in. All scavenged for employment under worsening conditions as industry, but also competition for jobs, grew. The average person's buying power fell. Real wages were stagnant or worse. Many working one- or two-parent families could barely feed and clothe their children.

The misery, including workhouses, debtors' prisons, orphanages, and other brutalizations, was described by Victor Hugo and Charles Dickens. Today's students of eighteenth- and nineteenth-century Europe maintain, however, that novelists of the period "prettied up" the poverty. English literature professor Elizabeth Langland says that actual conditions were worse: the slums dirtier, the mortality higher, the degradation more profound. Dickens told the gentler tragicomic parts of it because his installment novels had to sell.

CHILD ABANDONMENT

At the same time that fertility remained high in the countryside and public health measures attacked infectious disease in the cities, poverty led parents to walk away from tens of thousands of children. Babies throughout Great Britain and Europe were placed in foster care. Boarding arrangements often amounted to abandonment and murder. "Killing nurses," so-called, administered Godfrey's Cordial, a concoction of opium and treacle, as a tranquilizer for babies. In the British town of Coventry, states Langer (1972), Godfrey's Cordial sold at up to the rate of ten gallons a week, enough for twelve thousand doses. Bottle feeding with rubber nipples was still in the future, so most women could not honestly have thought that their babies would be nourished. Mothers must have been desperate to believe that wet-nurses could do enough for all comers.

Orphanages had sprung up by this time as public-spirited innovations to reduce infant mortality resulting from outright abandonment. Most of Frans Hals's group portraits (around A.D.

1640), now housed in the Haarlem, Netherlands, public museum, depict solid Dutch citizens who acted as trustees of local institutions that cared for the homeless young, infirm, or elderly. Orphanages' very success in giving infants a chance soon led to their overuse. An eighteenth-century London orphanage had so good a record that Parliament designated it as a refuge for children from all England. Conditions became chaotic, and after a short time it was again allowed to turn away all but Londoners.

Napoleon also tried to improve conditions for infants. He installed turnstiles at the entrance of orphanages so that babies would not be abandoned outdoors. This reform brought more foundlings into the facilities and overwhelmed service. In orphanages in England and the Continent, the death rate climbed to 80 percent within the first two years of life.

Unmarried women had no good choice if they became pregnant. Abortion endangered their lives; putting an infant into an orphanage almost certainly increased its suffering in life and still doomed it; keeping it, mother and child might both die. Within families, extra children could transform gentility into poverty.

RESPONSIBILITY REVIVES

In this context, marriage again came to depend on having a livelihood. Priests and pastors forbade imprudent marriage, and they were heeded. Local (city or cantonal) governments in Germany and Switzerland made a man's right to marry conditional on his not having been in debtors' prison, proving a two-year employment history, and/or demonstrating the means to provide housing. Individual accountability revived.

Awareness of limited resources as a bar to marriage and childbearing is possibly nowhere better shown than in the fictional "downstairs" of the British Broadcasting Company (BBC) television series *Upstairs, Downstairs*. Recall the cook's and butler's renunciation of romantic inclinations, and the debate (downstairs) over allowing entry to a former housemaid—disgraced after her seduction by the young master of the house—even though she arrived pitifully exhausted, on the brink of childbirth.

One may speculate that Victorian prudishness grew out of desperate fear of unplanned childbearing. Rejection of sexuality, the double sexual standard, and prohibition of female premarital sex were no cultural accident. These self-protective attitudes toward sex and family size reflected stark realities that exposed the limits of European wealth. Fear of poverty was the stimulus for abstinence, celibacy, coitus interruptus, abortion, infanticide, and delayed marriage. Careless love was a self-indulgence few dared to risk. The definition of liberty as "the right to discipline one's self" was rediscovered, reviving the dignity of the working class. Self-restraint helped individuals survive and prosper, and those values were passed on. Thus, cultures tend toward adaptation.

Throughout Europe, the average age of marriage rose. Fear of poverty, and the joint religious and secular demand for individual economic responsibility, revived tradition. Late marriage or nonmarriage again shaped lifestyles for large sectors of the population. In 1865, for example, Norwegian first-time brides averaged 26.7 years of age. Demographer Etienne Van der Walle (1968) estimates that by the nineteenth century, only 35 to 40 percent of European women married at an age when they could still have children. Thus, an enormous part of Europe's reproductive capacity was unused.

The modern pattern of nearly universal marriage but small completed family size developed first in France around 1850. It arose not from affluence but from misery, conditions that Victor Hugo recorded. England and other European countries, including those of Scandinavia, also began the shift to small family size during (not after) the era of sweatshops and high infant and child mortality. Recall John Knodel's conclusion for Germany that the "decline in infant mortality could not have been an initiating cause of the fertility decline in most areas" because the change in fertility came first!

THE VALUE OF LABOR REVIVES

By the turn of the twentieth century, after a long generation of low average fertility, the rate of growth of the labor force began to decline. When labor ceased being cheap and easy to exploit, industry began to look for labor-saving technology. Labor productivity (product per labor-hour) rose because of investment in technology. Profits, reinvestment, and expansion rose apace. So did the number of jobs. Slowly, the demand for labor overtook the supply. Real wages stopped falling. After a while, labor acquired a bit of bargaining power and successfully negotiated a larger share of the economic pie.

Nevertheless, a rigid social order in which most people were glad to sell their services cheaply to a small upper class dragged on. It took years (and maybe the manpower losses of World War I) before ordinary people became empowered to bargain for higher wages. Slowly, the sum of individual family-size choices restored a better balance between labor supply and jobs, and between population size and resources.

CODA

The oversupply of labor was the legacy of high fertility inspired by the industrial revolution, colonization, trade, welfare (the Speenhamland system in England), and a generation or two of real prosperity. Fertility was highest in the countryside, made briefly rich and ever hopeful by new crops, cottage industry, and the possibility of migration.

Long after the rural labor market was saturated, belief in urban opportunity persisted. Rural-to-urban migration was the eighteenth- and nineteenth-century pattern: "Turn again, Dick Whittington." Turn toward London, that is. This centuries-old children's story ends, of course, happily: The destitute country boy finds fame and fortune and becomes Lord Mayor of the City. Expanding opportunity continued as a cultural myth long after its promise escaped most people. The country fantasizes about the city. The more distant the destination, the easier to believe in its glamour and wealth. So long as excess rural population is regurgitated into cities, destitution remains remote and, to some extent, hidden.

Correct information does, of course, eventually percolate to the remotest places. Sterner visions of reality replace vague expectations. First in the cities, then in the countryside, European fertility fell.

In even the worst of times, however, there are those who encourage high fertility and *in*migration. Some population growth benefits landowners and investors in almost any society. Economist Ronald Lee (1980) estimates that a 10 percent growth in population in preindustrial England had the effect of raising rents (investment income) by 19 percent—at the same time that it depressed real wages by 22 percent.

The lower and middle class usually do not benefit from population growth. Economist David Ricardo, early-nineteenth-century advocate for free markets, warned that the power elite benefit from excess labor—therefore, cheap labor—at the expense of almost everyone else. The majority, who depend on wages and salaries, end up being worse off. Demographer Alfred Sauvy also foresaw how interests differ. Here is Nathan Keyfitz's paraphrase (1990) of Sauvy's reflection on the ideal population: "The farmer calculating the number of cows to raise in his pasture will always arrive at a larger number than the cows themselves would prefer."

The struggle, often based on a misperception of one's true interests, goes on. In the United States, the right-wing Heritage Foundation apparently identifies with Sauvy's farmer, advocating population growth and more immigration. Economist Julian Simon is the Foundation's champion. Simon asserts that there cannot be such a thing as too many people.

Chapters 16 through 20 address the basis for judging if population growth—whatever its source—serves America. The next chapter continues to explore the idea that prosperity raises family-size targets, whereas pessimism or harder times lower them. Our laboratory for this test is the United States of America.

History Does Not Stop

The U.S. baby boom after World War II is another example of economic and population build and bust. The account borrows from economist Richard Easterlin (1962, 1971), who is the foremost interpreter of cycles in U.S. fertility. His work embraces the colonial period and continues today with D. J. Macunovitch (1990) and others.

FERTILITY AND LAND

Recapping some history, U.S. fertility rates fell steadily from the colonial period through the Great Depression of 1929–1936. The fertility decline tracked the eastward to westward settlement of land. Family size fell as free or cheap land was taken up. High fertility characterized regions where access to land was easy. Low fertility gradually became established in New England, in East Coast cities, and on more settled farmland.

New England towns where textile mills employed women and children from very early in the nineteenth century were among the first to value smaller families. Some demographers emphasize the effect of development (urbanization and industrialization) or of women working outside the home, but Easterlin demonstrates that the trend toward smaller family size followed disappearance of the frontier. With little regard to degree of industrialization, the constant factor in declining fertility from east to west, north to south, was the *diminishing opportunity* to settle cheap land.

FERTILITY AND DEPRESSION

Superimposed on this pattern, on-farm fertility fell suddenly in the early 1920s when the bottom fell out from under agricultural markets. Hard times hit the farmer because of retrenchment from World War I. Production had been revved up as part of the allied war effort, but demand for American crops dwindled as armies dispersed and European farm production came back on-stream. The U.S. farm depression, signaled by a series of price collapses, began in 1919. Farmers' efforts to maintain income by cultivating all possible fields, including hillsides, probably worsened the natural disasters—drought, dust storms, and locusts—which came later.

The Great Depression hit the remaining half* of the population in October, 1929. Armies of urban unemployed joined the farmers on the road and in the breadline. Stories abound of personal struggle and stratagem for getting through these hard times. For example:

- In the first months of the emergency, families gathered around colleges where a child's board was prepaid for the semester. At Wellesley College, breakfast service lent itself to smuggling out hard-boiled eggs and bread.
- Fifty cents a week, enough to buy soup bones for her family, is the actual amount of help one New England mother requested and gratefully received from her church.
- A fourth child would have meant disaster to the family of a small building contractor in Maryland, so the mother had an abortion from which she nearly died.

*The 1930 census was the first to find over half of the U.S. population in urban settings. By 1990, about 75 percent of Americans were urbanized.

- Another intact family, in Ohio, rented out their home and moved to smaller quarters while the father, an architect, took out-of-town work, lumbering.
- One formerly prosperous Tennessee seed merchant abandoned his wife and three children, leaving the mother to take in sewing. Her struggle to adapt succeeded, but the eldest son recalled that she wept over her hungry children.
- In the intermontane west, drought, dust storms, and locusts finished the grass. Wyoming ranchers gratefully sold their weakest cattle to the government at $10 a head.
- John Steinbeck tells how it was in California. Babies died. Grown men starved.

Not so surprisingly, the fertility rate plummeted. The birth cohort of the 1930s was minuscule. It seemed at the time that the U.S. population would shrink. For some years it hovered at 135 million people. With this number, America fought World War II—and did not do too badly.

PROSPERITY AND A FERTILITY REBOUND

Post-World War II economic activity vastly improved employment prospects for younger men. The labor force was small because of earlier low birth rates. The G.I. Bill of Rights (which gave veterans the opportunity to attend college instead of going straight to work) kept some men out of the pool of job seekers. Immigration, which would have damped the market, was virtually nil because legislation during the 1920s had shut it down. With an expanding economy, a strong seller's market in labor was inevitable.

Wages went up quickly from Depression and World War II levels. Unions successfully pressed demands which, until then, had been easily shunted aside despite 1930s legislation that greatly favored labor over management. Home ownership became easier than at any time since the closing of the frontier. A pat-

tern of newlyweds moving in with one of the couple's parents,
which formerly had been prevalent, disappeared.

Housing costs did rise rapidly. A four-bedroom house in
Scarsdale, New York, resold three times in two years: From
$14,500 in summer, 1945, it jumped to $19,000, and then to
$32,900. But wages and salaries rose faster. In 1950, home
ownership took only 14 percent of a typical wage-earner's income,
compared with the 44 percent it ate up in 1990. Steadily rising real
income and the ease of home ownership persuaded most people
in the 1950s that each couple could look forward to greater
opportunity than had been enjoyed by their parents *and* that
growing prosperity was to be a continuing trend. Except for the
nuclear threat, the pervasive national mood was one of optimism
and confidence.

Demographic transition theory predicts that fertility should
fall under these circumstances. After all, urbanization continued.
Educational level rose broadly. Mortality fell for all ages because
of wider access to health care, better nutrition (pellagra and
rickets essentially disappeared), and new drugs (penicillin).
Racial discrimination remained an injustice to blacks but did not
keep a vital merchant and professional class from flourishing
within black communities. Development, as measured by per
capita use of energy, accelerated at the most rapid rate the world
had ever seen. Prosperity spread through almost every sector of
American society. Positives on every one of the demographic
transition model's factors should have further brought down
fertility. But did it? Did fertility even stay steady?

No. The United States had a baby boom. Age of marriage fell
dramatically. Indeed, marriage was a woman's goal.* Demographers Leon Bouvier and Carol De Vita (1991) observe that, "In
1956, women's median age at first marriage stood at just over 20
years. Half of all women marrying for the first time in the early
part of the baby-boom era were teenagers."

---

*Yours truly, married in 1955 at age twenty on college graduation day, with no
further plan in mind, was typical.

Most people were gripped by the culture of sex-role stereo-typing. Teachers' and parents' repeated, not-so-subtle signals promoting female domesticity were hard to miss or misinterpret.* As quickly as they could, newlyweds began to fill up their single-family homes with children. No one doubted that these children were affordable, because upward mobility was everyone's expectation. Bouvier and De Vita continue, "Close to 60 percent of women . . . who were in their prime childbearing years during the peak of the baby boom had borne three or more children by the time they reached their late 30s." This number of births represented an 80 percent increase from twenty years earlier.

FERTILITY AND MODERATING EXPECTATIONS

Yet, the lifestyle was bound to disappoint. The bloom was soon off the rose of playing house in the suburbs. Children began to feel like an emotional as well as economic burden. Betty Friedan's message (1963), derision of the feminine mystique, resonated with thousands of American women—and others already had read Simone de Beauvoir's *The Second Sex* (1953). At about the same time, male employment opportunities began to dim. The 1960s were prosperous by today's standards, but opportunities had narrowed by comparison with expectations set in preceding years.

Family-size preferences fell when upward mobility stalled, schools got overcrowded so that new ones had to be built, and taxes rose to pay for new schools and other infrastructure. Women saw themselves as victimized and infantilized by constant childcare, but nursemaids were beyond most budgets. Most people in the 1960s saw their standard of living rising at a slower rate. They sensed that children cost a lot relative to their present

*If someone told you, "If you go to Vassar, you won't get married," would you doubt that (1) you should marry, and (2) Vassar is too far from Yale?

and future value. Soon, middle-class couples concluded that two children were about right.

One may distinguish here between women in tight, often kin-based social networks and those whose closest ties are with friends in nonintersecting networks. Women in tight-knit networks get constant help with childrearing, and child-centered social occasions affirm a mother's closest ties. These mothers feel confident, secure, and enriched through childcare. In contrast, women in loose networks—that meant most women in America so long as the average family moved once every five years and surpassed their parents in education, creating social distance— have a different, often negative experience; these women value labor force opportunities as relief from childcare and are reluctant to increase family size beyond one or two children.

One sees how in the 1960s social arrangements reinforced economics. By 1964, many couples were ready for the contraceptive pill. Without it, sterilization might have become popular more quickly; and the pressure for legalized abortion, far greater.

FERTILITY AND THE WAR ON POVERTY

Fertility rates soon took on a very marked bimodal distribution: low in the middle class and substantially higher among the poor. Expectations were rising in the lower class in the 1960s because President John F. Kennedy had begun, and President Lyndon Johnson continued, making the war on poverty a national priority. The United States was to have butter along with guns.*

The 1964 Civil Rights Act alone would not have falsely raised expectations because it addressed advancement through equal opportunity and achievement. Blacks, probably much more than poor whites, who were held back only by their own values and talents, were prepared to work; and a large majority deeply

---

*John K. Galbraith must take credit(!) for financing the Vietnam War with debt, so that the United States would have "guns and butter, too."

valued education. Many were entrepreneurially or professionally active even though limited to opportunity within the black community.

Entitlement programs were different. The war on poverty, with promises of an easy and sufficient lifestyle, set the poor—white or black—on a road toward dependency that did them no favor. Great expectations without individual responsibility are a formula for disaster. It can be no surprise that fertility did not fall, and even rose, among the poorest Americans. Assessing the demographic picture, Lee Rainwater entitled a book, *And the Poor Get Children* (1960). Comparison is everything: What are your prospects compared to what they were? Or compared to a reference group of friends and parents? It is not a matter of being rich or poor, but rather, the *direction* you think you are moving.

FERTILITY AND THE COSTLINESS OF CHILDREN

As the economic burdens of childrearing increased for the middle class during the 1960s, men were sometimes ahead of women in preferring fewer, rather than more, children. As recently as 1980, only 38 percent of women with children under one year of age were in the work force. Now that 59 percent of married women are in the labor force while still taking major responsibility at home, and 53 percent of women with children under one year of age are at work, women are again more likely than men to prefer small families. Averaging together all sectors of the society, U.S. fertility fell like a stone through the sixties and seventies. In the late 1970s, it hit a low of 1.7, a rate well below what is needed for replacement.

Young men and women adjust to diminished employment and promotion opportunities. During the late 1970s and 1980s, they tried to continue affording goods by both cutting housing expense and taking on debt. The American Bankruptcy Institute reports that consumer debt exploded between the early 1980s and 1991: from 60 percent to 82 percent of personal income. The yuppie generation also adjusted by moving in with their own parents, sharing a household with same- or opposite-sex friends, delaying marriage, and delaying birth of the first child. In 1990, women married at age twenty-four, on average. That is three years later than the average age of marriage just twenty years before.

The last decade of the twentieth century begins with 22 percent of women in their thirties having never had children, compared with 13 percent in 1976. In connection with a 1991 Census Bureau report, sociologist Philip Morgan (1991) notes that childbearing patterns "look startlingly similar to those that prevailed during the Depression. . . . Half the women over age 25 were childless at the height of the Depression, roughly the same as today."

Fertility this low is not a surprise. Desired family size contracts along with opportunity, and real disposable personal income (after-tax income adjusted for inflation) has been nearly stagnant since 1973 (the first oil shock). Some economic indicators show an 8 percent loss in men's real hourly pay since the peak rate in 1972. Through the 1970s and 1980s, new jobs increasingly were in the low-paying service sector. Noah (1991) reports that average earned income among black Americans fell in the 1980s. For men without college degrees, inflation-adjusted median income has fallen since 1973.

FERTILITY AND THE BUSINESS CYCLE

Bottoming out of the 1980–81 recession, white fertility was 1.4 and black fertility was 2.09; that is, both rates were below replacement level. By the late 1980s, however, the longest-running U.S. economic expansion since World War II was underway and paying off for some families. Although wages barely kept pace with inflation, more family members entered the work force. Income in established (not youngest) families rose. Predictably, fertility rates went up, too. Black fertility rose from 2.09 in 1982, to 2.4 births per woman in 1990. White non-Hispanic fertility rebounded from 1.4 to 1.7 by 1990. The recession beginning in the summer or fall of 1990 had the reverse effect: By summer, 1991, demographers in the Census Bureau could see that the number of births was falling! The economy affects fertility.

FERTILITY AND LONGTERM TRENDS

So quick a response to recession is remarkable. For the foreseeable future, perhaps, fertility will be most sensitive to downturns in economic activity because business-cycle fluctuations appear to overlie a deep, national unease. For the first time in our history, many (if not most) native-born Americans do not expect to be financially better off than their own fathers and mothers. We are prepared to believe bad news.

Longterm trends are at work. A congressional study cited in the *Wall Street Journal* (Longer Hours, 1992) "shows that adults in 80% of two-parent American families with children worked more hours in 1989 than in 1979, but that their incomes didn't rise commensurately." In 60 percent of families, "decline in the husbands' pay was greater than their wives' wage increases" even though wives had upped their work hours by 13 percent.

The stagnation or loss in wages is a result of the labor force growing faster than the economy as a whole. The causes of slower economic growth can be debated (see Chapter 16); but baby-boomers and women of all ages entering the job market for the first time contributed much of the labor force growth and downward pressure on wages. The rest of the labor force growth came and increasingly comes from immigration.

Whatever the future of immigration, the rapidly growing labor force already means that Americans face continuing job insecurity, loss in buying power, and less opportunity relative to expectations absorbed from an older generation. The number of workers age twenty-two to sixty-four who earn less than poverty-level wages rose by 44 percent between 1978 and 1987, two benchmark years when the economy was expanding and touted as healthy. The growth in the number of working poor came from erosion of hourly wages, which were lower in 1988 than in any other year since 1966 after adjusting for inflation. Some observers conclude that, for the first time in recent American history, sons are doing worse financially than their fathers. The "Brazilianization" of America is justifiably a fear of the so-called X generation, those entering the labor force after 1980.

To take just two signs of a falling median standard of living: A smaller proportion of Americans owned their own home in 1990 than in 1950, and the disparity between rich and poor appears to be increasing. Young people and less-educated families bear the heaviest burden from competition for entry-level jobs, but the middle class is also struggling to protect its economic position. Thus, native-born Americans are unlikely to shift to a much larger family size in the foreseeable future.

FERTILITY AND IMMIGRATION

Even as native-born fertility falls because of bleak economic prospects—which seem about to become a constant backdrop to short-term movements in the business cycle—immigrant fertility may push the total fertility rate (TFR) upward. That is, if high immigration persists, the rapidly changing composition of the nation will dominate other effects so that native-born American fertility contributes less and less to the total. By A.D. 2020, non-Hispanic whites will account for just one-third, and blacks for under 7 percent, of California's projected population. The fertility rate of immigrants will increasingly determine the California fertility rate; and progressively, the national rate. Since immigrant fertility rates are high, constant upward pressure on the blended rate is inevitable if present immigration patterns continue.

Demographer Francine Blau (1991) is one who expects immigration to affect the U.S. fertility rate: "In the case of high fertility source countries, immigrant women's fertility is expected to

initially exceed their native-born counterparts." Demographer
Leon Bouvier (1992) shows that Hispanic fertility rates (and those
of other immigrant ethnic groups) are rising in part because
newcomers make up a larger and larger share of the total. That
is, as the proportion of newcomers rises, their fertility rate
increasingly dominates the statistic for the category. Hispanic
women born in the United States have a rate close to the national
average, but their performance contributes a smaller and smaller
share to the total Hispanic rate.

The effect of changing proportions between and within
ethnic groups appears in microcosm in New York City and
California. In California, where immigration from Mexico is a
potent factor, Hispanic fertility rose from 3.16 in 1982, to 3.5
by 1988, and to over 3.9 in 1990. Newcomers increasingly drive
the blended fertility rate for Hispanics as a group.*

Newcomers daily become a larger share of the whole demographic picture. For example, direct legal immigration accounts
for 28 percent of California's population growth, and two-thirds
of the 800,000 people a year who come to California are foreign-
born. Some are illegal. Some move to California after spending
time in other states. This progression is particularly evident
among refugees (mostly Vietnamese, Cambodian, and Russian)
because they often do not choose their first destination and, due
to refugees' automatic entitlement, are attracted to California for
its generous health and welfare benefits.

The California fertility rate reflects this growing third-world
and Russian presence. The Demographic Research Unit (1990)
shows the statewide TFR rising from 1.95 in 1982 to 2.33 in 1988
and to 2.5 by 1990. That is, the fertility rate is well above
replacement level (2.1) and rising. Indeed, the growing share of
foreign-born in California is likely to carry fertility a great deal
higher, a foretaste of what can come throughout America.

---

*The finding implies that Mexican women who move to the United States have
significantly higher fertility than those who remain in Mexico (where, according
to the 1991 official census, the TFR has declined to 3.2).

Large cities such as New York are similarly affected. Demographers Laurie E. Banks and Joseph J. Salvo stated in a paper presented at the 1990 meeting of the Population Association of America that

> For areas where native fertility is generally low, an influx of immigrants can have a major impact on the future population. Population projections for such areas must cope with both population growth due to immigration itself as well as the higher fertility of many foreign-born persons. . . . An analysis of fertility differentials by nativity, race and Hispanic origin indicate that, foreign-born women have higher total fertility rates than native-born women regardless of race and Hispanic origin.

That is, native-born black and Hispanic (mainly Puerto Rican) women in New York have strikingly lower fertility than their foreign-born counterparts. Native-born black women average 1.8 children, but foreign-born black women have 2.7 children. Native-born Hispanic women average 1.9; the foreign-born, 2.5.

The process occurring within ethnic categories is analogous to the effect of growing proportions of newer immigrants within the national population. Thus, foreign-born rates are the wildcard in guesstimating what will happen to U.S. fertility as a whole. In 1990, it already had reached replacement level, 2.1 children per woman. The 1991–1992 recession exerted temporary downward pressure, but in the long run, if immigration continues at present rates, replacement-level fertility is sure to give way to some higher number.

In 1991, Hispanic women accounted for 13 percent of births in the United States although they were, at that time, only 10 percent of the female population. Mexican-born women in the United States average 119.3 births annually per 1,000 women. This rate compares with 78 births per 1,000 among black and 65 births per 1,000 among white, native-born American women. Indeed, two-thirds of deliveries in hospitals operated by Los Angeles County are to women (primarily Hispanic) who are in the United States illegally.

Immigration also drives a worrisome upsurge in teenage pregnancy: "In California, Hispanic girls accounted for 75 percent of the increase in teen births between 1986 and 1989." Similar increases in births among Hispanic teens are seen in other southwestern border states, and "experts now say this growing birthrate is largely responsible for the surprising increase in national figures" (The Teen Pregnancy Boom, 1992).

All told, Hispanics (particularly of Mexican and Central American origin) have disproportionately high fertility and are also the most rapidly growing ethnic group in America on account of immigration. In California, their number grows 40 percent faster than the state average. Their representation in the U.S. population as a whole almost doubled, to 10 percent, between 1980 and 1990. The Hispanic proportion of total population is growing rapidly and will quickly surpass the black minority if present immigration policy continues in force.

Many immigrant groups besides Hispanics bring with them large family-size preferences. Filipino families are very large. Some Russian refugees have arrived lately with families of ten. Hmong and other South and Southeast Asians also have extraordinarily large families. (Some Asian nationalities have very small families.)

Immigrants tend to bear children at the rate idealized in their country of origin and facilitated by the jobs, health care, subsidized housing, and welfare benefits in the United States. One should take into account that, where native-born Americans see deterioration in the standard of living, most newcomers perceive themselves as much better off than before. Relative to their previous experience, immigrants find opportunity in the United States. Despite the poor housing and sweatshop ghettos developing in Southern California, Texas border towns, Florida, and major metropolitan centers, conditions are usually better than in the third world. Opportunity acts as an enabling factor in immigrant fertility: Life in the United States presents a golden time to have a baby. Immigration allows families to realize the family size they had wanted all along but could not afford. And the baby is an American citizen!

U.S. FERTILITY AND DEMOGRAPHIC THEORY

To summarize, total U.S. fertility was 2.0 births per woman in 1989. It was 2.1 in 1990. It fell in 1991 in response to recession. Births in the foreseeable future are expected to reflect the presence of immigrants from third-world countries, the larger family-size ideals they bring, and the higher fertility enabled by opportunity in the United States. The connection between prosperity and fertility in America is evident in all sectors. Economist Richard Easterlin (1961, 1971) was a pioneer in identifying the pattern and can show that economic opportunity—particularly at entry-level positions—consistently causes fertility to rise, while harder times make it fall.

Astonishingly, this ongoing analysis is seldom leveled at the demographic transition model. The two, entirely different, interpretations of an economy's influence on fertility are allowed to coexist. Demographers almost apologetically admit to using the Easterlin hypothesis to explain U.S. phenomena. None, including Easterlin, take up the cudgel to show how the analysis explains much else in human fertility. Yet the insight that prosperity causes fertility to rise even in an industrialized society is the *coup de grace* to received wisdom.

Much damage has been done to third-world countries by misunderstanding what causes fertility to change. Good intentions do not excuse continuing to do harm so easily foreseen. Certainly no time should be wasted in demolishing a belief that fertility declines in response to rising affluence.

Not optimism, but loss of optimism brings down fertility. The history of U.S. fertility since 1960 confirms it. Just like Irish having to farm peat bogs and Indonesians scratching a living from eroded mountain slopes, native-born Americans started to seriously limit family size precisely when the average person's economic prospects began to stagnate. Fertility among native-born Americans of every race and ethnic group will stay low so long as events threaten to make them poorer.

America's future need not be bleak, although it will be if

population growth continues. Chapter 16 suggests that rapid growth in the labor force is the factor preventing real wages from rising in many occupations. We take into account both competition for jobs and the role of labor-force growth in delaying innovation and introduction of technology which raises productivity and thence, wages. Fertility, immigration, population growth, international competitiveness, and standard of living are linked in a feedback loop that can work for, or against, America.

16

The Path to Poverty

When a population grows, not everyone does worse right away. The value of capital goes up, and wages go down. People on the right end of those transactions do well. Alfred Sauvy's farmer (1963) can retire, and the cows, well, they go on getting milked. Gradually, capital concentrates into fewer and fewer hands. Pretty soon, a thin top slice of the country is better off; the vast majority are worse off, owning little and selling their labor in a more and more competitive market.

INCREMENTAL LOSSES

The majority lose from population growth because of its effect on wages, benefits, workplace safety, and educational opportunity. The poor lose still more because the public health care and social services on which they depend are stretched thinner. That happens even while taxpayers cough up more and more to try to maintain quality services. All lose eventually because no sector escapes rising taxes and environmental degradation. Writes Olsen (1989), "While U.S. industry generally applauds increased immigration, some critics say it keeps wages and benefits unfairly low for American workers while environmentalists charge immigration is lowering the quality of American life."

The society also polarizes, just as in the most impoverished of third-world countries where the very-few-rich are really rich.

In the United States, the trend nibbling away at the middle class began in the 1970s. Movement up or down, but in either case out of the middle class, has been substantial and has affected all racial and ethnic groups. The U.S. Bureau of the Census (1992) reports that, during the 1980s, the middle class shrank for the first time since World War II, falling from 71.2 percent of the population in 1969 to 63.3 percent in 1989. Moreover, the poor no longer benefit to the degree they once did during economic recovery. Between 1983 and 1990, the poverty rate declined less than 3 percentage points compared with a poverty-rate decline of 9 percentage points in the 1961–1970 economic expansion. The U.S. Bureau of Labor Statistics (1991) states that 50 percent of black, 38 percent of Hispanic, and 30 percent of white twenty- to twenty-four-year-olds in 1990 were out of school but had not found jobs.

As a matter of equity *and* to preserve democracy and domestic markets, no one wants a polarized society. Decline in median, real disposable personal income means breaking faith with most Americans. The least that native-born Americans deserve, as their birthright, is a way to work and be paid a fair wage. But labor can be generously paid only if its productivity (product per worker-hour) is high and rising. Without rising productivity, higher wages are inflationary. A prosperous labor force is also good for business because it stimulates construction as well as the durable-goods and consumer-goods markets. On the contrary, a downward spiral eventually squeezes business; industry loses the ability and the incentives to invest in high technology; productivity stops rising; and the nation loses its competitive edge.

AN OVERSUPPLY OF LABOR

How does so much come to pass? The question reaches deeply into American values. Begin, however, with a fact: We live in a world of too much labor. The world's working-age population is expected to grow by 700 million persons during the 1990s, creating a need for 400 million new jobs. The United States cannot change that reality, but it can mitigate the effect at home. Rapid growth in the U.S. labor force is a principal factor that keeps real wages from rising. The result—many Americans unable to make a living wage—left two-thirds of the middle class worse off at the end of the 1980s than when the decade began, and America's poor stymied before getting a foot on the first rung of the employment ladder.

Rapid growth in the labor force began in the early 1970s when women in the "empty nest" stage of life, and the baby-boom generation, came simultaneously onto the market. The surge from middle-aged women and baby-boomers passed in a decade. However, immigration provides a large new source of labor-force entrants. Legal and illegal immigrant numbers have increased in every year since 1965. By 1990, immigrants were 10 percent of the total U.S. labor force and were a quarter of all workers without a high school diploma. Competition from this influx of unskilled labor weighs most heavily on young and least-educated Americans and helps explain unemployment as well as low wages.

Labor economist Vernon Briggs, Jr. (1990) of Cornell University testified before the Congressional Judiciary Subcommittees on Immigration, Refugees, and International Law that the lower end of the U.S. labor pool is victimized by immigration. Economists George Borjas and Richard Freeman (1992) see a double-edged sword falling on labor: They show that competition from immigrants is a direct cause—and net imports of goods manufactured by unskilled labor outside of the United States are an indirect cause—of the deterioration in economic position of U.S. workers who hold a high school diploma. The impact is still more severe in the high-school-dropout sector, where immigration and the trade imbalance together raised the 1988 effective supply of labor by 28 percent for men and 31 percent for women. The large labor supply, these economists say, is sufficient to account for up to half of the 10-percentage-point decline in the relative weekly wage of unskilled labor.

Economist Donald L. Huddle (1992) of Rice University is skeptical of "econometric models purporting to show that legal and illegal immigration has only a slight, if any, negative effect on U.S. labor." Huddle asks if models and field studies which do show "significant wage depression and job displacement [are] ignored and distorted . . . treated as taboos because immigration as a win-win situation is such a powerful myth?" Frank Morris (1990), Dean of Graduate Studies and Urban Research at Morgan State University (Baltimore), testified in the same vein before the House of Representatives Subcommittee on Immigration, Refugees, and International Law, stating:

> My first concern is that the black community, in looking at the slow rate of growth of our numbers in the labor force and our increasing need for higher skills, may find that any encouraging assumptions we had about opportunities for young black workers and prospective workers have been sidetracked by hasty immigration policies. . . .
>
> It is clear that America's black population is bearing a disproportionate share of immigrants' competition for jobs, housing and social services.

Richard Estrada (1991), editorial writer for the *Dallas Morning News*, concurs: "Apologists for massive immigration appear to blame the large-scale replacement of black workers by Hispanic immigrants in the hotel-cleaning industry of Los Angeles on the blacks themselves, instead of acknowledging the obvious explanation that the immigrants depressed prevailing wages and systematically squeezed thousands of citizens out of the industry."

Earlier immigrants also lose, even when an influx is their own ethnic group. Estrada (1990) attributes unemployment among established Hispanics to new arrivals who undercut wages, that is, will work for less and with fewer benefits. He writes, "Whatever the impact on other segments of society, there can be little doubt that the massive influx into the Hispanic community since the late 1960s has undermined U.S. Hispanics in the labor market, as well as in access to social services and affordable housing." Jobs are systematically downgraded by labor competition so that the nostrum, "There are some jobs that Americans won't do," becomes a self-fulfilling prophecy. Bring in fresh third-world labor and, indeed, the wage, benefit, and safety conditions to which jobs devolve attract neither native-born Americans nor established immigrants. Whitmire (1992) sums up: "A surge in immigration guarantees that the less skilled service-sector jobs remain low paid."

COMMUNITY AND ETHNIC GROUP

American voters—and businesses that pay into unemployment compensation funds—might take note that every area which is highly impacted by immigration has unemployment rates substantially higher than the nation at large. Dade County, Fla., had a December, 1991, unemployment figure of 9.5 percent at the same time that unemployment was 7.1 percent for the country at large. In 1980, one of four Miami residents fell below the federal poverty line; by 1990, after steady Haitian immigration and the 120,000 of the Mariel boatload from Cuba, it was one in three!

Newcomers are often entrepreneurial and start new enterprises. Communities are sometimes upgraded. Nevertheless, benefits may be narrow because immigrants tend to hire workers of their own ethnic group. Indeed, some businesses are not new but displace American-owned operations. In 1960, blacks owned 25 percent of the gas stations in Dade County (which encompasses Miami). By 1979, black ownership had dwindled to 9 percent, and Cuban ownership accounted for 48 percent of the total. This shift in an already developed region is not adequately explained as a net gain in enterprise. A county supports just so many gas stations!

Moreover, immigration is making blacks a minority in communities such as Watts, Calif., that until recently were predominantly black. Black Americans often hold the majority of jobs—from menial to high-level professional—but Hispanics have organized to demand access to public employment on the basis of a group-rights formula called *population parity*. At Martin Luther King Hospital in Watts, the result would be to displace blacks. Growth sufficient to retain old employees and absorb new ones is not in the cards for cash-strapped city and state facilities.

NO LABOR SHORTAGE IN THE UNITED STATES

No economic consideration justifies present U.S. immigration policy. America is not now, and never since the closing of the frontier has been, threatened by insufficient labor. Labor shortage is a myth promulgated by those who want fresh immigration as a source of cheap labor, as a way to consolidate political power by increasing the representation of their ethnic group, or out of a misguided humanitarian motive. Labor shortage is simply a convenient assertion. In fact, not even skilled labor is in short supply.

"Fifteen percent" seems seared into the collective brain of corporate America. This was said to be the proportion of labor force entrants through the year 2000 who would be white and male, the traditional pool of skilled labor. The statistic, which appeared in 1987 in the Hudson Institute's *Executive Summary of Workforce 2000*, is in error. Baldly, it is dead wrong.

On Nov. 19, 1990, three years later, *U.S. News & World Report* published the correct figure for white males entering the labor force through the year 2000. It is 31.6 percent—more than twice as large as the figure stated in the *Executive Summary* and authoritatively quoted by any CEO worth his or her salt. Omission of the word *net* made all the difference. The original document, but not the *Executive Summary*, conveyed the fact that 15 percent *more* white males are expected to enter the labor force than retire from it by the year 2000 (A Second Look, 1990).

The media, including *Science* staff writers, did not check the *Executive Summary* rendition. A correction, a letter to the editor of *Science* by Chancellor Richard C. Atkinson (1989) of the University of California (San Diego), was duly published but mainly passed without remark. The correction caused barely a ripple even after being picked up by *U.S. News & World Report*. Executives and government planners continue to believe "15 percent." The additional 16 or 17 percent of work-force entrants who will be white males has yet to figure in most people's calculations.

The incorrect number gave rise to dire predictions of labor shortage, an acute skilled labor shortage in particular. One wonders if this memory haunted anyone in the midst of middle-management layoffs in 1991–1992. Also unemployed were several hundred (out of fewer than 1,000) new Ph.D.s in mathematics who could not find jobs in the spring of 1991. *Science* (Math Ph.D.s, 1991) reports that they were competing with Chinese students seeking asylum and professionally established Russian mathematicians: Among the latter, "as many as 300 have sought employment in the United States in the last 2 years." Mathematicians are not the worst off; they may again be employed as mathematicians when the insurance industry recovers. Worst job prospects are in the humanities and basic sciences (e.g., astronomy). It cannot bode well for baccalaureate- or doctorate-granting programs and the country that skilled graduates have difficulty finding suitable work. The human as well as economic cost of underemployment may be felt for years to come.

False alarm though it was—and causing as it did an executive-suite panic verging on hysteria—reactions to the *Executive Summary* of Workforce 2000 were not all bad. For example, broad-based efforts to upgrade the language and technical skills of minorities and expand childcare facilities (for working mothers) benefitted both the economy and workers.

THE IMMIGRATION FIASCO

But the *Executive Summary* error also caused mischief. It prompted the business community to support passage of the 1990 Immigration Reform Act, a body blow to America if ever there was one. The 1990 legislation increased legal immigration by 40 percent. The flows of regular immigrants plus refugees and asylees now combine for a total of about 1 million arrivals annually. Permanent settlers who immigrate illegally add 400,000 to 1 million more. Against this total, approximately 160,000 persons voluntarily leave the United States each year. Thus, a net of at least 1,300,000 new settlers come each year intending to stay. This mass movement across borders has increased in every year since 1965. The Center for Immigration Studies (1992) estimates that 1972–1992 immigrants, including their descendants, account for half of U.S. population growth during this period.

Each year's immigrants added to the number of young Americans (both sexes and many-hued) just entering the labor market are straining the economy's capacity to create high-quality jobs. Even in a nonrecessionary economy, one cannot imagine anything but a buyer's market in labor. Most new jobs are expected to be in the service sector, and the majority will be low-paying. Think hamburger flipper; productivity: medium to low. Historically, the service sector has not been a leader in productivity growth, and this introduces a second reason that median, real disposable personal income is flat or falling.

THE CAPITAL-TO-LABOR RATIO AND LABOR PRODUCTIVITY

An inadequate ratio of capital to labor is the accepted explanation for slow gains in labor productivity. A 1 percent growth in the labor force requires business to generate a 1 percent growth in capital investment just to maintain the going capital-to-labor ratio. Less than an equivalent investment actually drags down per capita gross domestic product (GDP) because, in industrialized countries, total output is expected to increase by just 0.7 percent for every percentage increase in labor alone (see Rukstad, 1989, for the source of this estimate, the Cobb-Douglas equation). The Cobb-Douglas equation implies that, with labor characteristics and capital investment unchanged, a larger supply of labor leads to less output per worker. That is, when the labor supply grows, capital investment must increase just to keep labor productivity from falling.

So far, the United States has matched growth in the labor force with growth in capital investment but has been hard-pressed to put much extra capital behind each worker. From 1973 to 1989, *capital per employee* grew at a rate of just 0.6 percent; thus, the United States is not optimally backing both new and old jobs. Growth in labor productivity is on a slow track because labor does not have access to the best or to all possible technology. Economist Paul W. McCracken (1992), a former chairman of the president's Council of Economic Advisors, puts it this way:

> While the sources of our poor basic economic performance are many, one of the causes is clearly inadequate investment. And low investment means inevitably a slower introduction of new technology. Both the slower rates of increase in the stock of capital backing up each American worker and the more sluggish introduction of technology simply mean arthritic increases in productivity, real income and our international competitive position.

In fact, U.S. investment is proportionately the lowest among G-7 countries (the industrial superpowers). The United States invested 12 percent of GDP in 1990. By comparison, Japan invested 23.4 percent of its GDP in new factories, office buildings, machinery, and other capital goods. Our rate of investment and consequent slow growth in productivity put America behind every country in the world with which we care to compare ourselves. It is enough to say that from 1988 through late 1991, growth in U.S. labor productivity was flat zero.

Inadequate growth in the capital-to-labor ratio can be explained by too little saving or too much labor. Most traditional economic analyses pillory too little saving. If the labor factor is mentioned, it is usually to say that the bulge in new labor traceable to women and baby boomers has been absorbed. Economists engaged in studying productivity rarely take immigration into account. Thus, little is made of capital investment's having to play catch-up with a still rapidly growing labor supply.

INDUSTRY INCENTIVES AND CAPITAL INVESTMENT

Aside from its direct impact on productivity, a burgeoning supply of labor lowers the wages that labor commands (see above), and this development alone can change producer incentives. Whereas industry in a healthy economy will spend on automation and innovation in order to maximize output per worker-hour, lower-cost labor damps this incentive. The front-end investment needed to raise productivity may not seem justified when the labor factor is cheap. A tight labor market has the reverse effect, as one sees in Japan. Although more saving and better preparation of the labor force may account for much of the faster growth in productivity in Japan compared to the United States, the fundamental question is: What lies behind those factors? The explanation may be demography.

The contrast between Japanese and U.S. population trends could hardly be more stark. Some observers say that Japan's nearly stationary population—the result of low fertility and closed borders—accounts for a crucial difference in industrial strategy. With a nongrowing labor force, the Japanese compete by investing heavily in technology. See, for example, from the *Wall Street Journal*:

> A key motivation for Japan's current spending spree is a population trend. For the first time in a century, some economists predict, the country's working-age population will decrease later this decade as

more and more people reach retirement age. If its economy is to continue growing, the smaller labor pool must be more efficient than international rivals. The way to get productivity is to spend. That the rest of the world may get left behind in the process is an almost accidental result (Japan Slows, 1991).

Howard F. Van Zandt (1991), who is said to be "the foremost authority on Japanese business today," explains Japanese successes in similar terms. Promotion of quality control, high productivity of workers, a lifetime employment system, and cooperation of management, labor, and government go far toward explaining Japan's success. These are (as Van Zandt wrote originally in 1986) "all good reasons, but as yet unexplained is why the Japanese were motivated to do these things. Now the answer to this all-important question is emerging. Nippon's highly restrictive immigration policy is being given the credit as the stimulus that caused the others to fall into place."

In the 1960s, business interests in various countries prevailed upon their governments to import labor. The Germans took Turkish guest workers; the British took Jamaicans; the United States opened the door to third-world immigration. But the Japanese Diet withstood pressure to import labor. Other rapidly developing countries in Asia, including Korea, Singapore, and Taiwan, are said to have a labor shortage today; but, states Finnish director of the International Labor Organization Juhani Lonnroth, they "are not eager to increase the inflow of cheap labor because of the fear that this would slow down productivity and hinder the process of technological advancement" (Expert, 1992). Japan is, and others are becoming, economic powerhouses today because scarce labor promotes a technological response.

A similar conclusion emerges from a seminal study of factors which contribute to international competitiveness. Prevailing wisdom counts labor scarcity as a handicap. But Michael E. Porter (1990) concludes that it can be a springboard to success if it "prods" industry to compensate with innovation and automation. Indeed, the post-World War II Swiss and U.S. economies reached

new heights with a constant-size labor force. Subsequently the
United States, contrary to its own recent history and that of both
the Japanese and Swiss, embarked upon a policy of rapid labor-
force growth. Cheap labor has been substituting for capital
investment ever since. Now, the United States is rigidifying into a
mode of low growth in productivity, from which follows stagnation in real wages.

Other factors may indeed contribute to the slow growth in
U.S. productivity. However, it stretches the imagination just too
far to blame low productivity on U.S. workers' characteristics,
that is, low skills, low work ethic, and lack of commitment. A
nuclear scientist could not become an efficient street-cleaner if
his best tool was a pushbroom. The American worker needs tools.
No single other factor is so potent as the capital-to-labor ratio.

Incentives to save and incentives to invest savings in tangible
capital and technology (rather than in financial speculation) are
elements in planning for the future. The key is that, no matter
what the savings rate, the American worker will not get sufficient
tools until labor ceases to be cheap. The economy needs a return
to the condition where investment in technology is the most
profitable way to increase output.

THE SOCIAL FABRIC

Considering both U.S. competitiveness in international markets and the outlook for labor, the present situation is untenable.
The social fabric is in jeopardy in part because, at the socioeconomic bottom, discouraged workers do not search for work at
all. Limited job opportunities distort incentives straight through
developmental milestones: Why stay in school? Why apply
oneself? Why not get pregnant? Rationally, welfare and criminal
activities including drug-dealing *do* offer better opportunity.

Both native-born Americans and immigrants find that crime
may pay: The Triads, an import from Hong Kong, outdo the
Mafia; Southeast Asian gangs battle for turf and sales territories

against Hispanic gangs, and both battle blacks in Southern California; chronic rioting in Long Beach, Calif., pits Hispanics against Cambodians; the fall, 1991, Washington, D.C., riot erupted when a novice black female police officer attempted to arrest a drunkenly abusive Hispanic. Asians account for 10 percent of inmates in California's juvenile detention system. Chicago police are fighting Greek, Filipino, Syrian, Chinese, Cambodian, and Vietnamese as well as longer-established black and Hispanic gangs. Ethnic gangs are spreading to more and more U.S. cities, where they both intimidate and hide among established, law-abiding ethnic populations.

All things considered, and even if the *Executive Summary of Workforce 2000* had been right, immigration is not the answer for any conceivable labor shortfall in the United States. What is the problem with educating American youth in order to fill the hoped for high-tech, more productive jobs of the future?

A high standard of living—the American dream—means that everyone who wants to work should prosper. A prosperous labor force contributes more to the polity than it takes away. Growth of markets and a sound base for government revenue are clear benefits. The buying power and confidence of working Americans—of every race and national origin—are the cornerstone of a strong domestic market on which all depend and for which there is no substitute. But population growth which systematically undercuts the value of labor is not consistent with the national ideal. Prosperous Americans, not just lots of Americans, make the market—and the dream.

Thus, population stabilization is a key building block in integrated economic and social policy. With present policies, population cannot stabilize, productivity gains will be negligible, and the American standard of living cannot help but fall.

Per capita GDP slipped in 1991 to its lowest level since 1982. Other countries were also suffering from recession; nevertheless, a World Bank tabulation of countries by per capita gross national product put the United States in sixth place. Even without further overpopulation, the apparent prosperity of the late 1980s is unlikely to be repeated soon. It was built on debt. The country enters a new decade and a new century with red ink on federal, state, local, and consumer ledgers, and with vast international trade imbalances.

Members of Congress, mostly with legal (not business) backgrounds, might be advised to learn that when labor is cheap industry forgoes the expense of capital investment, even though it raises productivity in the long run. George Borjas and Richard Freeman (1992), Vernon M. Briggs, Jr. (1990), and Donald Huddle (1992, 1993) are among the growing number of economists who conclude that labor is cheap because of rapid growth in the labor supply, and that immigration is largely responsible for this trend. Ten percent of the U.S. labor force are not native-born Americans. The Immigration and Naturalization Service (INS) counted 1.9 million legal immigrants in 1990 (including some newly processed, formerly illegal immigrants who received amnesty under the 1986 act to control illegal immigration). "Over half, or 1.04 million of the 1990 immigrants are estimated to have entered the labor market. Of these, one third have less than a high school education," states the Center for Immigration Studies (1992).

It is up to policymakers in Washington to cease flooding the labor market via immigration. Only Congress and the president can pull the policy levers which will make a difference. If they do it, a tightening labor market will restore the confidence of American youth and also draw investment into innovative and sophisticated technology. This, in turn, will make jobs more productive and better paid, and the country more competitive internationally.

MIDDLE-CLASS AMERICA: IN FOR THE LONG HAUL

Adjustments take time, but at least a goal would be in sight. The transformation of housewives and baby boomers into workers long ago passed its peak. Were it not for high immigration, the labor market could now be coming into healthy balance, stimulating industry to raise capital investment and, concurrently, productivity. After two decades of stagnation, the buying power of average Americans would slowly begin to pick up.

In contrast, continued population growth is a long-run threat to a good quality of life for all. The issue is not so much number of jobs, but the quality of jobs created in an environment of very cheap labor. For how much longer must underemployment and part-time employment mar the future?

The 1980s saw the greatest redistribution of wealth away from the middle class that this country has ever known. Indeed, the middle class in America—the part which cannot afford to flee to the few still uncrowded oases—is threatened from all sides. Signs of unease suggest that, in amenities, the quality of life in America has fallen already: Traffic and overuse of recreational areas are growing aggravations; access to health care worries many; water is scarce in some locales and more expensive; garbage and pollution are problems in every population center; children go armed to school; crime is exploding, and men as well as women fear to walk alone under more circumstances; government budgets are strained by education, health, and welfare services and the construction of new prisons; the poor and homeless are more numerous and more visible. And all are becoming hardened—as though coldness and self-centeredness were the American way. Chapters 17 and 18 address these concerns from the perspective of America's longterm carrying capacity.

Nevertheless, Americans are fortunate. It will be some time before our poverty approaches the level of degradation from which immigrants are fleeing. The United States seems like the land of opportunity to immigrants even as it ceases to be a place of hope for its own citizens. Continuing pressure from those who wish to come to America means that Americans need to order their priorities in the light of conflicting goals and principles.

One question is: Do we wish to set aside our common interests, even stepping over other Americans, in order to accommodate new arrivals? Lindsey Grant (1991) suggests that choosing will not be easy. He writes, "Eventually, we are all hurt if we destroy the purchasing power of the working class. [But] there is, perhaps, a real conflict of moral goals involved in this blindness to one's fellow citizens. A generation raised on the idea of a shared planet, for whom the only 'aliens' are from outer space, may find it hard to value a U.S. worker's prosperity higher than a foreigner's."

Globalists are among us, but they will not be the only ones to choose. American taxpayers, business, labor, educators, and administrators—all who vote—can have a voice. The lesson is not only for the United States. Negative consequences from rapid growth in the labor force extend beyond America. The majority of citizens in any country can be impoverished by desperate competition for jobs. No country can escape poverty so long as population growth fuels rapid increase in the labor supply.

17

All Our People

Americans are generous. A genuine commitment to educating and caring for the less fortunate pervades public and private decisions. Sacrifices have been made. So Americans do not understand why they are not getting good results—and, indeed, are going backward.

Americans from every walk of life have striven to help, paid their taxes, and wished to see the fruits of plenty spread through the land. After 350 years of nation-building, what is the result? By result, Americans mean whether communities are safe and clean; children educated; families fed and housed; soil, air, water, forests, and wetlands protected. The result Americans want is a healthful, sustainable, equitable system.

A SICK SOCIETY

Results are in and they are not good. The homeless are on the streets of every large and middle-sized city—worse than before the war on poverty started. Twenty percent of the nation's children live below the poverty line. The schools fail to teach— or is it that children fail to learn? Medicaid and Medicare cost the taxpayer more and more, but many people in the United States have no health care coverage.

Public spending on social programs, health care, and education increased steadily from the 1960s through 1990; but results in terms of school dropout rates, poor achievement, premarital pregnancy, babies born addicted to crack, access to health care, and the dangerousness of schools and neighborhoods give small grounds for hope. City services deteriorate, crime spreads to more neighborhoods and cities, and social safety-net programs let families, including children, fall through the cracks. One in five children in the United States lives in poverty, and a much higher proportion live in one-parent households. Premarital pregnancy and drug addiction are just two of many ills brought on by voluntary self-destructive behavior. Conditions are uniformly worse, not better.

Disintegration of the social fabric may explain why money has not solved problems and seemingly, in any amount, is not enough. Giving food, health care, or educational opportunity does not reach the root of the problem. Personalized efforts to help occasionally bear fruit, but the required scale and depth of such interventions preclude helping more than a fraction of the many dysfunctional youth in our society. Public institutions including schools cannot, in the final analysis, substitute for family and community bonds. Both family and community, however, are swallowed by the monster city.

The infirmity, developmental failure among America's youth, from which no shade of white, black, brown, red, or yellow is exempt, may mean that our residential pattern has exceeded some optimal limit. Perhaps human societies remain healthy and function well only when their size and density provide for both spacing and primary face-to-face interactions governed by family and neighborhood norms. Thus, the concept of carrying capacity, usually applied to the physical environment, may be relevant to social systems as well.

Children learn high standards of behavior in moderate-size, stable communities where interactions are expected to persist, possibly over generations. Mutual reciprocity—sometimes seen as altruism—is an evolutionarily successful behavior *only* when individuals recognize each other, expect repeated encounters and opportunities to exchange favors, and can detect cheating on the implicit deal. These conditions are typical in the smallish, stable communities which characterized America through World War II, but they are often absent in large, impersonal cities.

The faster cities grow and the more impersonal they become, the less people can count on repeated exchanges where one good turn begets another. The greater the anonymity, the more daunting is the task of creating an environment in which decency is rewarded. Reputation, except in business or professional circles, counts for little. Credit bureaus know one's personal business before the neighbors do. In effect, children may not see that their parents value respectability and the esteem of their fellow citizens.

With effort, a semblance of community may be constructed around religious, sport, or club activities, and conscientious parents often try. These are only partial substitutes for small-town America. Real communities built the quintessential America character. Suburbs and cities have a track record which is, so far, uncertain.

PARTIAL REMEDIES

Desperately, citizens and policymakers are searching for solutions. Some know that the real search is for functioning families and communities. Substitutes (too often the school is cast in this role) are overburdened, ineffective, and expensive. Even though money is not the solution, because public institutions cannot substitute for family and community, efforts to help are costing money. Additions to health care, education, welfare, and housing programs continue.

Taxes (or inflation) have to rise so long as demands for infrastructure multiply, all users contribute to environmental stress, service recipients begin to outnumber taxpayers, and government tries to provide a minimum level of services to everyone. Taxpaying Americans may find that increases in their wages and salaries do not mean much. Real disposable personal income, as well as quality of life, are likely to fall because of inflation, rising taxes, and crowding.

GROWTH IS THE PROBLEM

California is a type case for rapid population growth. It is the fastest growing state in the Union, with an annual rate of nearly 3 percent. It is growing faster than most third-world countries. Population growth puts the educational, welfare, health care, utility, police, court, and transportation systems at risk of collapsing. This partial list of overburdened public systems explains why fees and taxes rise at the same time that services are curtailed. In 1991–1992, California projected a $13 billion budget deficit.

It is a myth that greater business activity due to population growth offsets the costs of growth. Another way to say it is: A larger gross domestic product (GDP) because more people are working does not translate into higher per capita gross domestic product or higher *real disposable personal income*. The 25 percent increase in population which California experienced during the 1980s has *not* made it a more prosperous state.

Moreover, commuting distances and costs for housing at convenient locations rise as cities grow. Commuting times of four hours a day are no longer rare in Southern California; traffic congestion is as likely a culprit as distance between home and job. Work performance and family time both suffer. Businesses as well as commuters begin to feel the shoe pinch because the most valuable employees have to be well paid to compensate for their time and/or expense.

The large concentrations of people and industry have also led California to enact the toughest air-pollution-control standards in America. Businesses are being forced to pay for the air pollution they cause and are held to standards higher than those of the federal Clean Air Act. With fewer businesses or people, one can often ignore the pollution that each one emits. When population density rises, the identical individual behavior becomes part of a noxious mess.

Especially in California, emitting pollution is no longer treated as a free good; it is (appropriately) internalized as a business cost. But again, one finds that a growing population costs money.

Robert McConnell (1992) observes that much of California's growth comes in sectors that put pressure on the welfare system. California sought to buffer its poor against the disamenities of growth, but benefits now draw people to California. Freeloading is a booming cottage industry. Welfare costs increase by 12 percent a year, and 7 percent of California's 1991 welfare recipients did not live there one year earlier.

Currently, every six California taxpayers bear the burden for five welfare recipients. But wage-earners in the thirty to fifty-six-year-old age brackets and businesses are fleeing the state, while more and more who need services are entering. By 1995, there will be more tax users than taxpayers. Gov. Pete Wilson has said that California is headed for a "fiscal train wreck" by the year 2000, when projections show that education, health, and welfare costs alone will exceed the entire tax collections of the state.

Clearly, business has a disincentive to stay in congested, high-tax, highly regulated areas, so growth eventually costs jobs. Loss of amenities, rising taxes, fees for polluting, and the higher wages required to attract skilled employees motivate many large corporations to relocate. The aerospace industry is but one of those which had begun to pull out of California before the 1992 Los Angeles riots. The Chamber of Commerce is concerned that 41 percent of companies polled in 1991 are expanding operations outside of California, and another 14 percent are thinking of relocating both headquarters and operations—pulling up stakes entirely. Thus, major employers as well as the self-employed are trying to escape the consequences of population growth. But no taxpayer, employer, or employee escapes all the consequences.

The reasons that population growth is impoverishing California should be evident by now. Infrastructure has to grow and that is expensive; large systems become unwieldy and begin to waste; all levels of government, which are among the biggest systems, take an increasing share of wealth; taxes and fees rise, and almost everyone pays more. Without even counting that a rapidly growing unskilled labor force drives down wages, impedes growth in productivity, and probably increases the welfare burden, population growth costs almost all citizens real money.

THE CORNUCOPIANS

Only with difficulty can one conclude that population growth is the gold brick road to prosperity. But some still try. The cornucopians assume that the Earth's resources and capacity to accept pollution are effectively infinite. They maintain that man-made capital can substitute indefinitely for natural capital and reject outright the concept of carrying capacity. Unshaken by evidence, cornucopians also take a longterm view of population growth and human well-being. While not disputing that the short-run effects may be painful, or that wages are depressed by rapid growth in the supply of labor, cornucopians simply contend that hardships should be discounted because economic misery is an incentive. In *The Economic Consequences of Immigration*, Julian Simon (1989) says that population growth both increases the supply and lowers the cost of resources, and ends by raising the standard of living for all.

By cornucopian reasoning, Dickensian conditions in England contributed materially to the glory of the British Empire, and illegal sweatshops in Los Angeles and New York, *pari passu*, will enhance the economic and environmental health of the United States—in the long run. The cornucopians do not care for the average American—the working man or woman who wants to live in a safe neighborhood, is trying to make ends meet today, and is not much comforted by the long sweep of history.

Cornucopians discount the working poor who may be one paycheck away from homelessness. Yet, the number of these Americans appears to be on the rise. Increasingly, often reluctantly and briefly, longtime middle-class Americans also turn to public assistance. No one begrudges them the helping hand.

SOCIAL SAFETY NET FOR ALL COMERS

Nevertheless, some public services have grown so burden-some to the tax-paying community that they are in themselves a factor nudging taxpayers into poverty. Among the largest pro-grams that use federal and state monies to benefit the needy are Medicaid, uncompensated care in public hospitals,* Aid to Families with Dependent Children (AFDC), public education, earned income tax credit, food stamps, school lunches, housing assistance, and general assistance. The number of people covered by Medicaid, a shared federal and state program, grew by 3.1 million in 1990.

Most Americans assume that the beneficiaries of these programs—which are supported by taxes or deficit spending—are other Americans. It may come as a surprise, therefore, that the annual cost of services for just one year's additional *legal* immigrants is nearly $2 billion.

Illegal immigrants absorb additional sums, more difficult to trace. The Center for Immigration Studies (CIS) estimates, how-ever, that $5.4 billion of 1990 expenditures on thirteen major federal and state programs can be traced to illegal aliens. Public education (K–12) is the largest expense category attributable to illegal aliens: The CIS (1991) estimates that kindergarten through high school plus Headstart accounted for over $2.5 billion in 1990: "Other major programs used by illegal aliens are uncompensated medical care in public hospitals ($963.5 million), criminal justice and corrections ($831 million), and Medicaid ($665.3 million)."

America now has subsidized immigration. Today, welfare is used by proportionately more immigrants than native-born Americans, and the gap appears to be widening. Economist George J. Borjas (1990b) writes that "By 1980, immigrants were more likely than natives to take welfare: 8.8% of immigrant households as against 7.9% native." This greater dependence on

---

*These costs are paid by the taxpayer, too. Uncompensated costs in *private* hospitals are shifted to private patients and their insurance carriers.

welfare reverses the traditional pattern—and our continuing image of immigrants—in which the country benefitted from the work ethic of committed newcomers. Borjas (1990c) further notes that "There really is a fundamental conflict between the welfare state and immigration."

Urban centers which are growing especially fast are interested in just how large a subsidy they pay to immigrants. Los Angeles County commissioned the Urban Institute to study its cash flow. The county learned that during the late 1980s it had provided an average of $2,245 a year more in social services per immigrant family than it collected in taxes. U.S. Rep. Elton Gallegly (R-Calif.) states that in 1990, Los Angeles County spent $276.7 million in services to *illegal* aliens—representing a 34 percent increase from the previous year. Statewide, Gov. Pete Wilson's preliminary estimate was that immigration—illegal, legal, and refugees—accounted for $1 billion of California's projected $13 billion 1991–1992 budget deficit.*

A subsequent report on illegal immigration (Rea and Parker, 1992) prepared for the California Auditor General's office estimates that undocumented immigrants residing in San Diego County in 1992 accounted for 9 percent of the total population and a vastly greater percentage of the county's health, justice system, education, and welfare costs. "Using the San Diego data, the Auditor General extrapolated that illegal aliens statewide generate a net cost to state and local governments of 'approximately $3 billion' per year" (Walters, 1992).

All told, "Almost a third of current [California] residents migrated here within the last 10 years, many from foreign countries and without substantial resources," write Chase and Dolan (1992). They expect that in the "coming year," illegal aliens will account for an additional 315,000 beneficiaries of state Medicaid assistance, increasing the roll by 25 percent.

---

*Cuts in programs and a tax increase would have left California with less than a $2 billion deficit for the 1991–1992 fiscal year, but for the unanticipated costs associated with rioting.

Wherever concentrations of immigrants—most of whom are designated minorities—are found, significant public monies are used or requested for services. In St. Paul, Minnesota, for example, members of the Hmong tribe from Southeast Asia take up a significant portion of public housing, police time (on account of wife abuse), and educational funds. In Montgomery County, North Carolina, 25 percent of the health department's 6,000-person caseload can be traced to Mexicans. Another situation, involving the 85,000 Hispanic immigrants in Washington, D.C., has become explosive but can be remedied by money, according to an interview given to Sanchez (1992) by a spokesperson for a U.S. Commission on Civil Rights. The 12,000 Washington residents of Asian descent may be better served: A position, special assistant for Asian and Pacific Affairs, is filled by a Chinese-American woman whose duty it is to advise the mayor.

Massachusetts (1992) is under fire for providing too little: It tightened eligibility criteria to make it more difficult for illegal aliens to qualify fraudulently for welfare benefits. Soon, an advocacy group charged that the state Welfare Department was hiring too few bilingual employees. The specific complaint was that people who cannot cope with the English language have had benefits denied or delayed. The federal government was called in to investigate.

CITIZEN CHILDREN

An unintentionally favored category of illegal immigrants is women who give birth in the United States. Their children, automatically U.S. citizens, cannot be deported, and reluctance to separate families effectively means that the mother gets to stay, too. As citizens, the children are entitled to AFDC payments. The 1991 bill for this category of recipients was $125 million in Los Angeles County alone. Indeed, children born to women who are in the United States illegally account for 25 percent of the welfare caseload in California. And California accounts for 26 percent of welfare payments in the United States!

EDUCATION

Another especially entitled category is school-age children. A U.S. Supreme Court ruling requires the states to educate all children regardless of legal or illegal status. In Florida, the influx of illegal immigrants adds about $100 million annually to the education budget. In Dallas, Texas, 2,000 to 2,500 *additional* non-English-speaking children enroll in the public schools each year. In 1987 (long ago in terms of the rapid rise in numbers), 90 percent of the 600,000-plus non-English-speaking children in California had been born outside of the United States.

Educating our children is one of America's primary goals. But take education as it is today: The problems are so bad that it is not clear where to start reform. Limiting the discussion to population growth, consider this: The United States is entering another cycle where the schools are not large enough to accommodate all the children. Temporary outbuildings are being pressed back into service. Building out will mean bond issues for construction and more teachers. If immigration into California increases in the 1990s as projected, one elementary school would have to be built every day of every year for the next thirty years to keep up with demand! The alternative is much larger class size.

Apart from class size, common language is an issue. Assimilation to American culture depends on English. But the courts initially, and now politics, mandate teaching children in their own language. The policy known as *English as a second language* (ESL) is supposed to bridge a transition into English-language classrooms. But, in fact, the foreign-language lobby perpetuates itself, and many children complete secondary school without ever having to learn in English. ESL is an obstacle to assimilation and is a problem for this reason alone. But when public school budgets are strained so that American children—often the poorest—are shortchanged, how can one justify the extra cost of teaching in a special-language classroom?

Do the arithmetic for your community. Each ESL classroom needs a teacher. Teachers cost their salary plus benefits (usually 20 to 25 percent of salary). How much is that? Nashville is not a major immigrant destination. But in 1991 its public schools employed forty teachers to teach children who spoke thirty-four foreign languages (up from twenty-six languages in 1988), plus three counselors who managed liaison between the schools and Cambodian parents. At an average salary of $29,000 and benefits of $7,250, the forty ESL teachers cost Nashville $1.45 million a year. Not bad for a city education department that has increased class sizes; cut staffing, including teachers' assistants; eliminated electives; and is lobbying hard to raise taxes!

Los Angeles is a worst case. This metropolis teaches children speaking 140 foreign languages—in many age groups, of course. Black parents in some districts complain that their children are the losers. What happens to American children when resources they should get—and need in order to become productive citizens—go to others? Ask also if the taxpayer intends to have public monies spent on American children or on anyone who is in America? How high are we willing that taxes should go, or how low will we allow standards to fall?

HEALTH CARE

Health care for persons illegally in the United States is unexpectedly high, considering the youth of most illegal migrants, because women routinely use public hospitals for delivery. Taxpayers pay for this, although the hospital is not technically compensated by Medicaid. A Texas hospital was close to bankruptcy due to the numbers arriving for obstetrics care; the flood was reduced to a trickle when admitting clerks dressed in green uniforms resembling those worn by Immigration and Naturalization Service (INS) personnel.

New York is the one state where pregnant women are entitled to Medicaid services, including prenatal care, regardless of legal status. The federal government challenged this provision of state law and, as of 1992, the case was being litigated (*Lewis v. Grinker*). Whatever the outcome, any person can receive *emergency* care in any county hospital in the United States.

Entitlements for illegal immigrants are disputed on various levels. Some officials of the Health Care Financing Administration (HCFA) insist that no Medicaid funds are used for illegal immigrants. Except for New York State and in emergency cases, perhaps they are not. As in Massachusetts, however, social-service and health-care workers do appear to collude at times in order to defeat regulations that are intended to screen out illegal immigrants. Indeed, individual cases *are* pitiable. But is it fair to use limited resources this way when native-born Americans are also in need?

Whatever the sentiment with regard to illegal aliens, experience in Oregon during planning stages for a proposed alternative to Medicaid suggests that—as of 1990—most Americans wanted to extend benefits and welfare to immigrants who are in the United States legally. The stereotype of the immigrant as one who works hard, contributes much, and takes little dominates the thinking of many Americans.

Generosity might be tempered, however, by attention to the adequacy of health care for ordinary Americans. How are we doing with the native-born American poor? Or the American middle class? Thirty-seven million people in the United States are without health-care insurance. Many of them are employed.

Extension of coverage that results in higher costs seems unaffordable because the United States already spends more per capita on health care than any other country in the world. Thirteen percent of gross national product (GNP) goes for health care. That is more than *one dollar out of every eight*; how much does that leave for education, housing, food, infrastructure, pollution abatement, criminal justice, transportation, defense, interest on the national debt, and new investment? The total health-care bill in 1991 was $700 billion. To be concrete, about $900 of the cost of every new U.S.-built car goes to pay for auto workers' health care. Capitalism is not a cow fed in heaven to be milked on earth, and this level of expenditure is unsustainable.

Some health care—often called *primary*, as opposed to high-tech chronic care—is preventive or curative. Our society would like to afford this level of care for all Americans. Therefore, perhaps we need to know who the 37 million uninsured are. Fourteen percent of non-Hispanic whites, 22 percent of blacks, and 40 percent of Hispanics have no health-care insurance. Do we know how many are citizens or how many are legally or illegally in the United States? Maybe we have to ask.

How many of the world's poor and sick are affordable in the United States, without driving publicly subsidized health-care costs much higher? What about the 20 percent of children in America who are poor? Who are these poor children? How many are immigrants and non-English-speaking children of immigrants who were poor before coming to America? How many were born here to women illegally in the United States? How many are themselves here illegally? And who pays for them?

CONGRESSIONAL LARGESSE, LOCALITIES' DEBTS

Congress appropriates funds for the District of Columbia. Other municipalities as well as states bear proportionately much more of their own costs. Therefore, a source of growing friction between governors and mayors on the one hand, and the federal government on the other, is that the federal government mandates programs which result in state and local expenditures. The federal government also sets refugee and legal immigrant numbers.

The 1980 Refugee Act, which created the refugee category, provides that the executive branch will annually set an admissions ceiling. Initially, refugee numbers hovered at about 50,000 admissions, but more recently (under pressure from Congress), the ceiling has risen by large annual increments. Numbers totaled 131,000 in 1991, and 142,000 in 1992. On an individual basis, refugees are the most costly immigrants by far. The federal government's upfront cost to settle the average refugee is $7,000 (a U.S. State Department estimate). The greater costs are downstream and, except for Social Security, these are mostly borne by state and local government. Refugees are automatically entitled to all benefits available to citizens plus, at the same age as those who have paid into Social Security, Medicare coverage, and a monthly pension. California is a favored destination because of its benefits package. Gov. Wilson's ballpark figure is that 70 percent of Russian refugees who have settled there remain on welfare.

Those eligible for refugee status prefer it to coming as a regular immigrant. Certain groups singled out by Congress are exempt from having to prove "a well-founded fear of persecution" with the result that, in 1991, the Russian regular immigration quota was unfilled. Travel writer Don Barnett (1992) describes the "cottage industry" which has grown up around teaching prospective refugees in Russia and those newly arrived at their U.S. destinations "how to work the ropes of U.S. social services." One Russian paper carried a letter within an article detailing benefits: " 'My mother-in-law lives in her own [subsidized] apartment and receives a full [U.S.] pension, which surprises even me. . . . This is a poor man's paradise.' "

PRIORITIES

Are our priorities properly placed when we neglect American children in order to accommodate others? Would it not be proper to help native-born American children (born to women legally in the United States), even at the cost of denying many, many deserving others?

People cannot be faulted for taking whatever is offered. But America may have to reevaluate what can be offered to its own citizens as well as whether they deserve to be first in line. Generosity and trust can become unintended largesse.

Abuse of welfare disgusts most Americans, but the system that encourages it was enacted by Congress. Refugees and other immigrants simply respond to the incentives and may believe they have found the American way. Continuing down the present path, however, quickly sponges up monies intended to help our own.

A newsletter from Population-Environment Balance (1991) reports that the 1990 Immigration Reform Act creates about $3 billion of additional funding obligations annually, for each year's complement of immigrants, in federal and local programs already experiencing dire funding shortages and slated for cuts. School- and child-centered programs are prominent on the list. Costs are borne largely by state and local taxpayers.

Former Tennessee Gov. Winfield Dunn (R) presented his 1972 budget to the state General Assembly with the words, "Those societies which have not been benevolent toward their own offspring have not been well regarded by history." Without attributing an opinion to Gov. Dunn with respect to immigration, one may ponder his words. What if emphasis were placed on the phrase "*own* offspring"?

The Carrying Capacity of the United States

The carrying capacity is the number of individuals that an area can support without sustaining damage. Carrying capacity is exceeded if so many individuals use an area that their activities cause deterioration in the very systems that support them. Exceeding the carrying capacity sometimes harms an environment so severely that the new number who can be supported is smaller than the original equilibrium population. The carrying capacity would then have declined, perhaps permanently.

Any number of elements or systems can be hurt by overuse. A field can be grazed down until the root systems of grasses are damaged; or so much game can be hunted off that food species are effectively extirpated. Now, the foragers that ate the grass or the predators that killed the game have lost a food source. In effect, the carrying capacity has been exceeded so that the population dependent on the area's productive systems is worse off than it was originally.

Animal populations that destroy their niche come and go. If not too many examples come to mind, it is because they rather quickly go. The miniature ponies on Assateague Island illustrate a point on the continuum. They would overgraze their island, seriously depleting their future food supply, except for the fact that a portion of each year's colt crop is removed. Without human intervention (there are no predators and apparently no reservoir of infectious disease), the pony population would explode. Probably it happened in the past. Their very small size today is a vestigial effect of starvation, when only the tiniest, for whom the least blades of grass were lifesaving, survived.

A population cannot be stable if, by its size or behavior, it destroys the very life-support systems on which it depends. Sooner or later, degradation of the environment is felt in inadequacies of the food or water supply, shelter, or havens where individuals can be safe and the young can develop. Sustainability requires human or animal populations to stay at or below the carrying capacity of their physical environment.

PHYSICAL AND CULTURAL CARRYING CAPACITY

Humans are a little different because of wanting more than bare subsistence. Humans value their aesthetic, intellectual, cultural, and political creations. People want more than a loaf of bread and processed grape juice. For humans, then, *carrying capacity* refers to the number who can be supported *without degrading the physical, ecological, cultural, and social environments*. Carrying capacity relates to the desired quality of life.

The carrying capacity of the United States depends upon standard-of-living targets, including high-quality recreational opportunities, coexistence with an abundance and diversity of wild species, tolerable work-to-home commuting conditions, favorable conditions for childrearing, and safe neighborhoods. Where population size detracts from the capacity to provide these amenities, overpopulation exists.

RECOGNIZING STRESS

One may discern overpopulation quite apart from large systems and specific resources. Overpopulation shows up in quality of life and cost of living. Repeatedly one sees—at least those who wish to, will see—that more people mean more problems from pollution, crowding, and resource scarcity because even conservationists pollute and consume. The costs of adjusting (i.e., decently accommodating more and more people in the same amount of space and with the same fund of natural resources) are monetized. Garbage is the topic of the hour. In just a few years, dumping fees in U.S. cities have skyrocketed, from $5 or $10 a ton to an average of over $150. Burning questions are whether to incinerate or not, how to recycle, and how to make money from one's ash heap.

The rising cost of water in areas that are not naturally arid makes the same point. Even if the quantity of water is sufficient, purity tends to suffer when population density grows. It costs money to keep clean or clean up. A 1992 *Wall Street Journal* account (Poor Pay, 1992) states that "Boston water and sewer bills have risen 39% in the past two years as the costs of cleaning up Boston Harbor have been phased into rates." In 1991, the average household paid $500 a year in water and sewer bills, and "water shutoffs as a result of nonpayment of water bills . . . tripled."

Demands on the public sector also increase as population grows. Taxes invariably rise to meet the higher demand for education, social services, health care, law enforcement, infrastructure such as schools, hospitals, prisons, systems for human transportation, and disposal of sewage and other wastes. Concurrently, systems are often left to deteriorate, an attractive option because taxpayers and users may not see meaningful gains even with higher spending. Infrastructure is decaying nationwide, but goes unnoticed until a bridge collapses, sewers leak, or tunnels cave in.

The disappearance of natural capital is equally silent, but it is continuing at a great rate and is compromising future production. Iowa has lost 50 percent of its topsoil since the advent of farming in the nineteenth century. The drawdown of U.S. aquifers is also proceeding quickly and, so far, has led to abandonment of over 300,000 formerly irrigated acres in Arizona alone. Seventy-five percent of irrigation is threatened in Nebraska. Good air, land, water, and energy are the nuts and bolts of carrying capacity. It is not trivial for the sustainability of our society that, as summarized by Carrying Capacity Network (1991), the United States is "currently losing topsoil 18 times faster than [it is being replaced; or that] groundwater, . . . much of which was stored during the Ice Age and is non-renewable, is currently being pumped out of the ground 25 percent faster than it is being replenished."

Substitution for very basic inputs such as soil and fresh water will be difficult. Moreover, there may be an interactive effect: Up to now, irrigation and petroleum-based fertilizers have compensated for deterioration in the innate productivity of the land. But even a temporary rise in the price of petroleum, if it led to cutbacks on fertilizer use, could unmask the hidden cost of topsoil loss. When farmers recognize that their longterm income stream is jeopardized by present farming practices, they are likely to shift toward a more sustainable process. Holding farmers' capital—their soil—intact will have the immediate result of lowering production to below what can be realized by current, soil-depleting agricultural methods.

Recognition of true costs and adoption of alternate (sustainable) agricultural technologies could come suddenly, wiping out food surpluses in just a few growing seasons. Some farmers already forgo maximizing the size of crops in order to preserve soil. But a prudent farmer might not switch all his acreage at one time. He knows that prices will not rise to compensate him for the decreased size of his crop until virtually all farmers make the transition. Changes will come when the cost of production on depleted soils rises, that is, ever-larger fertilizer and pesticide requirements and/or higher-priced petroleum force a reduction in production targets. This paradigmatic shift in agricultural accounting will be a cultural as much as an economic phenomenon.

The price of food might rise if the crop got smaller, but that effect would be limited by market mechanisms. Demand falls when prices rise, keeping downward pressure on prices of even the most essential commodities. This constitutes price elasticity, and it implies a question: Can people *afford* to buy?

Commodity prices are an unreliable indicator of scarcity, in fact, because workers in rapidly growing populations command less and less for their labor and thus have little to spend. Poor people do not buy much. They exert negligible effective demand. They go without. Thus, rapid population growth causes very little pull on most commodity prices. The price of food might not go up even if the crop were small and the number of hungry people, large.

Most of the world's 5.5 billion people are becoming poorer as they compete against each other for jobs. Most lose purchasing power on a yearly basis. Increasing numbers drop out of the consumer market altogether, exerting no effective demand. Thus, it was a fact that December, 1990, oat and wheat prices sank to their lowest levels since 1972 while more people than before starved or lived on the edge of famine. The multitudes do not bid up prices. Quality of life and environmental health, not commodity prices, are clues that the carrying capacity is being exceeded.

ENERGY AND CARRYING CAPACITY

Energy security is a key element of America's long-run, sustainable carrying capacity. Estimates of the carrying capacity assume a particular standard of living. The focus on energy recommends itself because, except for amenities provided by nature and our communities, per capita energy use is a good proxy for *standard of living*.

The eighty years between 1890 and 1970 were marked by the fastest rise in the standard of living that a whole country has ever seen; indeed, the first three-quarters of the twentieth century saw real disposable personal income rise at an average rate of 2.2 percent per year. This same period, according to energy specialist John Holdren (1991) of the University of California (Berkeley), saw a record 7 kW per capita *increase* in use of energy (from about 4 kW to over 11 kW). That works out to about 1.75 kW per twenty-year period, which is important for comparison with the latest twenty years: From 1970 to 1990, per capita energy use increased just 0.18 kW. Growth in inflation-adjusted after-tax income also stalled, averaging about 0.5 percent per year from 1973 to 1990.

The link between energy use per capita and standard of living is clear enough in concrete terms: Energy in the form of petroleum is the base for fertilizer, pesticides, on-farm mechanization, and much food processing and distribution. Energy lets us live somewhat distant from our place of work. Energy is the basis for heating, cooling, lighting, much communication, and most labor-saving devices in the home. Without plentiful energy, would your job exist?

To judge if we are within the carrying capacity of the United States, given the present standard of living, ask if our rate of energy use is sustainable. The related policy question is: Does the United States enjoy energy security? Geologists, computer modelers, petroleum industry analysts, and life scientists largely concur in projecting a bleak future.

A 1986 book, *Beyond Oil: The Threat to Food and Fuel in Coming Decades* by John Gever *et al.*, develops the concept of "energy/profit ratio": How much usable energy comes out for every unit of energy put in? That is, how much energy does one get for the energy used to find, produce, refine, and distribute energy? Long before all petroleum is used up, the best and easiest to recover deposits will be gone. Thus, the cost in energy associated with recovering petrochemical energy (oil and natural gas) will rise so that the profit ratio becomes less and less favorable. This ratio will be reflected partly in higher prices and partly in lower use of oil-based products.

In the decade or so after World War II the supply of oil seemed inexhaustible. John Gever and his coauthors point out that oil fuels were easy to tap because fields lay close to the surface; the wells were shallow and cheap to drill. Prospecting revealed so many good sites that dry wells were few and far between. The energy/profit ratio for domestic petroleum stood at about 50 to 1. But by the mid-1980s, the situation was far different. The energy/profit ratio of domestic oil was 8 to 1; of foreign oil (because of greater distribution costs), 5 to 1.

The 1991 Gulf War made the energy/profit ratio of foreign oil dramatically, if somewhat temporarily, still less favorable: Add together the investment in transporting and operating allied tanks, planes and all else. How much energy did it take just to save future units of energy from Kuwaiti fields?

When the energy/profit ratio reaches 1 to 1, there will be little point in going back to the well. Effectively, we will be out of oil; the cost of production will exceed the value of the goods and services derived from oil. New domestic oil production will reach this point, predict Gever and company, between 1995 and 2005. Although older wells will continue to pump profitably for some years longer, the diseconomies of new production signal the beginning of true energy insecurity. The point of vanishing returns for foreign producers extends out for another fifty years.

Geologists with the U.S. Geological Survey do not contradict John Gever or others' similar conclusions. *Beyond Oil* appeared in 1986. In 1991, C. D. Masters *et al.* of the U.S. Geological Survey wrote that

> The next several decades will not likely experience just a gradual exhaustion of oil as the primary energy source. Rather, the supply of oil likely will be periodically disrupted owing to its increasingly narrow geographic distribution into the single dominant area of occurrence—the Middle East.
>
> We can be substantially confident that new, large occurrences of oil, such as would be necessary to alter the proportional contribution of the Middle East to world petroleum, are not likely to be found; certainly, no such occurrences have been found in the several recent decades of intense worldwide petroleum exploration.

Fleshing out scientific overviews, Gutfeld (1992) reports the American Petroleum Institute's early 1992 estimate that "Total United States output is currently declining at an annual rate of

300,000 barrels a day." That is, the year by year decline represents 300,000 barrels less production each day. Speaking for the institute, Edward Murphy warned of this "substantial and largely unanticipated" trend: "The evidence indicates that the exploration and production sectors of the petroleum industry in the United States have entered a period of accelerated decline." The output picture is not expected to "brighten unless the oil industry wins greater access to public lands such as the Arctic National Wildlife Refuge in Alaska and certain offshore areas."

Mention of the Arctic National Wildlife Refuge (ANWR) in Alaska arouses environmentalists. For good reason, says Jan C. Lundberg, former publisher of the *Lundberg Oil Letter* and founder of Fossil Fuels Policy Action (Arcata, Calif.). A large and pristine environment would be put at risk for an amount of oil that would make only a small contribution to U.S. security. At best, the ANWR field would extend domestic oil supplies by two years.

Energy security is in far greater jeopardy from our population growth than from denying access to the few remaining pools of oil in the northern hemisphere. Indeed, population growth in the United States *drives* the increasing use of energy: From 1970 to 1990—while per capita use hardly budged—total energy consumption increased by 24 percent. John Holdren (1991) states that 93 percent of the increase in the United States' use of energy in this twenty-year period can be traced to population growth. With population growth, planning for energy security means taking aim at a moving target.

OIL FOR FOOD

Even without figuring in population growth, consensus among experts about the steep decline in domestic oil production means that we should evaluate oil's most essential uses. Perhaps domestic production for use in those most essential sectors will have to be subsidized by the society at large. That is, other energy sources might be diverted to production of oil even from wells where the energy profit ratio is 1 to 1 or less. The policy question now becomes: Where is fossil petrochemical fuel most productive, and where is substitution most difficult?

Agriculture is Gever *et al.*'s selection for this most sensitive sector of the U.S. economy. Food is essential. It generates much of our foreign exchange. No good substitutes for petroleum- and natural-gas-based pesticides and fertilizers exist, although a switch to organic farming (and avoidance of removing crop residues for alcohol-based fuels) would preserve soil fertility and minimize demand for artificial fertilizer.

These changes will be driven by the rising price of petroleum-based agricultural inputs. Supply will be in jeopardy when new wells cannot be brought in with better than a 1 to 1 energy/profit ratio, and old wells peter out. The prediction is that 2007–2025 will become the watershed years for agriculture. By this time, say Gever *et al.*, 10 percent of all U.S. oil consumption (from domestic and imported sources combined) and 60 percent of all natural gas will be required for on-farm uses. Not coincidentally, the United States will have ceased by then to be a net exporter of food.

POPULATION SIZE AND THE STANDARD OF LIVING

Now for the bad news. Depletion of soil, water, and fuel at a much faster rate than any of these can be replenished suggests that the carrying capacity of the United States already has been exceeded. David and Marcia Pimentel (1991) of the College of Agriculture and Life Sciences, Cornell University, take these three factors into account to estimate that, at a standard of living only slightly lower than is enjoyed today, the sustainable population size for the United States is less than half its present number. Beyond this, we abuse the carrying capacity and should expect sudden shocks that will massively drive down the standard of living.

The Pimentels embrace the desirability and potential for a

transition to clean, renewable energy sources as substitute for most uses of oil. The very breadth of their approach leads to their addressing *all* present and potential energy sources. They find:

> In the United States, humankind is already managing and using more than half of all the solar energy captured by photosynthesis. Yet even this is insufficient to our needs, and we are actually using nearly three times that much energy, or about 40% more energy than is captured by all plants in the United States [italics in the original]. This rate is made possible only because we are temporarily drawing upon stored fossil energy; the very use of these fossil fuels, plus erosion and other misuse of our natural resources, are reducing the carrying capacity of our ecosystem.

Evaluating land, energy, and water, the Pimentels conclude that the United States is rapidly depleting its nonrenewable or very slowly renewable resources and overwhelming the capacity of the environment to neutralize wastes. The present level of resource use is probably unsustainable in even the minimal, physical sense. If population increase and the present per capita use of resources persist, a crash becomes likely.

The Pimentels do, however, offer two alternate scenarios. Either one of them is stable and sustainable. They differ only in population size and standard of living. Both scenarios envision the United States moving to a solar-energy-based economy, that is, to total replacement of our current fossil-fuel energy dependence. Solar energy is a renewable, steady stream, so it meets a key criterion for sustainability. From renewable sources alone, however, only one-fifth to one-half of the present level of energy use would be available. To maintain a standard of living only slightly lower than we enjoy today, population size would need to decline to about 100 million people.

The estimate of maximum sustainable population size takes into account both the source and sink functions of Earth. At least two effects of pollution—greenhouse warming and the ozone hole—are poorly understood. One can only estimate the extent of change to which present levels of pollutants commit us already, the lead time before effects become manifest, and the damage that is being done. Nevertheless, the shift away from a fossil-fuel-based economy, adopted in order to minimize greenhouse gas emissions and/or as a market response to high prices, will be one of the severest constraints.

Others, more sanguine, peg the U.S. carrying capacity at a higher level. Economist Robert Costanza of the Marine Biological Institute (University of Maryland) and editor of *Ecological Economics* thinks the carrying capacity is closer to being 150 million persons (Carrying Capacity, 1991).

The Pimentels, Jan Lundberg, and John Gever *et al.* start from very different premises and institutional biases. But their conclusions accord well with each other and with earlier estimates. With twenty years' hindsight, respect for Dennis and Donnella Meadows's *Limits to Growth* is renewed. This computer model of global dynamics was published in 1972 by the Club of Rome. It traces five factors including population size, energy throughput, and pollution under different assumptions (values and feedback loops) to conclude that the system faces collapse before the end of the twenty-first century.

Fossil fuels still are being depleted at a faster rate than new discoveries are made (or likely to be made in the United States, which is thoroughly explored). Nuclear-waste disposal remains an intractable problem. Water for farmers and population centers is scarcer and more contaminated. Plus, threats the Meadows foretold in general, but could not have known specifically in 1972, now include possible global warming and the widening ozone hole. The time frame for experiencing "sudden shocks" is perhaps thirty to fifty years—beyond most legislators' lifetimes. But all our children and grandchildren should prepare, if our generation cannot reverse present demographic and environmental trends.

PLANNING AHEAD

The question is not whether the carrying capacity of land, air, and water ultimately limits how many people can subsist on

Earth and in the United States. The limits are real; the only discussion can be about whether we have passed them or how close they are coming. The ultimate question is: What combination of population size and standard of living is wanted in America?

We need ask only for ourselves. American influence truly extends little beyond U.S. borders. Sovereign nations brook no outside interference with population targets or the fertility of their people. Money, they take; pressure to democratize and free their economy is grudgingly heeded as the price paid for aid. But unsolicited advice on fertility? That is an affront!

So, for the United States and the *United States only* we may ask: What is the optimum population size? If a target is not chosen as a matter of policy, if we continue to grow by more than 3 million persons a year, one of the Pimentels' scenarios becomes academic, a nonpossibility. The larger we grow, the less likely we are to shrink gracefully back to 100 million or 150 million people; that is, we probably cannot hope, in the long term, to maintain a standard of living that much resembles what we now enjoy.

One need not accept the Pimentels' or Costanza's estimates of limits in order to see that overpopulation is not just a third-world problem. It is America's as well. Population stabilization was the target spelled out in the 1972 recommendations of the President's Commission on Population Growth and the American Future (the Rockefeller Commission). Citing considerations such as energy and mineral resources, water supply, agricultural land supply, outdoor recreation resources, and environmental pollution, the commission concluded that "Neither the health of our economy nor the welfare of individual businesses depends on continued population growth. In fact, the average person will be markedly better off in terms of traditional economic values if population growth slows down than if it resumes the pace of growth experienced in the recent past." The Commission closed with the recommendation "that the nation welcome and plan for a stabilized population."

TAKING STOCK

In 1972, the population of the United States had just passed the 210 million mark. In 1990, it passed 255 million. Because of immigration, population stabilization is a more distant goal today than in 1972, when replacement-level fertility was the issue. Moreover, the American future foreseen two decades ago appears to have arrived.

The standard of living has barely risen, and even this has come at the cost of borrowing from abroad. In many households, two earners are needed where one formerly sufficed. Home ownership and a college education are unaffordable for many Americans. Public parks and recreational areas are deteriorating from overuse. Wilderness, a refuge in thought even when not easily reached, is disappearing from America. The very poor are often "discouraged" workers, uncounted in unemployment statistics. Education, health-care, garbage-disposal, correctional, water, and highway costs have become more burdensome, while education, housing, social-service, and welfare monies are spread more thinly. The number of poor grows constantly. More children (and a larger proportion) than before live in poverty. Homelessness appears chronic.

Domestic population stabilization will not instantly cure these ills, but all become more intractable as population grows. Generations of Americans have been believers in abundance (their legacy from the frontier) and in immigration (to populate that frontier). National needs change, however. Events will show how long complacency with domestic population growth survives realization that overpopulation causes poverty; or that the poverty of the high-fertility-rate countries which send their unskilled emigrants to the United States *is being shared* with most native-born Americans.

19

And Away We Go

Few Americans get excited about population growth. It may be the starchiest subject going. Those who think of it at all often assume it is a problem for third-world countries but not America. Many believe that the U.S. population is not growing because we reached replacement-level fertility quite some time ago.

The reality is, U.S. population growth is moderate only by comparison with the third world. At a rate of 1.1 percent per year, we are growing two to ten times faster than any western European country except Liechtenstein and Iceland. Indeed, Denmark's population has stabilized and, before reunification, West Germany's population had begun to decline.

Growth in the United States can be traced to the two usual factors. The first is that more people are born each year than die (nearly 2 million more). The main reason for this imbalance is that so many females were born during the baby boom. Even if these women have only two children each, this rising generation will be larger than any ever before born here. The second reason for population growth is immigration.

AMERICA'S DEMOGRAPHIC FUTURE

Government data released in January, 1991, suggest that legal and illegal immigration will propel the United States population to 400 million by the year 2080. This is the middle projection within an array of possibilities. The Urban Institute (1992) has arrived at substantially the same figures by assuming a fertility decline to 1.9 children per woman and immigration stabilizing at under 1 million per year—highly conservative assumptions. The Urban Institute model projects 440 million people by 2090.

Both projections assume fertility and immigration below present levels and *still* suggest numbers far larger than envisioned just a few years earlier. These scenarios received very little attention in the media. Paradoxically, the U.S. Census Bureau's earlier (1989) array of possible population scenarios for the future received wide coverage. The bureau's middle projection in 1989 showed U.S. population *stabilizing* in 2020 at under 300 million.

Demographic projections extending beyond twenty or twenty-five years are fraught with uncertainty. Any one of several parameters—fertility, mortality, and immigration—can change far beyond what would be thinkable in the light of a country's recent history. For example, no 1930s demographer envisioned the baby boom that would sweep America just ten to fifteen years later.

Moreover, the media sometimes irresponsibly transform a projection into a prediction. This happened in 1989. *Prediction* implies certainty, which greatly increases the influence of scientific data on public policy. The potential to distort public policy is equally real. Public complacency over the 1990 Immigration Reform Act can be traced in part to the inaccurate portrayal of future U.S. population.

The Census Bureau's 1989 projections were criticized almost as soon as they appeared. Demographers Dennis Ahlburg and James Vaupel (1991) suggested at the time that the figure for net immigration used in computing the middle projection was too low because illegal immigration was being underestimated. Other of the Census Bureau's assumptions about immigration and mortality also seemed unwarranted. Ahlburg and Vaupel emphasize the possibility of much more variability and the probability of much faster growth than the Census Bureau had projected: "We conclude that their high projection might be treated as a reasonable middle forecast. . . . By 2080 our high projection is more than 300 million people bigger than their high projection. A U.S. population of 800 million may seem incredible, but the annual average growth rate that produces it runs at only 1.3% per year."

Indeed, so long as growth is above 0.0 percent, stabilization is pure fantasy. The tiniest bit of growth, if continued long enough, leads eventually to population doubling. At its present pace of 1.1 percent annual growth, the U.S. population will double in sixty-four years.

Assumptions about the future are based on best current information. In hindsight, it may turn out to have been misleading. For example, the 1989 middle projection assumed that net illegal immigration would fall to 100,000 a year because the 1986 Immigration Reform and Control Act (IRCA) would work as intended. For about one year, the law did have a deterrent effect, and attempts to cross the border more or less halved. However, when it became apparent that enforcement would be lax, illegal immigration resumed its pre-IRCA flow and is strengthening. Very conservatively, a net of 200,000 illegal, permanent settlers is arriving each year, so that even the Census Bureau now admits that the 1989 middle projection is an unlikely scenario. The 540,300 apprehensions of illegal immigrants at San Diego during the 1991 fiscal year were up 14 percent from 1990, and 50 percent from 1989.

Note that San Diego is just one of many hotspots for illegal crossings. Apprehensions across the whole border ran at about 1.2 million during 1991, and the Immigration and Naturalization Service (INS) estimates that three illegals cross for each one caught. The Census Bureau appears to consistently underestimate illegal settlers.

Nevertheless, one eagerly awaits publication of each new array of Census Bureau projections; regrettably, litigation over the 1990 Census delayed the most recent set by several years. Secretary of Commerce Robert Mosbacher ruled that the original figures of the disputed 1990 Census would stand for purposes of apportionment (for Congressional seats) but at the same time suggested that the amended estimates (which add 5 to 6 million people) might be used as a basis of postcensal projections and federal appropriations to states and municipalities.

A new array of projections will take into account the higher illegal immigration as well as the 1990 Immigration Reform Act, which boosts legal immigration to nearly 2 million a year when amnestied illegal aliens, asylees, and refugees are included. The bureau's estimates of fertility will probably remain close to 2.1 children per woman or higher, taking into account both business cycle fluctuations and the impetus to fertility which comes from the growing immigrant sector. The next middle projection may well estimate 200 million or 300 million more people within a century and no stabilization in sight.*

COMPONENTS OF POPULATION GROWTH

Stabilization can occur only with replacement-level fertility *and* replacement-level immigration, or some combination of the two. Biologist Paul Ehrlich (1990) suggests that Americans cut fertility still further below replacement level so that more immigrants can be accommodated. Others consider such substitution unfair to native-born Americans, who should be entitled to continue their present rate of reproduction—which is modest—as well as to enjoy the relative prosperity which low fertility helps to ensure. Since U.S. fertility is right at replacement level, the population would stop growing in about forty years were it not for immigration. Immigration into the United States is about six or seven times greater than the number required to replace those who voluntarily leave.

In terms of numbers, legal immigration is by far the largest flow (see below). It will command attention and a political

*The Census Bureau released a new report in December, 1992. No stabilization in sight and much faster, immigration-driven growth than formerly expected are key features of the new middle projection. This projection assumes illegal immigration of 200,000 annually, a number which many experts see as unrealistically low given current enforcement policy.

response when population stabilization is recognized as essential to the U.S. competitive position internationally and to the well-being of the American worker, as well as key to any credible environmental and national security policy.

Nevertheless, illegal immigration has captured media attention because it is dramatic and flouts U.S. law. Mass rushes across interstate highways on the United States–Mexico border have been broadcast nationwide on TV. Some of the media (e.g., public radio) freely transform illegal aliens fleeing poverty into "refugees" in order, one suspects, to elicit sympathy. (Recall that refugees from most countries must individually prove a "well-founded fear of persecution." Political turmoil in one's country of origin does not suffice as evidence of persecution, or much of the world would be potentially entitled to come to the United States under provisions of the 1980 Refugee Act. Revolutions and coups d'état are likely wherever there is poverty, so the numbers at risk are constantly growing.)

Airports are points of illegal entry second only to the land border with Mexico. The number caught at U.S. airports with fraudulent or no papers doubled, to 43,580, between fiscal years 1987 and 1990. The San Diego airport was a favored port of entry until a detention center was enlarged so that would-be immigrants without papers could be held pending a hearing. New York City's Kennedy Airport (JFK) replaced San Diego as the place to walk off a plane into the United States when word got around that its detention center had space for just 190 detainees.

The New York-area INS district director, William S. Slattery, tells how easy it is to crash the gate (Kamen, 1992). Illegal entrants typically board a plane using fraudulent documents; these are either destroyed en route or returned to the smuggler who is providing assistance. Once at the U.S. port of entry, the would-be immigrant has new, forged documents or is without documents of any kind. The INS then accepts, says Slattery, "whatever name they give us, whatever nationality they want to claim. So the fellow who purports to be a freedom fighter from Afghanistan could be a taxicab driver from Cairo. . . . Here's the irony. We then give them a U.S. government document . . . with a number and picture and fingerprint on it . . . to prove they are who they verbally represented to us." Most people whose papers are not in order are released on their own recognizance with a date, about fourteen months later, to appear in court. Kamen (1992) reports that 60 percent of 3,100 undocumented JFK arrivals scheduled for a court hearing June 26–December 31, 1991, did not appear. The most represented nations were India (921), Pakistan (463), and China (827). Of those who did not appear, 90 percent were Indians, 78 percent were Pakistanis, and 36 percent were Chinese.

Arrival in the United States on a visitor's or student's visa and then disappearance into the labor force—with or without falsified documents—is another means of becoming a permanent settler. Almost anyone who inquires will learn about specific cases. Moreover, many persons with temporary visas claim asylum and prolong their stay more or less indefinitely. The U.S. State Department estimates that 20,000 Cubans, out of 64,000 visitors in an eighteen-month period which includes 1991, will settle in south Florida. The market for work-authorization "green cards," to buy or rent, is well established and not particularly covert in some cities. The INS lets employers accept any one of seventeen different documents as evidence that a job applicant is legally in the United States. Some employers do not inquire too closely; they drive by street corners where illegals congregate in order to pick up day labor as needed.

Illegal immigration provides endless variety and engages a range of emotions—from pity to outrage. But individual cases are a poor guide for making policy. The statistical realities—how many come—should be of greater concern. At the same time that illegal immigration is brought under control—which can be done by enforcing employer sanctions, matching unemployed Americans to jobs which open up after an INS raid, and giving the INS resources to do their job—very high *legal* immigration will continue until new legislation is enacted. Recall that the 1990 Immigration Reform Act raised annual legal immigration by 40 percent.

THE 1990 IMMIGRATION REFORM ACT

The 1990 legislation increased visas in two family-reunification categories, increased employer-sponsored visas (but these are still less than 10 percent of the total), increased diversity immigrant visas (the former law discriminated against Europeans—35,000 Irish were legalized under this new provision), and awarded "temporary voluntary departure" from the United States (allowing them to stay here) to two categories of illegal aliens: 187,000 El Salvadorans and 12,000 others. Moreover, *relatives* of formerly illegal aliens granted amnesty under a 1986 law now, themselves, received amnesty.

Not counting refugees, asylees, former illegal aliens amnestied by IRCA, and the special amnesty categories, the Act caps immigration at 700,000 each year in 1992 through 1994, and 675,000 annually in subsequent years. However, the so-called cap is "pierceable." The law provides no true maximum because immigration demand by the immediate relatives of citizens pierces (i.e., raises) the number of visas by however much is needed to clear the waiting list. One may anticipate that immediate-family visa applications will sooner, rather than later, exceed the number stipulated under the legislation. As previous years' immigrants meet the five-year residency requirement which makes them eligible for naturalization, many will sponsor "immediate family," defined as the spouse, minor children, and parents of the seed immigrant. Moreover, children born in the United States are citizens and, at age eighteen, are also entitled to bring in their immediate family, effectively without limit.

All categories combined suggest that legal immigration is running at over 1 million a year. The Center for Immigration Studies (1991) projects a five-year total of 5.4 million, or 44.1 percent of U.S. population growth over the period (Table 2). The number of immigrants does not, of course, include their contribution to growth through high fertility.

With a 1991 population of about 31 million, California is growing by 2.7 percent a year, a rate higher than that found, say,

Table 2.   Total Projected Immigration, 1991–1995[a]

Family-related	2,574,000
Employment-related	614,000
Special categories	40,000
Diversity	200,000
Humanitarian	1,712,000
Illegal immigration	1,250,000
Emigration	−900,000
Net total immigration	5,440,000
Immigration as % of total population growth	44.1

[a]Source: Center for Immigration Studies, *Scope*, No. 6, Fall/Winter 1990/1991.

in India. California received the largest share of the 1980s immigrants and is projected to receive over 34 percent of the 1990s legal immigrants. Under provisions of the 1990 Immigration Reform Act and the 1980 Refugee Act, the addition to California's population by legal immigration and refugees is expected to be a minimum of 3 million and a maximum of 4 million-plus persons. Demographer Leon Bouvier's projections (1992) of state-by-state minimums and maximums in Table 3 were commissioned by the immigration-control activist organization Population-Environment Balance.

WERE THERE A WILL, THERE'S A WAY

Politicians will need more than a little prodding from constituents to revisit immigration legislation after having so recently "reformed" it to their own liking. Nevertheless, legal immigration is the principal destabilizer of U.S. population, and it will remain unchecked until Congress acts.

Even a concerted effort to stop illegal immigration will require congressional action. Appropriation as well as authorization of money is needed because, at present, Congress is starving the INS. The steps required for stopping illegal immigration all depend on backing up the INS both financially and morally. The American people need to *want* to take back control of their borders or it will not happen.

The INS is policing the southwestern border states with about 5,000 agents. Funding is needed both to increase the number of border-patrol and other agents and to build temporary detention centers for undocumented persons. All of the latter receive a hearing before either being deported or given a visa. Extra money could be made available to the INS by eliminating the public funding of legal counsel for illegal aliens who appeal deportation. More funding for the INS could be recovered by charging anyone crossing the border in either direction a $1 toll. A program like this would generate $500 million a year, according to Alan C. Nelson, former Commissioner of the INS. Major appropriations, however, depend upon congressional action.

A serious effort would entail *never* releasing an undocumented alien on his or her own recognizance and returning deportees to near the region of their country from which they came; not, as in the case of Mexico, just putting them back over the border. In addition, when undocumented aliens who have been convicted of criminal activity in the United States are released from prison, they should be automatically turned over to the INS for deportation. Our state prisons hold an estimated 8,000 illegal aliens at any one time. Bancroft (1991) reports that, after serving their time, these criminal illegal aliens are mostly released into the community.

The INS could also make better use of provisions in the 1986 Immigration Reform and Control Act (IRCA) which make employers responsible for not knowingly hiring illegal aliens. The law requires employers to inspect documentation but not to verify its authenticity. The present plethora of documents and the ease of forging many of them make it difficult for the employer to spot illegal aliens. If the system were improved, so that undocumented immigrants found themselves barred from both jobs and

Table 3.   State-by-State Projections of Migration from Foreign
Countries in the 1990s

| State | Immigrants settling in each state in the 1980s[a] | Percentage of total U.S. immigration to state | Projected immigration to each state in the 1990s[b] | |
			Minimum projected	Maximum projected
CALIF	2,331,300	34.54	3,108,000	4,144,000
NY	959,400	14.21	1,279,000	1,706,000
TEXAS	594,600	8.81	793,000	1,057,000
FLA	439,600	6.51	586,000	782,000
ILL	401,100	5.94	535,000	713,000
NJ	266,000	3.94	355,000	473,000
MASS	128,400	1.90	171,000	228,000
PA	119,100	1.76	159,000	212,000
MICH	108,900	1.61	145,000	194,000
WASH	107,200	1.59	143,000	191,000
VA	104,600	1.65	139,000	186,000
MD	94,000	1.39	125,000	167,000
HAW	82,800	1.23	110,000	147,000
OHIO	78,000	1.16	104,000	139,000
CONN	70,700	1.05	94,000	126,000
ARIZ	66,200	0.98	88,000	118,000
COLO	57,600	0.85	77,000	102,000
ORE	51,900	0.77	69,000	92,000
LA	51,600	0.76	69,000	92,000
MINN	51,200	0.76	68,000	91,000
GA	46,500	0.69	62,000	83,000
OKLA	40,600	0.60	54,000	72,000
WIS	39,100	0.58	52,000	70,000
IND	36,100	0.54	48,000	64,000
NC	34,200	0.51	46,000	61,000
MO	33,400	0.49	45,000	59,000
NMEX	30,100	0.45	40,000	53,000
KAN	29,900	0.44	40,000	53,000
NEV	28,000	0.41	37,000	50,000
UTAH	26,100	0.39	35,000	46,000
DC	25,600	0.38	34,000	45,000
TENN	23,600	0.35	31,000	42,000
IOWA	23,400	0.35	31,000	42,000

(*Continued*)

Table 3. (*Continued*)

State	Immigrants settling in each state in the 1980s[a]	Percentage of total U.S. immigration to state	Projected immigration to each state in the 1990s[b]	
			Minimum projected	Maximum projected
RI	20,500	0.30	27,000	37,000
ALA	18,500	0.27	25,000	33,000
SC	18,500	0.27	25,000	33,000
KY	16,800	0.25	22,000	30,000
NEB	13,000	0.19	17,000	23,000
IDAHO	12,100	0.18	16,000	21,000
MISS	11,000	0.16	15,000	20,000
ARK	11,000	0.16	15,000	20,000
AL	7,500	0.11	10,000	13,000
WVA	7,100	0.11	10,000	13,000
DEL	6,300	0.09	8,000	11,000
NH	5,300	0.08	7,000	9,000
MAINE	5,000	0.07	7,000	9,000
WY	4,000	0.06	5,000	7,000
MONT	3,800	0.06	5,000	7,000
NDAK	3,600	0.05	5,000	6,000
VT	2,800	0.04	4,000	5,000
SDAK	2,700	0.04	4,000	5,000
Total	6,750,200	100	9,000,000	12,000,000

[a]*Source*: U.S. Census Bureau, prepared for Population-Environment Balance by Leon Bouvier.

[b]The 1990s figures are projections, not predictions. Events could substantially increase or decrease the actual numbers. For example: (1) actual number of immigrant settlers could *increase* if pending legislation to repeal employer sanctions for hiring illegals is enacted because these sanctions serve as a deterrent to illegal immigration; (2) actual numbers of immigrant settlers could substantially *increase* if the United States experiences one or more Mariel boatlift-type waves of immigration; and (3) actual numbers of immigrant settlers could *decrease* if Congress enacted legislation to substantially reduce legal immigration from current levels of about 1 million per year. No such legislation is currently pending.

receiving health and welfare benefits, two magnets currently drawing people to the United States would lose force.

One provision in IRCA which could help save jobs for American workers is Systematic Alien Verification for Entitlements (SAVE). SAVE is intended to screen out illegal aliens who apply for Aid to Families with Dependent Children (AFDC), Medicaid, unemployment compensation, food stamps, publicly assisted housing, and education grants and loans. The guts of SAVE are an INS computerized index (ASVI) which already holds the records of 22 million aliens. Nationwide, 80 percent of the agency offices which administer the six entitlement programs listed above were using SAVE by 1991, but the potential use of SAVE is greater. The Center for Immigration Studies (1991) suggests that SAVE "could prove useful as a data base for employers to determine work eligibility. The employer, who would access the system by calling, would be able to check the recently hired employee's name, work eligibility status, and a verification number against the information that the employee provided."

This use of SAVE sounds not much more complicated than the verification of a charge card. Moreover, a determined approach to using all the potential of SAVE could partially overcome loopholes in the employer-sanctions aspect of illegal immigration-law enforcement. The principal effect might be deterrence. This is difficult to track, but a reasonable expectation that the program would *prevent* fraud makes SAVE an attractive job-applicant-screening mechanism.

The proposal meets strong opposition from immigration advocates, who object even to using SAVE to screen applicants for welfare benefits. Critics say it is not cost-effective. Some illegal immigrants do, in fact, sidestep SAVE by presenting themselves as citizens. Critics of SAVE's effectiveness have, themselves, purposely undermined the system by having INS enforcement personnel, who originally ran SAVE, replaced with (presumably less enforcement-minded) data-processing and statistical personnel.

Probably the ultimate deterrent to illegal immigration is a national ID system. Any national identification program would have to be instituted by an act of Congress and is likely to be opposed by many Americans. Advocacy groups for immigrants strongly oppose a national ID. Nevertheless, draft-age men have been required to carry IDs, all Americans who receive earned or unearned income have a Social Security number, and most adults carry a driver's license. If SAVE is not used to its fullest capacity, or if it proves inadequate to the task, the national ID question is likely to enter the debate about how to bar illegal aliens from employment in the United States.

Refugee policy is an area also being debated. U.S. refugee policy was, until recently, sensitive to whether a person had fled a Communist regime. That underlying rationale resulted in nearly 1 million refugees from Vietnam, Cambodia, El Salvador, Cuba, and Russia arriving in the United States in the twelve-year period beginning in 1980. The most recent waves are Kurds and Haitians. Now, signs of growing worldwide turmoil including food shortage and dislocation in the former Soviet Union raise a different concern. Parts of the free western world already are flooded by applicants for asylum. As a consequence of generalized upheaval, millions of people are physically in danger from famine if not from the military, the police, or revolutionary militias. These crises create a danger that is real but, nevertheless, is not individually targeted political persecution. The 1980 Refugee Act was a creature of the Cold War, and perhaps it is time to revoke the special status it created. Refugees might better be folded into whatever new form and limit that national needs and politics dictate our immigration policy should have.

Leadership in government could entail funding an educational campaign to inform Americans of the harm done by the influx of immigrants who work at below the minimum wage and/or siphon off welfare, health, and education funds. Environmentalists might take note, as well, that more people simply mean more who pollute and consume. Growing population pressure inexorably strengthens the hand of those who argue for sacrificing environmental values in order to provide jobs, housing, drinking water, and more roads. Immigration control is a fundamental element of population stabilization and conservation.

Replacement-level immigration, an equitable complement to replacement-level fertility, is at present about 160,000 immigrants a year because that is the estimated number of persons who annually leave the United States. All-inclusive, replacement-level immigration is a political objective urged by a number of Americans. Regular immigrants, asylees, refugees, and an estimated illegal number totaling no more than 160,000 persons a year would put the United States on the path toward population stabilization.

AN INTERNATIONAL RESPONSE

It is time to learn from Turkey, India, South Korea, Hong Kong, Taiwan, Mexico, Japan, and all western European nations— nations intent upon securing their international borders. For example:

- India deported Bangladeshis from its province of North Assam during a 1984 famine in Bangladesh and is guarding a new fence built between the two countries. The fence is two-thirds the length of the Mexican-American border.
- Italy deported 20,000 Albanians in just one action in 1991.
- The Dominican Republic deported Haitian workers, also in 1991.
- In 1989, Nigeria abruptly deported several million workers back to a neighboring country.
- Malaysia sent back two boatloads of Indonesians fleeing political persecution, also 1991.
- Taiwan jails, then deports, refugees from the Chinese mainland.
- Hong Kong interns, then deports, Vietnamese boat people.
- The Japanese Diet decided in the 1960s against immigration

for any purpose. About 700,000 ethnic Koreans live in Japan. Some were forcibly brought to Japan during its occupation of Korea, but 90 percent are native-born. A handful of the children with Korean mothers have been granted Japanese citizenship. With exceptions for Korean and Taiwanese nationals, all foreign residents in Japan are fingerprinted.

- On one occasion, the Mexican government sent thousands of troops to seal off its border against illegal immigration from Guatemala. (Currently, Mexico appears to speed illegals on their way to the United States.)
- Ahead of other countries of the European Community, Germany rushed to recognize Slovenia and Croatia and supports massive aid to Russia; warding off immigration is the strategic reason behind all these moves.
- Twenty-seven eastern and western European countries are cooperating to detect falsified documents in order to foil gangs which smuggle asylum-seekers into Europe.
- Great Britain fingerprints all asylum-seekers so that they cannot disappear into the population at large.
- Australia, which flirted with a liberal immigration policy based on family reunification, reduced its 1992 limit by nearly 12 percent. Admissions were curtailed in response to public pressure and a 1985 study (see Smith, 1991) which concluded that average longterm real wages and economic activity would be higher in the absence of immigration.
- France and Sweden, which used to be open to refugees, are now among the most determined guarantors of European borders.
- Jobseekers in the European Community increasingly complain about competition from immigrants, and politicians who oppose immigration are acquiring a broad base of support in France, Germany, Austria, Italy, and the Scandinavian countries.
- European countries make reasonable allowance for for-

eigners who come with guaranteed employment; however, visas for work or study are understood to be temporary. Fingerprinting and secure documentation prevent foreigners from disappearing into the population at large.

But the United States:

- Admits well over 1 million legal immigrants and refugees each year. Legal immigrants are entitled to all health, education, and welfare benefits available to U.S. citizens.
- Provides refugees with every benefit available to U.S. citizens, including automatic entitlement to Social Security. The front-end cost of settlement in the United States is borne by the federal government at an estimated outlay of $7,000 per refugee. The number to be admitted is set annually by the president. In 1992, it climbed to 142,000, of which 50,000 were Russian. Congress exerts constant pressure to admit more and, in 1990, enacted the Morrison-Lautenberg bill which creates a "presumption" that Jews and Christian Evangelicals in the Soviet Union are subject to persecution. That is, persons in these categories are exempt from having to prove political persecution.
- Underfunds the Border Patrol. Congress authorized a larger force in 1986 but, as of 1991, had not appropriated funds. Just over 5,000 agents are assigned to the border with Mexico; not all can be on duty at any given time. An unknown number of illegal immigrants slip past. Apprehensions in 1991 had climbed to 1.2 million, and probably only one of three is stopped. Anyone caught is put back just across the border.
- Awards citizenship on the basis of birthplace. The Fourteenth Amendment provides that any child born in the United States automatically becomes an American citizen. The amendment was passed after the Civil War to protect the rights of native-born black Americans. This rationale now seems superfluous. An amendment to limit citizen-

ship to children whose mothers are citizens or legal
residents has been introduced by U.S. Rep. Elton Gallegly
(R-Calif.).

About two-thirds of births in the Los Angeles County
Hospital are to women who are in the United States
illegally. The children, as American citizens, are entitled to
the full range of social, health-care, and welfare benefits.
AFDC for the *citizen children of illegals* costs Los Angeles
County taxpayers $250 million annually.

- Is lax about identification. Illegal immigrants who get past
  the border can easily rent documentation which shows that
  they are legal (any one of seventeen different documents is
  acceptable), so in many settings they compete on an equal
  footing with American workers. Employers are required
  only to check the documents of newly employed workers.
  Verification is not required or facilitated. If both worker
  and employer are aware of fraud, the minimum wage
  becomes a joke. Some cities try to get unemployed illegal
  aliens off the streets by providing employment halls to
  facilitate hiring. Illegal workers are a major presence in
  the food and construction industries—as any American
  kitchen worker or subcontractor will attest.

- Releases would-be asylees on their own recognizance.
  Applicants for political asylum are not detained but told
  to turn up for a hearing; few keep the appointment. Until
  recently, they were given an interim work permit.

- Educates all who apply. School districts are under court
  order to educate all children. Illegal immigrants are admitted to the University of California in competition with legal
  residents and citizens. In 1991, the California legislature
  voted to further extend the welcome mat by granting illegal
  aliens reduced, in-state tuition, but Gov. Pete Wilson
  vetoed that!

- Puts safety first. In summer, 1991, the California Department of Transportation closed off the four inside, passing
  lanes of eight-lane Interstate 5 just north of the Mexican

border. Traffic is funneled into just two lanes in each direction. The purpose of creating the traffic jam was to make it safer for illegals who are crossing the highway into the United States. The number of crossings quickly doubled to 2,000 per day.

- Regulates business in order to accommodate non-English speakers. Hispanic populations are growing rapidly in the midwest as well as in southern states. In 1990, the Iowa legislature required companies to hire interpreters if the same foreign language was spoken by more than 10 percent of their work force.
- Encourages everyone to expect the same benefits. Jack Kemp, formerly Secretary of Housing and Urban Development, defends illegal aliens' having the same right to public housing as do U.S. citizens. Federal policies already require states to provide illegal immigrants with health care in emergency settings, with bilingual education, and with free legal aid to appeal deportation if they claim asylum.
- Is loath to deport anyone. The 8,000 or so illegal immigrants in California state prisons will probably be released to the surrounding community when their terms are up unless current practice changes.
- Extends Constitutional and civil rights protections to those who would not be in the United States except for having broken U.S. immigration law. In 1991, a federal district judge in California "ruled that an undocumented worker has the right to pursue a discrimination suit against an employer—regardless of [the worker's] legal residency status" (Carlton and Marcus, 1991). The decision arose from a sex discrimination suit brought by the Equal Employment Opportunity Commission (EEOC) on behalf of a woman who was fired, allegedly for filing the complaint which impelled her employer to take her back after a pregnancy leave.

Bringing illegal aliens under the protection of civil

rights and minimum wage laws diminishes their attractiveness to employers and thus, somewhat ironically, helps
American workers compete. Of much greater concern is a
policy which further hampers border control and which
took effect in July, 1992. This policy resulted from a suit
brought against the INS by the Mexican Legal Defense and
Educational Fund (MALDEF). It requires the INS to inform
every person apprehended that he or she is entitled to free
consultation with an attorney; all those apprehended must
also be asked if they face political persecution in their
country of origin. Anyone who says yes can apply for
political asylum (and receive free legal aid with the application at the expense of the U.S. taxpayer).
• Raises legal immigration numbers. In October, 1990, the
U.S. Congress increased annual immigration by over 40
percent, to over one million annually when refugees,
asylees, and new amnesty categories are counted. The Act
provides for legalizing several million relatives of immigrants who had themselves been illegal until legalization
under IRCA, in 1986.

Legal immigration could go much higher: The Clinton-Gore
1992 Democratic party platform adopted a plank to accelerate
admission of extended-family relatives of U.S. residents and
citizens (i.e., eliminate the present fifteen-year backlog).

However, executives and professionals trying to enter the
United States for high-level, temporary employment have a hard
time gaining entry. Our rigidity in this domain gives rise to a
booming legal subspecialty in immigration law and to the convic-
tion in some quarters that U.S. immigration policy is restrictive.
Schizophrenia reigns.

The question for the 1990s will be: Do Americans care? Poll
results suggest that they do, and public response to the 1991–1992
return of Haitian boatpeople is another indicator: The vast
majority of Americans gave tacit support to the Bush administration's policy of requiring would-be asylees to apply at the U.S.

embassy in Haiti; not on the high seas; not at Guantanamo Naval Base; and not after arrival in the United States. Floridians, waiting at the Haitians' first intended destination, had evidently learned from the arrival of 120,000 Cubans in the Mariel boatload that refugees are not easily absorbed. Some political analysts suggest that accepting the Mariel Cubans lost President Jimmy Carter Florida's electoral votes and was, therefore, a factor in his failed 1980 bid for reelection.

Before Americans act, however, they will have to *know*. Good information is the basis of self-government. Therefore, let us second Dennis Ahlburg and James Vaupel's conclusion: "Population projection is not a bloodless technical task, but a politically charged craft of great interest to policymakers and the public. Consequently, it should not be left to a single agency. A livelier competition of alternative assumptions and innovative methods not only would further the development of demographic analysis but also would serve the public interest."

20

Let Freedom Ring

Some people do not believe that population growth, by itself, erodes freedom. Whether or not it does depends, in part, on definitions. Whether overpopulation harms our liberties and form of government depends partly upon what one means by the words *freedom* and *liberty*.

In fact, there can be more freedom to act as one wishes in a large, anonymous city. No one knows you. You can be weird. Many find that they can even be criminal. In a small town, you might not dare divorce, have an affair, or be rude. Being rude to someone you will never see again is one of the particular joys of big-city living.

But freedom means more than license. As conceived in America, freedom includes economic opportunity, civil liberties, and our democratic form of government. Freedom from interference by government is part of the concept, which brings up the first way that population growth cuts into freedom. When a place starts to get crowded, people look to government to protect them against their fellow man.

LIBERTY REDEFINED

The protection sought from government concerns more than crime. Protection starts to anticipate harms; it is preventive. But one woman's social good is another woman's government regulation. The changes come in small ways. Everyone's right to cleanliness, quiet, and order restricts what everyone can do. Many choices vanish when we live close to other people. Your right to swing your fist ends where my nose begins.

At first, swinging one's fist in a smaller arc seems no great price to pay. Population growth in a medium-size American city has few early downsides. Small inconveniences that come with more people can be disregarded because growth rides in on a beguiling breeze of prosperity. The good parts of growth include more cultural and educational opportunities, better restaurants, people making money, and being an airport hub city.

But consider Nashville, Tenn.—Music City, the Athens of the South, the big guitar (say *gui*-tar). As a sign of things to come, the expense of parking at the airport quadruples. Stop signs and lights multiply. Four extra stop lights on a nine-mile drive to downtown—and many more cars—add thirty minutes to rush-hour commuting compared to fifteen years ago. One has to wait in lines. At work, employees pay to park, another change from 1975. A dog cannot legally roam free; garbage cannot be burned. Nowhere may leaves be burned. No one gets to be buried in his or her back forty, and some might have liked that.

The amenities go next. In Denver, Colo., one cannot light a fireplace on an overcast winter's day (the smog alert). In Los Angeles, the outdoor grill might as well be scrap iron. One-passenger cars are barred from the fast lane. Regulation becomes a way of life.

Nashville and many other cities have a garbage problem. Even with recycling and thermal plants, more people mean more waste. Arguments wax and wane over expanding thermal capacity, but the main attention-grabber is landfill space. One landfill in Nashville stayed in use two years after reaching capacity. The community that had it was promised relief, but no one else wants a landfill either—especially since every part of the county is now densely residential and the amount of garbage keeps growing. Will the next dump be sited by power of eminent domain? Ah, growth. Let freedom ring.

California and several other large states are adding bar codes to licenses to encode formerly private information. Bar codes on licenses are part of an identification system that will help enforce the 1986 Immigration Reform and Control Act (IRCA), legislation which prohibits employers from knowingly hiring an illegal alien. Enforcement of immigration law must be weighed against infringement on the privacy rights of citizens. But without enforcement at some point, citizens go on losing jobs, most people's real income falls, energy security becomes a bitter joke, the environment suffers, the carrying capacity is exceeded, and Americans lose cherished values along with their privacy right.

TO NURTURE DEMOCRACY

Further, population growth puts distance between Americans and their elected leaders, so consent to regulation goes by way of more and more distant proxy. Lobbyists rather than ordinary citizens call the tune. "Inside the Beltway" seems remote. In the first fifty years of the republic, an elected member of the House of Representatives stood for 30,000 people. Today, he or she represents 570,000. Government by the people and for the people is less a truth and more a memory as a larger and larger multitude must be ruled. We, the people, know that a lesser commitment to one person, one vote risks freedom. We know that voting is our precious right and solemn duty. But does one vote out of 255 million feel like self-government?

Too large a government, by itself, is an enemy of freedom, but another factor may be more potent. Population pressure—not politics—may take the measure of democracy. Some observers say that a healthy ratio of resources to people is the bulwark of freedom. Historian David Potter (1954) quotes nineteenth-century observer Alexis de Tocqueville, who wrote that "The chief circumstance which has favored the establishment and maintenance of a democratic system in the United States is the nature of the territory that the Americans inhabit. Their ancestors gave them a love of equality and of freedom; but God Himself gave them the means of remaining equal and free by placing them upon a boundless continent." Potter continues, "Abundance has influenced American life in many ways, but there is perhaps no respect in which this influence has been more profound than in . . . strengthening equality, with all that . . . implied for the individual in the way of opportunity to make his own place in society and of emancipation from a system of status."

The American system of government will be in increasing jeopardy, if de Tocqueville and David Potter are right, as population growth presses ever more relentlessly against carrying capacity.

POLITICIZING ECONOMIC COMPETITION

Political power rests on coalitions. So long as coalitions are fluid, democracy is safe. But coalitions based on permanent group membership become increasingly likely as the stakes rise.

The stakes do rise as more sectors experience a fall in their standard of living: Resource scarcity provokes resource grabs, which can sometimes be made to succeed by escalating economic competition into the political realm. That is, feeling pressed, one tries to use political clout to further economic goals. The threat to the United States is that individual equal opportunity may give way before the potentially greater advantage to be gained from membership in permanent coalitions channeled into political activism.

The threshold which could propel America into reliance on political avenues to economic success may not be distant. Some commentators allude already to a zero-sum game, where privilege for some entails loss to others. Frederick R. Lynch (1991) writes in this vein about strains inherent in governmental efforts to equalize economic results. Polls of randomly sampled Americans suggest that 1 in 10 white men has been injured by affirmative action. Various data suggest a militant white working-class response to contract set-asides and race-norming programs which appear to discriminate against them. Lynch attributes the "fury over quotas for blacks and immigrants . . . [to] more intense zero-sum problems wrought by a shrinking blue collar jobs market."

Affirmative action in the zero-sum job market is paralleled by competition for limited places in major U.S. colleges and universities. Race-norming admissions tests—where separately scored racial and ethnic curves are melded into a single rank order (i.e., where rank depends on one's place on one's own curve rather than on a comparison with all scores) are resulting in whites being underrepresented on some campuses. White claims of present discrimination clash with black and Native American grievances over past discrimination. Asians may be overrepresented because of belonging to an accepted minority category.

Numerical underrepresentation of blacks and Hispanics in California's public universities and colleges would be redressed by quotas if California Assembly Speaker Willie Brown prevails. Brown has won over the state legislature and only the executive branch stands in the way: Gov. Pete Wilson vetoed a 1991 bill which would have mandated that the proportion of minorities graduating from California's high schools be exactly reflected in the freshman classes of the state's institutions of higher learning. The bill also mandated the college graduation of this proportion, as well as job-performance evaluation of faculty and administrators on the basis of meeting these admission and graduation requirements.

So advantageous is it today to qualify as a minority protected by civil rights legislation that many rush to resurrect a long-forgotten pedigree. *The Economist* (The Landless, 1991) reports that the 2 million Americans who claimed to be Native Americans in 1991 represent a 38 percent increase since 1980. As group rights shortcircuit individual opportunity, one wonders if being the best for the job matters anymore.

The January, 1991, dispute in the San Francisco Fire Department was about this exactly. It had been decided that the next fire chief would be Hispanic. It only remained to determine whose Hispanicism could stand up to scrutiny. A man who placed fortieth on the qualifying exam claimed that the two Hispanics who placed above him (his only politically viable competition for the job) had faked their ethnic credentials. The city formed an Ethnic Purity Review Board to mediate. Only in San Francisco could this happen, you say. You hope!

This example shows how political power shortcircuits economic competition. This path leads far from the objectives of fairness, equal opportunity, and evaluation of individuals on merit. Thus, population pressure and alignments based on noneconomic criteria both raise the stakes and alter the nature of competition.

HISTORICAL PERSPECTIVE

The original 1964 civil rights legislation was designed to guarantee equal opportunity to blacks and Native Americans. It never was anticipated that the politics of color and ethnic group would be seized upon as group entitlements or by ever-larger contingents of other minorities. Many who voted for the 1964 legislation must be surprised by the large number and variety now claiming protected status, especially immigrants who came voluntarily (and even illegally) *after* 1964. Indeed, the first immigration act to open the United States to substantial numbers of other minorities was not passed until 1965.

Proliferation of enclaves where each group claims minority status should alert us to future divisions. Although whites will be relieved of automatic guilt in every ethnic clash, no American has cause to celebrate. Shifting the battle lines from white/black to black/Hispanic or black/Korean still leaves America disunited. The American dream does not advance when middle-class blacks complain of unassimilated Hispanics who move into their neighborhoods, or when Hispanics commit hate crimes against Cambodians. A strong society is not built on victimization; nor is it built on enshrinement of victims' rights.

MULTICULTURALISM

Growth of ethnic enclaves is also undercutting the American consensus on history, language, and core values. Inspired by the new power blocs, values including free speech are under systematic attack. The new mode of thinking is called *multiculturalism*. Multiculturalism has altered educational curricula in many universities and secondary schools and is an attempt to define acceptable fact, attitude, and speech according to what is politically correct (PC). Students at Brown University coined the term *PC* to deride their administration's attempt to regulate how one should speak, think, and feel about minorities, women, the handicapped, homosexuals, and so on. Similarly, at Smith College, students are warned during orientation to avoid "lookism," that is, placing undue emphasis on physical attractiveness. "Temporarily abled" is recommended lingo for describing the healthy, normal person at other campuses. Thus are students prepared for earthly mortification and mortality. But politics—not philosophy or religion—inspires such gibberish.

Although multiculturalism is easy to satirize, its purpose is deadly serious. It aims to elevate group rights over individual rights, that is, politics again. In schools, multiculturalism is becoming *the* issue of the day. Much uncertainty in education is created by confusing diversity, which may refer to individuals who have different cultures, with multiculturalism, which asserts that the cultures of all groups have equal relevance and validity for America.

Multiculturalism in the educational system is about criteria for deciding what is taught and who teaches it. These decisions determine what information, analytic competence, and values are transmitted to future generations of students. Faculty, students, parents, alumni, and citizens all have a stake in the debate.

Multiculturalism has little in common with free—liberal arts or scientific—inquiry. The principle underlying multiculturalism is that there is no reality except in the eyes of the beholder. Words like *deconstructionism*, *postmodernism*, and *hermeneutics* identify the intellectual wellsprings of this bizarre premise. Deconstructionism and these other terms imply that each group or person is entitled to create, even invent, his or her own reality—including history. Whose reality prevails is then determined by political power. Is this scholarship? Many critics of multiculturalism would agree with sociologist Anne Wortham (1991): "Universities will simply have to stop giving each little ethnic group its own playroom."

LANGUAGE

Our language, unifying us in the past, is also under siege. The schools are, again, in the front rank in disuniting America. In the past, the public schools were a principal force for transmitting the common culture. But that is no more. In 1972, finding in favor of a Chinese immigrant's son, a court in San Francisco mandated classroom teaching in a student's native language.* Multiple-language teaching, or ESL (English as a second language), now seems enshrined in educational systems across America. An entrenched bilingual teaching cadre fights for its niche in the bureaucracy, making common cause with advocates of multiculturalism and immigration.

In this new climate of public opinion, initiatives to have English made the language of official government business have even subjected proponents to abuse. Consider this: Supporters of the activist organization U.S. English were evicted from their booth at a March, 1991, California Democratic Party (CDP) convention after becoming the butt of a demonstration. The attack against the U.S. English exhibit was unprovoked, except by its

Lau v. Nichols.

message. Demonstrators shouted threats, "You are a White Caucasian. . . . You are the intruder. Spanish should be the official language." Democratic Party officials evicted U.S. English rather than the demonstrators (Hearing Date Set, 1991). U.S. English charged the CDP with a civil rights violation and won the first round of litigation. Appeals may follow.

Resistance to multiculturalism and multiple-language teaching is sometimes attacked as "racist." This charge is nonsense on its face. Every country is entitled to define certain features of nationality, including official language. Native-born Americans, whether black, white, red, brown, or yellow, all speak English. The losers when education funds are diluted by ESL programs are often English-speaking racial minorities. The children toward whom resources are diverted are often not identifiable by race: Many Hispanics are white; Kurds necessarily belong to some race and it may be Caucasian (many have green eyes), *et cetera ad nauseam*.

ESL could well be revisited in the courts. Communities are straining their tax base to teach basic skills, so replicating effort, teacher time, and classrooms as many times as students have different native languages is a poor use of resources. And to what end? Students ultimately do not benefit from being sheltered from learning English in America. Moreover, diversion of resources to ESL deprives children who are native English speakers. It is unclear, as well, how a country can have a proficient, skilled work force if there is no *lingua franca*. Incompetence in basic literacy and numeracy skills is handicap enough. Should United States workers be unable now to communicate in one language? Finally, what will happen to national identity without a language in common?

AN AMERICAN IDENTITY

Human nature itself impels people to search for criteria which create identity. Distinguishing oneself from others is part of the search for identity. Amazon rainforest tribes use diet to set themselves apart. Some groups eat monkey meat; others do not. Either way, one group looks down on the other. Why, in America, should we take a natural human tendency and do our best to create identity at the level of the smallest possible unit? What is wrong with a *national* identity, an American identity?

Concessions to group rights and non-English classrooms in the public schools strike at the very core of the American value system and culture. Group rights, as pressed in many esteemed quarters of academia and public life, have the potential to lead this country down the path of tribalism. Writes Arthur Schlesinger, Jr. (1991), "High minded but wrong-headed multicultural zealots propose to use the educational system to protect and perpetuate ethnic and racial communities. The currently fashionable attack on the old American ideal of a 'melting pot' is an attack on the concept of an overriding American nationality."

The divisiveness of language as in Quebec or of ethnic group as in Yugoslavia, Iraq, and the former USSR should be a warning. Tribalism could plunge America into a dark night of self-doubt, combat, and misery and might extinguish forever in the world the light of democracy. Americans cannot ignore the possibility of ethnic conflict. Current educational and immigration policies increase the risk. Enlarging ethnic enclaves and enshrining different languages and cultural backgrounds guarantees preparedness for drawing up battle lines should the fatal spark be struck.

Until now, unity has been the American theme. Biblical, Graeco-Roman, and Northern European traditions, enriched by the contributions of Native American and African peoples, produced a fabric that has served this nation well. The American values of individualism, conscience, self-reliance, the work ethic, and community service are a combination unique in today's world. Our culture is the basis of a form of government that, while not perfect, is widely envied. One of its strengths is its capacity for measured, evolutionary change. All citizens are able to contribute, benefit, and succeed within this system. Ever-changing in detail, its core values are an American birthright, to be cherished and protected.

Multiculturalism and language separatism are frontal attacks in part because they would stop evolutionary change. They aim to stop assimilation and accommodation, freezing society into political power blocs based on ethnic or racial group membership.

The demographics which give edge to this redefinition of American politics are fast developing. If present immigration trends persist until the year 2000, Hispanics will have surpassed blacks as the largest minority group in America. Indeed, various racially, religiously, or ethnically defined groups will be numerically strong enough to bid for power, and they will have the incentive to do so if "group rights" become legitimate political currency in the United States.

CONSTITUTIONAL GOVERNMENT REDEFINED

Certain Hispanic advocacy groups have signaled already their intention to operate as a power bloc. La Raza Unida (The United Race), LULAC (League of United Latin American Citizens), and MALDEF (Mexican-American Legal Defense and Educational Fund) spearhead Hispanic activism. Their claims, framed in the language of civil rights, aim to advance group entitlements and access to resources of many kinds including jobs, promotions, education, bilingualism, open borders, health care, housing, and welfare benefits. Indeed, a strident irredentist theme permeates the leadership of some Mexican enclaves in Southern California: The land was theirs (although it belonged first to Native Americans—where does one start history?) and they intend to have it back. Activists deny any meaningful distinction between Mexican and U.S. citizenship.

Unsurprisingly, some immigrants are assimilating less willingly than was true in earlier generations. Perhaps the ease of travel back and forth encourages new arrivals to retain roots and loyalties that do not feel American and sometimes do not serve the United States. Most immigrants have benign motives. Many simply seek a better life and settle within ethnic enclaves where the language and culture of the old country envelop them. Nevertheless, many accept the economic advantage available through group-rights-based claims.

American culture and the Constitution are being not so much rejected as redefined and accepted piecemeal. Civil liberties become group rights. Group rights are elevated at the expense of individual opportunity. "Freedoms from" become group entitlements. And entitlements are conflated with affirmative action.

U.S. Supreme Court Justice Clarence Thomas defined affirmative action in his Supreme Court confirmation hearing before the Senate. He described affirmative action as searching out minorities and encouraging them to apply for openings; beyond that, he said, admissions, hiring, and promotion should be blind to race, ethnicity, and gender. Affirmative action is a way of breaking down divisions based on group membership. Affirmative action means opposing discrimination on the basis of color, age, gender, and so on. It is designed to provide opportunity for individuals, not entitlements for particular groups.

Discrimination is wrong because people are judged on traits that are irrelevant to their competence. Group rights implies a similar disregard for individual competence, so how can it be proper? Civil rights do not entail adoption of any system of preferences, be it a multicultural curriculum or hiring and advancement based on group membership. During the Senate confirmation hearings, Justice Thomas made it clear, and other sensible Americans also know, that it is not racist, or an attack on civil rights, to advocate *individual rights*.

Equal protection under the law, as a principle, is also threatened when ethnic enclaves grow so large as to overbalance American values. In 1989, a Chinese immigrant (Dong Lu Chen) received only five years' probation after being convicted of murdering his wife. She confessed to adultery, he bashed in her skull with a claw hammer, and the defense successfully argued to a New York City judge that the husband's action was understandable within the context of his own culture and community. But is a uniquely Chinese value system relevant in an American courtroom? Do Americans need more of this justice?

DISUNITY AND CARRYING CAPACITY

An anthropologist would be the last to dump on the values and institutions of other peoples. But values, assumptions, and behavior that seem appropriate to others, and elsewhere, are not appropriate in the United States. We should be proud of what we have and feel entitled to defend it. Individual opportunity and equal protection under the law are integral parts of the system. Group rights and multiculturalism are aberrations that could sink our form of representative self-government. Why give up the ship? Divisions—the other face of permanent coalitions—become more dangerous in the face of limits to the carrying capacity. Warns Schlesinger, "If the United States goes into depression, it will not be a melting pot. It will be a boiling pot." The preeminence of ethnic and racial identity could "disunite" America, preventing us from meeting the challenge of environmental limits honestly, courageously, and together.

An infinitely growing economy would allow a nation to give a sufficiency to all without taking away from any other. But the essential nature of limits is being discovered, even in America. Inescapably, the current running through all negotiations and accommodations is the ratio of population to resources, and what sacrifices must be made. We are engaged in a zero-sum game, but no longer are most Americans unwitting players. Ironically, the reality emerged first in the system of higher education, where admissions numbers are traditionally limited. They will remain limited, not because of arbitrariness, but because the resources to greatly expand the number of spaces are not available. Scarcity

is of the essence. Admissions slots, jobs, promotions, and benefits may expand, but not so quickly as to accommodate our much
more rapid rate of population growth.

Accommodations among permanent, ethnically based coalitions will become a matter of government regulation unless
determined citizen action prevents this further distortion of
American values. The difficulty of legislating privilege for some
without infringing on others' freedom should alert all Americans
to the dangers inherent in there being (1) further replacement of
individual opportunity with group entitlements; (2) more divisions among us; and (3) more of us. All these threaten liberty.

Taking Hold

The humanitarian cause is perennially popular. Compassion is a call to action. An urge to do good prompts us to take more and more of the world's homeless and destitute. And if taking the world's poor really helped, the opportunity to do good would be nearly limitless. The United States could take 100 million people a year, every year for many decades, without easing population pressure abroad from its present excruciating pitch.

POPULATION PRESSURE

The perceived moral imperative to take in the needy arises in the context of an exploding world population: 2.5 billion in 1950, 5 billion in 1987, and a sixth billion to be added perhaps as early as 1996. Worldwide population growth is accelerating because of the increasing number of reproductive-age women and the frustratingly slow decline in their average fertility.

As recently as five years ago, 90 million people were said to be added annually but, by 1990, the more generally accepted number for annual increase to world population was 93 million. By 1992, the U.N. Population Fund estimated that it was 97 million.

The ever-larger base (i.e., total world population) contributes to the mathematical result that the *rate* of growth appears to be slowing. It may have declined over the past fifteen years from 1.8 to 1.7 percent per year. Thus, rates and absolute numbers are moving in opposite directions. This has to temper somewhat a conclusion—heard in some quarters—that progress is being made. Celebration is premature.

Close to home, Mexico's population is expected to reach 109 million by the year 2000, and 154 million by 2025. Over 900,000 young adults will enter the labor pool each year during the 1990s. In Central America the population growth rate is somewhat higher, so that, write demographers Leon Bouvier and David Simcox (1989), "These nations face the staggering task of creating productive employment for their estimated 2.8 million citizens already unemployed or underemployed and for more than 300,000 new job seekers who will reach working age each year between now and 2000." Counting Mexico and Central America together, 1.25 million young people are entering the labor market annually.

A HUMANITARIAN CHECKLIST

With such need, say self-styled humanitarians, how can the United States shut the door even a bit? Indeed, why not let it be shoved wide open? The answer is that one must think through the consequences. Otherwise, the claim to beneficence and goodwill is simply vacuous.

The possibility of unintended and counterproductive effects exists in almost any course of action. As some sectors press for open borders and more international aid, it is time to make sure that the minimum humanitarian criterion (that our policy do no harm) is met. To find that past efforts to help have possibly done harm is disconcerting. Nevertheless, all evidence points that way. Fertility has remained stubbornly high and, with modernization, foreign aid, and other signals of better times ahead, may even at times have risen.

Vast experience with introduced family-planning programs shows that the availability of modern contraception is not enough; it misses the whole motivational aspect. Couples have to *want* small families or they accept modern contraception only for birth spacing and after many children. The desired and completed family size is likely to stay large.

The first sections of this book deal with motivation. We have shown that more children are wanted when parents think that opportunity is expanding. Thus, foreign aid and liberal U.S. immigration policies may retard acceptance of birth control. The harm is probably proportional to how much our policies lead the third world to discount signs of economic, social, or environmental limits. At the least, one concludes that the humanitarian case is flawed. Belief in abundance somewhere neutralizes local signs of limits. Perceiving poverty as a distributional problem that can be resolved by emigrating or by appeals to equity, people may not be motivated to plan realistically.

A further important political consequence of a liberal immigration and refugee policy should also concern us. The possibility of simply leaving a bad situation undercuts pressure for internal reform. The most energetic people, who are most likely to initiate change, may choose emigration if that option is easy; whereas they might otherwise engage constructively with conditions in their country of birth. Thus, emigration is a safety valve for excess population and retards change both because it fosters belief in expanding opportunity and because it lets a nation's dissident elements *out*.

Irrational governments have often tried to keep people even against their will: Fossilized political theory equates more people with more clout. But events in Eastern Europe and the former USSR reveal the effect of containing population, including dissidents, within their own country. People who are dissatisfied energize, lead, and structure internal reform.

Insightful governments which seek stability, including dictatorships, often try to rid themselves of population. When President Jimmy Carter pressed China on human-rights violations and demanded that emigration policy be liberalized, he got the answer he deserved: "Will you take 10 million?" From Cuba, Carter did get the Mariel boatload, a "boat" which held 120,000 people. And in the summer of 1991 why, except to be rid of

dissidents and the underemployed, did Fidel Castro precipi-
tously drop the age at which Cubans are allowed to emigrate?

It cannot be denied that most immigrants benefit from
settling in a country richer than the one they leave. But when
those remaining behind also raise their expectations, the consequences for birth control are poor. Moreover, populations in
countries to which immigrants come suffer a loss—often
substantial—in their standard of living.

Immigration in a too-crowded world is a zero-sum game.
Recent controversy over celebration of Columbus's discoveries
in the New World makes the point. The discrepancy between
colonists' and Native Americans' interests is all too clear. Native
Americans suffered impoverishment and culture loss. The intrinsic conflict is not diminished because some Indians colluded in
their people's debacle; this only shows that the threat was seen
too late. By the time some tribes tried to fight, the intrusion had
gone too far; the word had gone back to Europe that prosperity
beckoned. (Realistically, only the natives of Hispaniola had a
chance: They might have burned Columbus's ships.)

A reasoned humanitarian position must weigh multiple
interests: the wishes of those who would come, the effect on
those left behind, and the well-being of earlier immigrants and
citizens at the destination. These are competing claims—claims
which vary in legitimacy. All told, a strong case exists that liberal
immigration policies help relatively few but harm many. In the
long run, the destination countries will close their doors out of a
sense of responsibility for their own citizens and in recognition of
environmental limits. In the meantime, the number admitted will
never be more than a tiny fraction of the world's poor. Those who
can never come are, nevertheless, likely to be tragically misled.

A FOREIGN POLICY THAT SERVES THE UNITED STATES

The remaining questions for Americans are: How much
foreign aid to give and how many immigrants or refugees to
take? How much population growth—if any—is good for the

nation? Americans, including descendants of the earliest Americans, have every right to answer this question as honestly and clearsightedly as they can. Political theory is firm on one point: Every nation has the sovereign right to pursue a course leading to its own survival and territorial integrity.

E pluribus unum means that we, citizens of the United States of America, are morally obligated to act for, and avoid acting against, the best interests of our country and fellow citizens. The many become one. That is patriotism. It means loving and defending one's motherland and its people. Nothing is wrong with that. Patriotism does not have to be justified.

Much is wrong, however, with an apologist climate of public opinion which puts Americans on the defensive, obligating us to justify that which should be learned at home, in school, and in church and absorbed with the air we breathe. Charity begins at home. Why so great an outcry over abuses and want abroad when destitution visits our own streets? Believing it a matter of morality to take in the needy, start by taking a few deserving poor into one's own household. Those who want to do good should start at home. Save the poor? Start at home. Set an example? The rural and urban poor of America need you. Save the children? One-fifth of America's own live in poverty. Conditions here worsen, driving out hope. *God save America.*

The environment also sickens. Many communities are as polluted as a decade ago despite public and private efforts. Los Angeles spends millions on air quality, but the air is little better today than it was when cleanup efforts started. The Chesapeake Bay, three hundred miles of once-thriving coastland and estuary, may be dying as a life-support system. Assaults on the environment do not stop. Despite remedial efforts, how much net gain do *you* know about? Why is America going backward?

CARRYING CAPACITY

The President's Commission on Population Growth and the American Future (1972) had the answer. Although stabilizing population size would not in itself solve the nation's problems, the Commission stated that all would become harder to solve if the population grew. They were on the money. Take the environment, everyone's life-support system, and begin with pollution.

The nineties are forecast to be a decade of fighting nonpoint sources of pollution and garbage flows. The term *nonpoint source* describes the average American's contribution to the well-publicized environmental witches' broth. Our automobile emissions, our waste water, our refrigerator's chlorofluorocarbons, the agricultural runoff of fertilizer and pesticides, the fossil-fuel-based production and distribution of our food supply, toxics and CO_2 emitted by furniture makers and bakers and dry-cleaners, our packaging and "disposables"—the list goes on—are sources of such pollution. Nonpoint sources are us. The more of us there are, the more pointlets: not points of light, but pointlets of pollution.

This observation is not a criticism of character. At worst, Americans are guilty of innocence, generosity, belief in abundance and renewable wealth, and blithe denial that Earth's resources and capacity to absorb waste are finite. Americans also "pay" for their high consumption by limiting fertility to below replacement level. American women do not have four children each.

Third-world countries would mimic Americans' standard of living if they could. All struggle to reach a higher average level of consumption, which is to say pollution generation, and those of their citizens who can afford it are as consumption-oriented as any. The World Bank, the International Monetary Fund, various U.N. agencies, and national governments share the explicit goal of increasing consumption worldwide. Thereby they would enable all to become more like the industrial world in per capita emissions of atmosphere-altering gases and pollutants.

Immigration, also, has the principal objective of raising the migrants' standard of living. The average immigrant or refugee to Europe or the United States has no fonder hope than to adopt the host country's level of per capita consumption, that is, level of emission and garbage production. With 5 percent of the world's people, the United States consumes 25 percent of the world's energy, and many people understandably covet this standard of living.

The irony is that America will change. Despite ourselves, modesty in consumption seems about to be added to modesty in reproduction. In virtually no case will price-driven, voluntary, or compulsory measures to limit consumption and pollution be costless. Our grandchildren, if not our children and ourselves, will relearn Ben Franklin's admonition (from *Poor Richard's Almanac*):

> Use it up,
> Wear it out,
> Make it do
> Or do without.

One hopes for apt pupils because Americans' time, energy, and money are all about to be engaged in the struggle to prevent further downgrading of our standard of living and the environment. With good fortune (a grace period for, say, the "conservation revolution" advocated by Fossil Fuels Policy Action), with community effort, and with individual sacrifice, the United States will find a fair, efficient path.

ENVIRONMENTALISTS ON THE DEFENSIVE

If population growth can be stopped, we may, moreover, be spared some very tragic choices. The new trend in energy conservation (recall that in the whole time since 1970 Americans increased per capita energy use by less than 1 percent) means that without population growth we would have a much lower demand for oil today. Indeed, energy specialist John Holdren (1991) writes that "If the United States still had the population with which it fought World War II—135 million people—the 1990 level of per

capita energy use for this country could be met from its 1990
array of energy sources *minus* all the imported oil and all the
coal." Think of that. Maybe no Gulf War. And without population
growth to spur higher demand for oil, debate about test drilling
in the Arctic National Wildlife Refuge (ANWR) might be postponed indefinitely.

Think also of wetlands and diversity of species. Wetlands in
the United States are disappearing at a rate of 300,000 acres a
year. Former Housing and Urban Development Secretary Jack
Kemp thinks they should go faster. In 1991, he said that we should
set aside provisions of state wetlands protection legislation so that
builders could add to the nation's stock of low-cost housing.

Examples of clashing environmental and people-oriented
values put environmentalists on the defensive because of the
widespread presumption in favor of people. Thus, loggers need
jobs? Shrink the old forest reserve, home to the spotted owl.
People need oil? Explore ANWR. People need water? Drain the
Sacramento River dry and let the delta smelt and salmon adapt
to gravel. Concludes environmentalist Thomas Lovejoy of the
Smithsonian Institution: "There seems to be a coalescing of
different economic interests to fight the green devils" (Alexander,
1992).

Environmental battles are perennially refought because the
needs of people for jobs and housing grow in proportion to the
number of people. How long will the cycle go on? How long do
Americans intend to watch while population growth adds both to
poverty and to justification for taking more from Nature? Why
fuel Jack Kemp's use of "poor people" to front for the developers'
lobby?

With overpopulation, the clash of values grows both more
bitter and more illogical. Does Kemp support open borders *and*
housing the poor *and* preserving wetlands? Not possible. These
are mutually exclusive goals; clumping them together reminds us
that every environmental cause is a lost cause if population
growth continues.

Does Vice-President Albert Gore pose as an environmentalist

at the same time that he plumps for more immigration? He does. As a senator, Gore voted for the 1990 Immigration Reform Act, which raised legal immigration by 40 percent; and his Oct. 16, 1989, letter to a constituent states, "I believe there are real dangers in placing numerical caps on legal immigration visas." The 1992 Democratic Party platform reflected Gore's views: It called for higher legal immigration in order to eliminate the fifteen-year waiting list of extended-family relatives who are applying for immigration visas. As an environmentalist, Gore inspires neither confidence nor trust.

FALSE SOLUTIONS

Annual increases in the U.S. population mean that conservation and pollution-control measures become an accommodation to growth rather than a solution. All efforts at lasting environmental protection will be defeated by the claims of needy people. People need jobs, need water, need oil—and there goes the environment. Add enough people, and any potential gain from per capita conservation is overwhelmed.

Consider an example published by Population-Environment Balance (1991), a grass-roots membership organization headquartered in Washington, D.C. Start with "the potential energy savings of a compact fluorescent bulb":

> An 18-watt compact fluorescent can replace a 75-watt incandescent bulb, producing the same amount of light but using only 24% of the energy. If each of the 92 million households in America were to replace three incandescent bulbs with compact fluorescents, the United States would save 157 billion kilowatt hours (KWHs) of electricity over the seven-year lifetime of the bulbs. This annual energy savings of 22 billion KWHs—the result of doing no more than changing light bulbs—is equal to approximately 1% of the total annual electricity budget for the whole country!

During that same seven-year period, however, the United States would add at least 20 million people to its population (assuming current rates of population growth), all of whom will consume energy. If these individuals were to install compact fluorescents in their households, they would use, on average, a cumulative 193 billion KWHs of electricity over the seven years. *The net result: an increase in consumption of 36 billion KWHs over the lifetime of the bulbs.*

Apply this concept to America's population growth. Over 3 million more consumers and polluters each year means that each American must reduce emissions and garbage flow just to keep total waste production from growing. With continuing increase in population, the environment can recover only with difficulty and temporarily. Each American who debates location of the next community landfill and the costs of a new (added-capacity) town incinerator, who faces higher utility bills, who pays extra for pollution-control devices on a motor vehicle, or is told when and where that vehicle may not be driven experiences a cost of growth. Further degradation is a distinct possibility in the near term and inevitable in the long term.

GOAL SETTING

Demographer B. Meredith Burke (1991) recalls a 1970 National Academy of Science study which

urged Americans to consider explicitly how they wanted their future society to look and what this would necessitate in reconciling mutually exclusive goals. We were not ready to do this, then were appalled at the paving over of Southern California and the threatened collapse of Florida's fragile ecology. [Now] above all, we must announce that curtailed immigration and population policy are not taboo subjects for public debate. Otherwise, we cannot object if our politicians deliver us to a future we deplore.

Some Americans see only what cheap immigrant labor can do for them. David Rieff (1991) in *Los Angeles: Capital of the Third*

World describes the oblivious Anglo to whom immigrants appear mainly as maids and gardeners. Writes reviewer Samuel Taylor (1991), "Mr. Rieff has stumbled onto one of the most appalling mysteries of late-twentieth century America: that people who live face to face with the imminent dispossession of European America have scarcely given the future a thought."

Not everyone is surprised by the ongoing reconquest of the Southwest. Hispanic activists have renamed parts of Texas and the area of the Gadsden Purchase. The new name, Aztlàn, means the "bronze continent." Self-appointed Mexican-American spokespersons perennially call for tearing down the statues of white explorers and conquerors. Appealing to history ("This was Mexican land anyway"), others assert that California is a part of Mexico which will be reclaimed in due course by sheer weight of numbers.

Activism extends beyond the Southwest. In November, 1991, the Hispanic population in Takoma Park, Md., a suburb of Washington, D.C., helped pass a referendum which lets non-U.S. citizens (even those illegally in the United States) vote in their municipal elections. The campaign to give voting rights to noncitizens can be expected to surface in other places where concentrations of immigrants settle.

In this climate of opinion, the Immigration and Naturalization Service (INS) agents removing illegal aliens from residential complexes and job sites are likened to "storm troopers," and Anglos are called "racist." The same slur is aimed at California Gov. Pete Wilson for saying that immigration imposes financial burdens on state and local government. Bancroft (1991) cites State Sen. Art Torres (D-Los Angeles), who encourages casting the debate on immigration in racial terms: "I thought we rejected David Duke in Louisiana, but now he's raising his ugly head here in California. . . . It's clearly anti-Hispanic, and clearly the way of Republicans, which these guys are, to shift responsibility for their failed domestic policies. I can't believe the governor is part of this debate." In Wilson's case, the stakes are rising. A bomb was mailed to him at the state capitol, accompanied by a note which "denounced Wilson for linking the state's mounting budget problems to an influx of new Californians, who have increased demands for expensive government services such as welfare and Medi-Cal" (Lucas, 1992).

So far, Americans have been largely silent while state and federal governments try to accommodate growing and conflicting entitlement claims. Congress makes immigration policy and mandates most social, health-care, and education benefits; but costs are often borne locally so that the states and Congress have different incentives. The negatives associated with population growth have less immediacy for Congress. Congress dances to the tune of the shortsighted cheap-labor lobby and to immigrant-advocacy lobbies which see their political power increasing as constituencies grow. Other members of Congress respond to self-styled humanitarian arguments and to who knows what else.

CONGRESS UNRESPONSIVE TO THE AMERICAN PEOPLE

It is certain that Congress was not responding to the American people when, with the 1990 Immigration Reform Act, it raised legal immigration by 40 percent. A May, 1990, national Roper poll showed that 77 percent of Americans, including 78 percent of blacks and 74 percent of Hispanics, believed the United States should not increase immigration. Two Gallup polls in 1992 confirmed the breadth of sentiment. Dallas columnist Richard Estrada (1991b) makes no bones about the interests of the average American: "Labor economists . . . testified [before Congress] that there is not a labor shortage in the country. [But] Congress pretended not to hear and proceeded to pass a bill expanding legal immigration."

The Rev. Calvin Butts, pastor of New York's Abyssinian Baptist Church, is another who does not mince words. During television interviews in spring, 1991, he stated that the nation must limit immigration if New York City is to prosper or even survive (U.S. Cities, 1991). Butts observed that, "We have huge numbers from Eastern Europe, Asia, Africa, [and] the Caribbean. A city with dwindling resources and crumbling infrastructure will never recover if we don't get a grip on this. . . . Either you deal with this practically or you have chaos in the streets."

All Americans are *not* well-off, and all of us know it. Moreover, immigration hurts most those who can least afford it. Some Americans may feel guilty because of their own high consumption, but it is irresponsible for them to salve their consciences by bringing in more people who compete with our own least advantaged citizens. America *first* means, among other things, that Americans should take care of their own. Resources are limited. The Earth is finite. More for one is less for another. So it is not trivial to step over one's own working poor and middle class in order to accommodate new arrivals.

A decent standard of living for all is slipping away. America's growing population is the root cause of some troubles and an aggravating cause of many more. A fighting chance to solve our problems—instead of temporizing by treating symptoms—depends on stabilizing population size.

America's population cannot stop growing if immigration continues at a rate above replacement level. About 160,000 persons voluntarily leave each year. So, rounding out the numbers, an all-inclusive target of 200,000 immigrants a year would get America where it needs to be. *All-inclusive* means just that: regular legal immigrants, illegal would-be immigrants, refugees, and asylees.

Our present porous borders facilitate another source of population growth which is unconsented to by Americans: births to women illegally in the United States. These births are not honestly counted as American fertility. Yet the babies do count as Americans because the Fourteenth Amendment to the Constitution awards citizenship to anyone born in the United States regardless of the mother's nationality. Recall that two-thirds of births in the Los Angeles County public hospitals are to women who are in the United States illegally. Perhaps 90 percent of births are to women who are not citizens.

Bemused that Americans let themselves be taken for patsies, one returns to why the people have been so strangely reticent to debate the issue. Economist Donald L. Huddle (1992) of Rice University suggests that debate has been the victim of a myth. The myth, that immigration is a win-win deal, is perpetuated by the media. The London *Economist* (California, 1991), while decrying immigration for England and Europe, urges it on America as the antidote to recession: "Immigration has saved California before and will save it again." An exasperated Californian replies in a "Letter to the Editor" (1992): "Perhaps you could explain why California's recession is worse than the rest of the nation's after a decade of much higher than average immigration."

Americans' capacity for independent thought, as revealed in the polls, is the more remarkable considering how often they get "human interest" news. The plight of would-be immigrants and refugees is touchingly reported. The implicit instruction to Americans is that we should make all welcome. Immigration is almost never linked to damage we deplore. Yet, coverage of endangered species, jobless Americans, overcrowded schools, and overburdened systems of all kinds could alert people to the costs of population growth and its sources. Americans, given information, can decide for themselves if opposition to immigration is racist, if immigration hurts our own poor, if the middle class is undercut by population growth, if taxpayers end up holding the bag, and if all may someday suffer because of resource scarcity and environmental degradation. More Americans know each day that this debate is their business.

Jobs no less than environmental values are at stake. During the 1980s, the U.S. economy created 19 million net new jobs. But 8 million immigrants came in that decade, seeking jobs or benefits. Chapter 16 shows that young Americans entering the labor market in the same period were the principal losers.

With present liberal immigration policy, the future holds still less opportunity for the young. Immigration in the decade of the 1990s is projected to reach 12 million (Bouvier, 1992). At the same time, young Americans entering the labor market will outnumber their elders who leave it by at least 15 million. New job creation will have to be more rapid than ever before seen if severe unemployment is to be averted.

However, impediments to job creation will include the stricter conservation and pollution-control measures needed to mitigate the effect of more and more people: Pollution abatement is costly and thus works against business expansion. Nevertheless, Congress—which has just about exhausted local governments' capacities to pay for programs mandated at the federal level—is eyeing the business sector as the next sugar daddy. The burden of the Clean Air Act has been put on industry; health-care insurance for the poor is likely to follow. Whatever the goal, population growth and increasing poverty make its attainment more costly. If costs are socialized to the individual taxpayer or business, this itself makes it difficult to create high-quality, well-capitalized jobs. Thus, the 1990s and the twenty-first century promise endless conflict among incompatible goals; the dilemmas will worsen in proportion to population size.

Americans will also be interested to hear more from economist Gary Burtless of the Brookings Institution, advocate for the American worker and author of *A Future of Lousy Jobs* (1990). Burtless points out that three countries which allow virtually no immigration and have very little population growth—Iceland, Japan, and New Zealand—can boast of relatively small wage disparity between their highest- and lowest-paid workers. The U.S. pattern is different on all counts. The United States has the highest rates of immigration and population growth of any industrialized country, and the United States has also the greatest disparity between highest-paid executives and lowest-paid labor. Recalling Chapter 14, diminution of social equity is a real effect of less and less favorable population-to-resource ratios.

TAKING SIDES

Both legal immigration (which contributes about 40 percent of annual population growth) and illegal immigration are justifiably highly politicized issues. Already the lineup is more complicated than will fit into a simple dichotomy of liberal versus conservative. Liberal Democrats (the workers' supposed friends), Albert Gore (a Democrat from Tennessee and an unenlightened environmentalist), congressional immigrant advocates (what you see is what they are), and the Heritage Foundation (extreme right-wingers whose champions are Julian Simon and Ben Wattenberg) teamed up to ram through the 1990 Immigration Reform Act. Moderate Sen. Alan Simpson (R-Wyo.) and Sen. Ted Kennedy (D-Mass.) sponsored it in a bad Senate bill made worse by reconciliation with the House version. The coalition wraps itself in the flag of globalism, and most pretend to believe that it is possible to help everyone because capitalism is a cow fed in heaven to be milked on earth.

President George Bush signed the bill.

In opposition to the above, labor economist Vernon M. Briggs, Jr., of Cornell University testified before a Congressional committee that high levels of immigration prevent the poor from getting a first toehold on the employment ladder. Frank Morris (1990), graduate school dean at Morgan State University, testified before the same committee that "opportunities for young black workers and prospective workers have been sidetracked by hasty immigration policies." Former Colorado Gov. Richard Lamm, a Democrat, also testified against increasing legal immigration; Lamm warned that state and local governments were becoming insolvent and could not afford the added burden of meeting immigrants' health care, educational, housing, and general welfare needs.

California Gov. Pete Wilson, a Republican, opposes immigration on nearly identical grounds as Lamm. He states that the present high level of immigration is a principal factor busting his state's health care, education, criminal justice, and welfare budgets and, moreover, that this multibillion-dollar added burden deprives native-born Americans of benefits and services even as it raises their taxes.

On the federal side, Attorney General William P. Barr of the Bush administration used departmentally generated funds to raise the number of border patrol and drug-enforcement-immigration-liaison officers by about 11 percent. However, the number remains below 10,0000. Clearly, not all officers are on duty at any one time, and part of the INS's job is guarding a border where 4 million illegal crossings are attempted annually.

The major contenders in the 1992 presidential campaign had little to say about immigration. Pat Buchanan, alone, appeared informed on the labor, tax, educational, and welfare safety-net effects, and he brought lower limits on immigration into the primary campaign. On the margin, the widely reviled David Duke, who says he is for the common man, also wants to limit immigration; his involvement with the issue plays into the hands of those who cry racism, distracting Americans from what may well be their common economic and environmental interests.

A COMMUNALITY OF INTEREST

Illegal immigration is an issue for any sovereign state and must be speedily addressed. If no counter measures are taken, one may be assured that the number flouting U.S. laws will grow. Legal immigration accounts for by far the largest number, however, and is necessarily a part of integrated planning for a stable environment and society. All-inclusive replacement-level immigration—about 160,000 persons per year—is the most that the United States can accommodate if we wish to pass on to our children the opportunities and freedoms which we have long enjoyed.

Addressing all Americans in the Keynote Address of the 1984 Democratic Party's National Convention, Jesse Jackson said that Americans may have come here in different ships, but "we are all in the same boat now." Boats sink when they become overfull, and Jackson appears to be reconsidering his former proimmigration position.

No common ideological thread distinguishes among partisans or links allies in the immigration debate. But as an unresolved matter which is critical to the national interest, the immigration issue must not be allowed to drop from sight anytime soon.

Bibliography

1. Growth: Why We Love It

"Accounting for the Environment," *Science* Dec. 20:1724, 1991.

Atiyah, M., and Press, F., *Population Growth, Resource Consumption, and a Sustainable World*, Royal Society of London and National Academy of Sciences, Washington, DC, February 1992.

Auster L., "The Mondo Baffo of the New York Regents," *Measure* 100(1):3–5, 1991.

Barbier, E. B., *Economics, Natural-Resource Scarcity and Development: Conventional and Alternative Views*, Earthscan, London, UK, 1989.

Brown, L., *State of the World, 1990*, Worldwatch Institute, Washington, DC, 1990.

Culbertson, J., " 'Economic Growth,' Population and the Environment," *Population and Environment* 11(4):299–300, 1990.

Daly, H., "Population and Economics: A Bioeconomic Analysis," *Population and Environment* 12(3):257–258, 1991.

Ehrlich, R. P., and Ehrlich, A. H., *The Population Explosion*, Simon & Schuster, New York, 1990.

Green, C. P., The Environment and Population Growth: Decade for Action, *Population Reports*, Series M, No. 10. Johns Hopkins University Population Information Program, Baltimore, MD, 1992.

Harris, L., "Species and Habitat Preservation," address at the Vanderbilt Institute for Public Policy Studies, Nashville, TN, Nov. 20, 1991.

Hebert, H. J., "Wetlands Restoration," *Nashville Banner* Dec. 11:A12, 1991.

Keely, C. B., *Mexican and Central American Population and U.S. Immigration Policy*, edited by F. D. Bean, J. Schmandt, and S. Weintraub, Center for Mexican American Studies, Austin, TX, 1989.

"Last One Out of Gotham, Close the Door," *The Economist* Oct. 20:21–22, 1990.

Population-Environment Balance, "Executive Summary: The Costs of Population Growth in the Patuxent River Basin," Author, Washington, DC, 1985.

Potter, D. M., *People of Plenty*, University of Chicago Press, Chicago, 1954.

President's Commission on Population Growth and the American Future, *Population and the American Future*, New American Library, New York, 1972.

Rheinhold, R., "They Came to California for the Good Life; Now They're Looking Elsewhere," *New York Times* Oct. 16:A16, 1991.

Rose, F., "California Babel: The City of the Future Is a Troubling Prospect if It's to Be Los Angeles," *Wall Street Journal* June 12:A1, 1989.

Stipp, D., "Toxic Red Tides Seem to Be on the Rise, Increasing the Risks of Eating Shellfish," *Wall Street Journal* Nov. 22:B1, 4, 1991.

2. A Global Dilemma

"Border Protests Grow as Aliens Swarm Unchecked," *San Francisco Chronicle* April 29:A1, 1990.

Demeny, P., "Human Numbers and Standards of Living," paper presented at the Resources, Environment, and Population Conference, Hoover Institution, Stanford University, Palo Alto, CA, Feb. 1–3, 1989.

Draper, P., "Cultural Pressure on Sex Differences," *American Ethnologist* May:602–616, 1975.

Draper, P., and Buchanan, A., *Developmental, Symbolic, and Evolutionary Perspectives*, Aldine de Gruyter, New York, 1993.

Eaton, J. W., and Mayer, A. J., *Man's Capacity to Reproduce*, Glencoe Press, Glencoe, IL, 1954.

Gallup Poll, "Americans Respond to Immigration Queries," March 1, 1992.

"Immigration Unpopular in Poll," *San Francisco Chronicle* June 5:A-10, 1990.

Notestein, F., "Population: The Long View," in *Food for Thought*, edited by T. W. Schultz, Norman Wait Harris Memorial Lectures, 1945.

The Roper Organization, "Poll: American Views on Immigration," May 1990, May 1992.

Spaeth, A., "An Indian Lawyer and His Ruby as Big as the Ritz," *Wall Street Journal* Dec. 31:Arts and leisure page, 1991.

White, L., Jr., *Medieval Technology and Social Class*, Oxford University Press, New York, 1966.

3. Belief as Part of the Problem

Aswad, B., *And the Poor Get Children: Radical Perspectives on Population Dynamics*, edited by K. L. Michaelson, Monthly Review Press, New York, 1981.

Brittain, A. W., "Migration and the Demographic Transition: A West Indian Example," *Social and Economic Studies* 39(3):39–64, 1990.

Brittain, A. W., "Anticipated Child Loss to Migration and Sustained High Fertility in an East Caribbean Population," *Social Biology* 38(1–2):94–112, 1991.

Brooke J., "Births in Brazil Are on Decline, Easing Worries," *New York Times* August 8:A1,9, 1989.

Chowdry, A. K. M. A., and Khan, A. R., "The Effect of Child Mortality Experience on Subsequent Fertility," *Population Studies* 3(2):249–261, 1976.

Coale, A., and Watkins, S. (eds.), *The Decline of Fertility in Europe*, Princeton University Press, Princeton, NJ, 1986.

"DHS Documents Major Fertility Declines," Demographic and Health Surveys, *Newsletter* 4(1):1, IRD/Maco, Columbia, MD, 1991.

Díaz-Briquets, S., and Pérez, L., *Cuba: The Demography of Revolution*, Population Reference Bureau, Washington, DC, 1981.

"Fertility Declining among Younger Women in Sudan," Demographic and Health Surveys, *Newsletter* 4(1):5, IRD/Maco, Columbia, MD, 1991.

Friedlander, D., "Demographic Responses and Socioeconomic Structure: Population Processes in England and Wales in the Nineteenth Century," *Demography* 20:249–272, 1983.

Goldsmith, E., "The Population Explosion: An Inevitable Concomitant of Development," *The Ecologist* 19:2–3, 1989.

Gore, A., *Earth in the Balance: Ecology and the Human Spirit*, Houghton Mifflin, Boston, 1992.

Heilig, G., Büttner, T., and Lutz, W., *Germany's Population: Turbulent Past, Uncertain Future*, Population Reference Bureau, Washington, DC, 1990.

Hern, W. M., Book Review of *The Population Dynamics of the Mucajai Yano-mama*, by J. D. Early and J. F. Peters, *Population Studies* 45:359, 1991.

"Kenya: More Choice, Fewer Babies," *The Economist* July 11:39–40, 1992.

King, M., "Health Is a Sustainable State," *The Lancet* 336:664–667, 1990.

Knodel, J. E., *The Decline of Fertility in Germany, 1871–1939*, Princeton University Press, Princeton, NJ, 1974.

Lemsine, A., "God Guard Islam from the Islamists," *The Washington Report on Middle East Affairs* March:14,16, 1992.

Levine, N. E., "Differential Child Care in Three Tibetan Communities," *Population and Development Review* 13(2):281–304, 1987.

McGregor, J., "Jobless Peasants Swarm through China," *Wall Street Journal* May 2:A12, 1991.

Obbo, C., "HIV Transmission: Men Are the Solution," *Population and Environment* 14(3), 1993.

Pebley, A. R., Delgado, H., and Brineman, E., "Fertility Desires and Child Mortality Experience among Guatemalan Women," *Studies in Family Planning* 20:129–136, 1989.

Repetto, R., "Soil Loss and Population Pressure in Java," in *Population and Resources in a Changing World*, edited by K. Davis, M. S. Berstam, and H. M. Sellers, Morrison Institute for Population and Resource Studies, Stanford, CA, 1989.

Rollet-Echalier, C., *La politique à l'Égard de la Petite Enfance sous la IIIe Republique*, Presses Universitaires de France, Paris, 1990.

Stycos, J. M., "The Second Great Wall of China: Evolution of a Successful Policy of Population Control," *Population and Environment* 12(4):389–406, 1991.

Teitelbaum, M., "Relevance of Demographic Transition Theory for Developing Countries," *Science* 188:420–425, 1975.

"When History Passes By," *The Economist* May 12:4–26, 1990.

White, R. M., "Editorial," *Issues in Science and Technology* 1(3):6, 1990.

4. Cultural Brakes

Abernethy, V., *Population Pressure and Cultural Adjustment*, Human Sciences Press, New York, 1979.

Bugos, P. E., Jr., and McCarthy, L. M., "Ayoreo Infanticide: A Case Study," in *Infanticide*, edited by G. Hausfater and S. Hrdy, Wenner-Gren Foundation for Anthropological Research Inc., New York, 1984.

Center for Health Statistics, Tennessee Department of Health and Environment, "Gender Gap in the Diaper Set," *Vital Signs* 2(3):1–2, 1985.

Chaudry, M., "Role of the Social and Cultural Factors in Human Fertility in India," *Population and Environment* 12(2):117–138, 1990.

Early, J. D., and Peters, J. F., *The Population Dynamics of the Mucajai Yanomama*, Academic Press, San Diego, 1990.

"Poor Man's Plague," *The Economist* Sept. 21:21, 1991.

Riddle, J. M., and Estes, J. W., "Oral Contraceptives in Ancient and Medieval Times," *American Scientist* 80:226–233, 1992.

Segal, S. J., "Contraception Research: A Male Chauvinist Plot?" *Family Planning Perspectives* 4(3):21–25, 1972.

5. Where to Look for Balance

Abernethy, V., "Comments on Tibetan Fraternal Polyandry," *American Anthropologist* 84:895, 1982.

Demeny, P., "Early Fertility Decline in Austria-Hungary: A Lesson in Demographic Transition," *Daedalus* 97(2):502–522, 1968.

Demeny, P., "Social Science and Population Policy," *Population and Development Review* 14(3):451–480, 1988.

Drake, M., *Population and Society in Norway 1735–1865*, Cambridge University Press, Cambridge, UK, 1969.

Firth, R., *We, the Tikopia*, Beacon Press, Boston, 1936.

Hunt, E. E., "The Depopulation of Yap," *Human Biology* 26:20–51, 1954.

Keyfitz, N., "Population and Development within the Ecosphere: One View of the Literature," *Population Index* 57(1):5–22, 1991.

Low, B. S., and Clarke, A. L., "Resources and the Life Course: Patterns in the Demographic Transition," *Ethology and Sociobiology* 13, 1992.

Moran, E. F., "Human Adaptive Strategies in Amazonian Blackwater Ecosystems," *American Anthropologist* 93:361–382, 1991.

Ohlin, G., "Mortality, Marriage and Growth in Pre-industrial Populations," *Population Studies* 14(3):190–197, 1961.

Population Reference Bureau, "Man's Population Predicament," *Population Bulletin* 27(2):1–39, 1971.

Population Reference Bureau, "Survey Report: Jordan," *Population Today* Dec.:4, Author, Washington, DC, 1991.

Van de Walle, E., "Marriage and Marital Fertility," *Daedalus* 97(2):486–501, 1968.

Westoff, C., "Is the KAP-Gap Real?" *Population and Development Review* 14(2):225–232, 1988.

6. Which Incentives?

"China Hopes to Curb Births," *Wall Street Journal* June 14:A6, 1991.

Keyfitz, N., "Population and Development within the Ecosphere: One View of the Literature," *Population Index* 57(1):5–22, 1991.

Noonan, J. T., Jr., "Intellectual and Demographic History," *Daedalus* 97(2):463–485, 1968.

Weiner, M., *The Politics of Scarcity*, University of Chicago Press, Chicago, 1962.

Wyon, J., and Gordon, J. E., *The Khanna Study: Population Problems in the Rural Punjab*, Harvard University Press, Cambridge, 1971.

7. Development Alone May Spur Population Growth

Bairagi, R., "Food Crisis, Nutrition, and Female Children in Rural Bangladesh," *Population and Development Review* 12(2):307–315, 1986.

Bajpai, S., "India's Lost Women," *New Delhi Indian Express*, reprinted in *World Press Review* April:49, 1991.

Bose, A., *Population of India: 1991 Census Results and Methodology*, B. R. Publishing Company, Delhi, 1991.

Center for Immigration Studies, "Asencio Commission Reports: Trade and Development Are Long Range Antidote of Illegal Immigration," *Scope* 5, Author, Washington, DC, 1990.

Chaudry, M., "Role of the Social and Cultural Factors in Human Fertility in India," *Population and Environment* 12(2):117–138, 1990.

Coale, A. J., "Excess Female Mortality and the Balance of the Sexes in the Population: An Estimate of Number of 'Missing Females,'" *Population and Development Review* 17(3):517–523, 1991.

Commission for the Study of International Migration and Cooperative Economic Development, *Report*, U.S. Government Printing Office, Washington, DC, July, 1990.

Davis, K., "Human Fertility in India," *American Journal of Sociology* 52(3):243–254, 1946.

Davis, K., *Population of India and Pakistan*, Princeton University Press, Princeton, NJ, 1951.

Demeny, P., "Social Science and Population Policy," *Population and Development Review* 14(3):451–480, 1988.

"Development Alone May Spur Population Growth," *International Family Planning Digest*, International Planned Parenthood Federation, New York, 1976.

Freed, R. S., and Freed, S. A., "Beliefs and Practices Resulting in Female Deaths and Fewer Females Than Males in India," *Population and Environment* 10(3):144–161, 1989.

Hern, W., "Effects of Cultural Change on Fertility in Amazonian Indian Societies: Recent Research and Projections," *Population and Environment* 13(1):23–44, 1991.

Monroe, R. L., "Population Growth among the Margoli," Department of Anthropology, Pitzer College, Claremont, CA, n.d.

Nag, M., *Factors Affecting Human Fertility in Nonindustrial Societies: A Cross Cultural Study*, Human Relations Area Files, New Haven, CT, 1968.

Population Reference Bureau, "Man's Population Predicament," *Population Bulletin* 27(2):1–39, 1971.

Scheffel, D. Z., "The Dynamics of Labrador Inuit Fertility: An Example of Cultural and Demographic Change," *Population and Environment* 10(1):32–47, 1988.

Solis, D., "Corn May Be Snag in Trade Talks by Mexico, U.S.," *Wall Street Journal* Dec. 27:A5, 1991.

Stycos, J.M., "The Second Great Wall of China: Evolution of a Successful Policy of Population Control," *Population and Environment* 12(4):389–406, 1991.

Westoff, G., "Is the KAP-Gap Real?" *Population and Development Review* 14(2):225–232, 1988.

Wyon, J., and Gordon, J. E., *The Khanna Study: Population Problems in the Rural Punjab*, Harvard University Press, Cambridge, 1971.

8. Culture: Make or Break

Handwerker, W. P., "Women's Power and Fertility Transition: The Cases of Africa and the West Indies," *Population and Environment* 13(1):55–78, 1991.

Kohler, T. A., "Prehistoric Human Impact on the Environment in the Upland North American Southwest," *Population and Environment* 13(4):255–268, 1992.

Laughlin, C. D., Jr., "Deprivation and Reciprocity," *Man* 9:380–396, 1974.

Potter, D. M., *People of Plenty*, University of Chicago Press, Chicago, 1954.

Turnbull, C. M., *The Mountain People*, Simon & Schuster, New York, 1972.

Wilson, E. O., *Sociobiology*, Harvard University Press, Cambridge, 1975.

9. One-World: A Global Folly

Babbitt, B., "The New and Improved South America," *San Francisco Chronicle* March 20:Briefing Section, 1991.

Boulding, K. E., "One World," in *Finite Resources and the Human Future*, edited by I. G. Barbour, Augsburg, Minneapolis, 1976.

Harper's Index, *Harpers Magazine* March:12, 1989.

Harper's Index, *Harpers Magazine* Dec.:11, 1989.

Mathews, J. T., "Rescue Plan for Africa," *World Monitor* May:34, 1989.

Olasky, M., *The Tragedy of American Compassion*, Regnery Gateway, Washington, DC, June 9, 1992.

Population Reference Bureau, "Spot Light: Myanmar," *Population Today*, July/Aug. 12:4, Author, Washington, DC, 1991.

Smith, J. W., *The Remorseless Working of Things: AIDS and the Global Crisis, An Ecological Critique of Internationalism*, Kalgoorie Press, Canberra, Australia, 1992.

Steele, S., *The Content of Our Character*, HarperCollins, New York, 1991.

Umpleby, S., "Will the Optimists Please Stand Up?" *Population and Environment* 10(2):122–132, 1988.

Umpleby, S., "The Scientific Revolution in Demography," *Population and Environment* 11(3):159–174, 1990.

Umpleby, S., *GW Professor Disputes Decline in World Population Growth Rates*, George Washington University, Washington, DC, October 18, 1991.

Von Foerster, H., Mora, P. M., and Amiot, L. W., "Doomsday: Friday, 13 November, A.D. 2026," *Science* 132(3436):1291–1295, 1960.

Webster's New Collegiate Dictionary, G and C Merriam Co., Springfield, MA, 1975.

10. Potlatching Twentieth-Century Style

Durham, D. F., and Fandrem, J. C., "The Food 'Surplus': A Staple Illusion for Economics; a Cruel Illusion for Populations," *Population and Environment* 10(2):115–121, 1988.

Fletcher, J., "Chronic Famine and the Immorality of Food Aid: A Bow to Garrett Hardin," *Population and Environment* 12(3):331–338, 1991.

Grant, L., *Free Trade and Cheap Labor: The President's Dilemma*, Negative Population Growth, Teaneck, NJ, 1991.

Green, C. P., "Impact of Population on the Environment," Annual Meeting of the American Public Health Association, Atlanta, Nov. 11, 1991.

Hardin, G., "The Tragedy of the Commons," *Science* 162(13 Dec.):1243-1248, 1968.

Trivers, R. L., "The Evolution of Reciprocal Altruism," *The Quarterly Review of Biology* 46:35–57, 1971.

Unruh, J. D., "Transhumant Agriculture and Irrigated Agriculture," *Human Ecology* 18(3):223–246, 1990.

11. Helping While Not Harming

Bowers, B., "Third World Debt That Is Almost Always Paid in Full," *Wall Street Journal* June 7:B2, 1991.

Handwerker, W. P., "Women's Power and Fertility Transition: The Cases of Africa and the West Indies," *Population and Environment* 13(1):55–78, 1991.

Kapoor, R., "The Psychosocial Consequences of an Environmental Disaster: Selected Case Studies of the Bhopal Gas Tragedy," *Population and Environment* 13(3):209–216, 1992.

"Poor Man's Plague," *The Economist* Sept. 21:21–22, 1991.

"Women's Value, Men's Worth," *The Economist* Nov. 10:54, 1990.

12. Conservation, Incentives, and Ethics

"Capital Flight," *Business Week*, April 10:74, 1989.

Carlson, E., and Bernstam, M. S., "Population and Resources under the Socialist Economic System," in *Resources, Environment and Population*, edited by K. Davis and M. S. Bernstam, Oxford University Press, New York, 1991.

Cobb, J. B., Jr., and Daly, H. E., "Free Trade versus Community: Social and Environmental Consequences of Free Trade in a World with Capital Mobility and Overpopulated Regions," *Population and Environment* 11(3):175–192, 1990.

Cohen, R., "Brazil," *Wall Street Journal* April 10:A6, 1989.

Culbertson, J., " 'Economic Growth,' Population, and the Environment," *Population and Environment* 11(2):83–100, 1989.

Eder, J. F., "Deforestation and Detribalization in the Philippines: The Palawan Case," *Population and Environment* 12(2):99–116, 1990.

Fortmann, L., and Bruce, J., *Whose Trees? Proprietary Dimensions of Forestry*, Westview Press, Boulder, CO, 1988.

Goldstein, M. C., and Beall, C. M., *Nomads of Western Tibet*, University of California Press, Berkeley, 1990.

Green, C. P., "Impact of Population on the Environment," Annual Meeting of the American Public Health Association, Atlanta, Nov. 11, 1991.

Hardin, G., "The Tragedy of the Commons," *Science* 162:1243–1248, 1968.

Naipaul, V. S., "A Miraculous Achievement," *Newsweek* (European Edition) July 3:48, 1989.

Park, T. K., "Early Trends toward Class Stratification: Chaos, Common Property, and Flood Recession Agriculture," *American Anthropologist* 94:90–117, 1992.

Rawls, J., *Theory of Justice*, Belknap Press of Harvard University, Cambridge, 1971.

Russell, W. M. S., "Population, Swidden Farming and the Tropical Environment," *Population and Environment* 10(2):77–94, 1988.

Stroup, R. L., "Controlling Earth's Resources: Markets or Socialism?" *Population and Environment* 12(23):265–284, 1991.

13. Limiting Factors

Brown, L. R., *State of the World, 1990*, Worldwatch Institute, Washington, DC, 1990.

Durning, A. B., and Brough, H. B., "Taking Stock: Animal Farming and the Environment," Worldwatch Institute, Washington, DC, 1991.

"Farm Subsidies," *The Economist* June 8:104, 1991.

Fischer, C., "Energy Consumption and Limits to Global Emissions of Carbon Dioxide," *Population and Environment* 13(3):183–192, 1992.

Green, C. P., "Impact of Population on the Environment," Annual Meeting of the American Public Health Association, Atlanta, 1991.

Hallwachs, R., "Metropolitan Water District of Southern California," *Aqueduct* 1:6–9, 1991.

Kerr, R. A., "Geothermal Tragedy of the Commons," *Science* 253:134–135, 1991.

Lundberg, J. C., "The Oil Society Spins Its Wheels," *Population and Environment* 11(1):59–72, 1989.

McCoy, C., "Little Fish May Put California in Hot Water," *Wall Street Journal* July 10:1, 1991.

Myers, N., "Extinction 'Hot Spots,'" *Science* 254:919, 1991.

14. Kissing the Blarney Stone and Other Tales

Abernethy, V., *Population Pressure and Cultural Adjustment*, Human Sciences Press, New York, 1979.

Keyfitz, N., "Alfred Sauvy: In Memoria," *Population and Development Review* 16(4):727–733, 1990.

Knodel, J. E., *The Decline of Fertility in Germany, 1871–1938*, Princeton University Press, Princeton, NJ, 1974.

Langer, W. L., "Checks on Population Growth: 1750-1850," *Scientific American* 226:92–99, 1972.

Langland, E. Personal Communication, February, 1992.

Lee, R. D., *Population and Economic Change in Developing Countries*, edited by R. E. Easterlin, pp. 517–556, University of Chicago Press, Chicago, 1980.

Noonan, J. T., "Intellectual and Demographic History," *Daedalus* 97(2):463–485, 1968.

Simon, J. L., *The Ultimate Resource*, Princeton University Press, Princeton, NJ, 1981.

Van der Walle, E., "Marriage and Marital Fertility," *Daedalus* 97(2):486–501, 1968.

15. History Does Not Stop

Abernethy, V., "Social Network and Response to the Maternal Role," *International Journal of Sociology of the Family* 3(1):86–92, 1973. Reprinted in *Inventory of Marriage and Family Literature*, Vol. 1, 1975.

Banks, L. E., and Salvo, J. J., "Foreign Born Fertility: New York City Faces Its Future," Annual Meeting of the Population Association of America, Toronto, Canada, 1990.

Beauvoir, S. de, *The Second Sex*, translated by H. M. Parshley, Knopf, New York, 1952, 1953.

Blau, F. D., "The Fertility of Immigrant Women: Evidence from High Fertility Source Countries," *Working Paper #3608*, National Bureau of Economic Research, Inc., Cambridge, 1991.

Bouvier, L. F., *Peaceful Invasions*, University Press of America, Lanham, MD, 1992.

Bouvier, L. F., and De Vita, C., "The Baby Boom . . . Entering Midlife," Population Reference Bureau, Washington, DC, 1991.

Camire, D., and Willette, A., " 'Working Poor' Shatter Traditional Image of Poverty," *The Tennessean* July 30:3G, 1989.

Demographic Research Unit, "Fertility Rates," Department of Finance, Author, Sacramento, CA, 1990.

Easterlin, R., "The American Baby Boom in Historical Perspective," *Occasional Paper #79*, National Bureau of Economic Research, New York, 1962.

Easterlin, R., "Does Human Fertility Adjust to the Environment?" *American Economic Review* 61(2):399–407, 1971.

Friedan, B., *The Feminine Mystique*, Norton, New York, 1963.

"Longer Hours, Not Pay Rises, Boost Most Families' Income," *Wall Street Journal* Jan. 21:1, 1992.

Macunovich, D. J., and Easterlin, R. A., "How Parents Have Coped: The Effect of Life-Cycle Demographic Decisions on the Economic Status of Preschool Children," *Population and Development Review* 16(20): 301–325, 1990.

Morgan, P., "Census Bureau Study Finds Shift in Fertility Patterns," *Wall Street Journal* June 22:B1, 1991.

Murray, A., "Losing Faith: Many Americans Fear U.S. Living Standards Have Stopped Rising," *Wall Street Journal* May 1:1, 6, 1989.

Noah, T., "Urban League, in Bleak Report, Finds Black Americans' Income Fell in the '80s," *Wall Street Journal* Jan. 9:A2, 1991.

Rainwater, L., *And the Poor Get Children: Sex, Contraception, and Family Planning in the Working Class*, Quadrangle Books, Chicago, 1960.

Smith, J. W. (ed.), *Immigration, Population and Sustainable Environments: The Limits to Australia's Growth*, Flinders University Press, Bedford Park, South Australia, 1991.

"The Teen Pregnancy Boom: Solving the Mystery," *U.S. News and World Report* July 13:38, 1992.

16. The Path to Poverty

"American Survey," *The Economist* June 27:25–26, 1992.

Atkinson, R. C., "Letter," *Science* 245:584, 1989.

Borjas, G., and Freeman, R. B., *The Economic Effects of Immigration in Source and Receiving Countries*, University of Chicago Press, Chicago, 1992.

Briggs, V. M., Jr., "Testimony before the U.S. House of Representatives Judiciary Committee Subcommittee on Immigration, Refugees and International Law," *Congressional Record*, March 13, 1990.

Briggs, V. M., Jr., *Mass Migration and the National Interest*, M. E. Sharpe, Inc., Armonk, NY, 1992.

Campbell, E. K., "The Fading American Dream," Georgia Institute of Technology, Atlanta, 1992.

Center for Immigration Studies, "1990 Immigration Level Is the Highest in U.S. History," *Scope* 10:5, Author, Washington, DC, 1992.

Estrada, R., "Less Immigration Helps Hispanics," *The Miami Herald* July 24:13A, 1990.

Estrada, R., "The Impact of Immigration on Hispanic Americans," *Chronicles* July:24–28, 1991.

"Experts Paint Bleak Picture of World Labor Market," *San Francisco Chronicle* Sept. 19:B3, 1992.

Francis, D. R., "Imports, Immigrants Hurt the Unskilled," *Christian Science Monitor* Sept. 6:Editorial page, 1991.

Grant, L., "Free Trade and Cheap Labor: The President's Dilemma," Negative Population Growth, Teaneck, NJ, 1991.

Harrison, L. E., "America and Its Immigrants," *The National Interest* Summer:37–46, 1992.

Huddle, D. L., "Immigration, Jobs and Wages: The Misuses of Econometrics," Negative Population Growth, Teaneck, NJ, 1992.

Huddle, D. L., "Dirty Work: Are Immigrants Taking Jobs That the Native Underclass Do Not Want?" *Population and Environment*, in press.

Hudson Institute, "Executive Summary" of *Workforce 2000*, Author, Indianapolis, 1987.

"Japan Slows but Firms Still Invest Heavily," *Wall Street Journal* April 15:1, 1991.

Lamm, R. D., *Megatraumas: America at the Year 2000*, Houghton Mifflin, Boston, 1985.

Lamm, R. D., "Immigration Policy Ignores U.S. Poor," *Rocky Mountain News* Sept. 17:8, 1989.

Lamm, R. D., "Testimony on Legal Immigration Reform Bills S. 358, H.R. 672, H.R. 2448, H.R. 4165, and H.R. 4300 before the U.S. House of Representatives Judiciary Committee Subcommittee on Immigration, Refugees and International Law," *Congressional Record*, March 13, 1990.

"Living Standards Declined in U.S. in '90, Study Finds," *Wall Street Journal* July 10:1,5, 1991.

"Math Ph.D.s: A Bleak Picture," *Science* 252:502, 1991.

McCracken, P. W., "The Big Domestic Issue: Slow Growth," *Wall Street Journal* Oct. 4:A14, 1991.

McCracken, P. W., "The Best Recession Policy: Investment," *Wall Street Journal* Jan. 17:A10, 1992.

Morris, F., "Testimony before the U.S. House of Representatives Judiciary Committee Subcommittee on Immigration, Refugees, and International Law," *Congressional Record*, March 13, 1990.

Murray, A., "Losing Faith: Many Americans Fear U.S. Living Standards Have Stopped Rising," *Wall Street Journal* May 1:1,6, 1989.

Noah, T., "Number of Poor Americans Is Up 6%," *Wall Street Journal* Sept. 27:A2, 1991.

Olsen, D., "Immigration and Filling the Jobs of the Future," *The Subcontractor* 11(3):1–2, 1989.

Porter, M. E., "The Competitive Advantage of Nations," *Harvard Business Review* 90(2):73–93, 1990.

Reinhold, R., "They Came to California for the Good Life; Now They're Looking Elsewhere," *New York Times* Oct.16:A16, 1991.

Rukstad, M. G., *Macroeconomic Decision Making in the World Economy*, Dryden Press, Chicago, 1989.

Sauvy, A., *Théorie Générale de la Population*, 2 vol., Presses Universitaires de France, Paris, 1963.

"A Second Look at America's Workers," *U.S. News and World Report* Nov. 19:19, 1990.

Van Zandt, H. F., "Japan's 'No Immigration' Policy: An Important Factor in Its Economic Success," *Border Watch Special Report*, American Immigration Control Foundation, Monterey, VA, 1986, 1991.

U.S. Bureau of the Census, "Income Distribution in the U.S.," Author, Washington, DC, Feb. 19, 1992.

U.S. Bureau of Labor Statistics, "Employment and Earnings," *Report No. 170*, Author, Washington, DC, Jan. 1991.

Whitmire, R., "When Living and Wages Don't Meet," *The Tennessean* Jan. 5:1,4E, 1992.

17. All Our People

Allen, C., "America: Restricted Territory," *Insight* March 16:6–37, 1992.

Barnett, D., "Refugee Bonanza for Soviet Jews, Christians," *Christian Science Monitor* Aug. 28:19, 1989.

Barnett, D., "Free Pass to Disneyland," *Chronicles* Feb.:41–44, 1992.

Borjas, G., *Friends or Strangers*, Basic Books, New York, 1990a.

Borjas, G., "The U.S. Takes the Wrong Immigrants," *Wall Street Journal* April 5:Editorial page, 1990b.

Borjas, G., "Immigrants—Not What They Used to Be," *Wall Street Journal* Nov. 8:Editorial page, 1990c.

Center for Immigration Studies, "Estimated Annual Costs of Major Federal and State Services to Illegal Aliens," Author, Washington, DC, 1991.

Chase, M., and Dolan, C., "California's Beacon to Newcomers Dims as Services Are Pared," *Wall Street Journal* Sept. 1:1, 1992.

Dunn, W., "Tennessee State Budget Address, 1972," Nashville, TN, 1972.

Goldfarb, C., "Study: Miami a Poor City That Is Getting Poorer," *Miami Herald* Oct. 29:1B, 1991.

"Governor Tackles Welfare Reform," *San Francisco Chronicle* Dec. 15:Editorial page, 1991.

Gurwitt, R., "Back to the Melting Pot," *Governing* June:30–35, 1992.

James, D., *Illegal Immigration: An Unfolding Crisis*, University Press of America, Inc., Lanham, MD, 1991.

"Jewish Refugees Pour into U.S.," *San Francisco Chronicle* Sept. 29:A30, 1989.

"Massachusetts Accused of Denying Benefits," *San Francisco Chronicle* Jan. 21:1, 1992.

McConnell, R., "Population Growth and Environmental Quality in California: An American Laboratory," *Population and Environment* 14(1):9–30, 1992.

Page, C., "Failed Foreign, Urban Policies Called in Miami," *Nashville Banner* Feb. 15:5, 1989.

Population-Environment Balance, "How the 1990 Immigration Law Adversely Affects the United States," *Balance Data*, Author, Washington, DC, April, 1991.

Rea, L. M., and Parker, R. A., *A Fiscal Analysis of Undocumented Immigrants Residing in San Diego County*, Report by the Auditor General of California, Sacramento, CA, August, 1992.

Sanchez, C., "U.S. Official Calls for Federal Money to Help D.C.'s Hispanic Community," *The Washington Post* Feb. 2:B4, 1992.

Simon, J., *The Economic Consequences of Immigration*, Basil Blackwell, New York, 1989.

Smith, J. W., "Population, Immigration and the Limits to Australia's Growth: A Catalog of Criticisms," in J. W. Smith (ed.), *Immigration, Population and Sustainable Environments: The Limits to Australia's Growth*, Flinders Press, South Australia, 1991.

Walters, D., "Jobs Disappear but Not People," *Sacramento Bee* August 9:1, 1992.

18. The Carrying Capacity of the United States

Carrying Capacity Network, "Has the United States Already Exceeded Its Optimum Population Size?" *Clearinghouse Bulletin* 1(5):1–2,7, Author, Washington, DC, 1991.

Chin, A. S., and Furillo, A., "Viet Gangs a Growing Threat in State, U.S.," *San Francisco Examiner* April 28:A1, 1991.

Gever, J., Kaufmann, R., Skole, D., and Vorosmarty, C., *Beyond Oil: The Threat to Food and Fuel in Coming Decades*, Ballinger, Cambridge, 1986.

Gutfeld, R., "U.S. Crude Output during 1991 Was Lowest since 1950," *Wall Street Journal* Jan. 16:A6, 1992.

Holdren, J. P., "Population and the Energy Problem," *Population and Environment* 12(3):231–255, 1991.

Lundberg, J., Personal Communication, 1991.

Masters, C. D., Root, D. H., and Attanasi, E. D., "Resource Constraints in Petroleum Production Potential," *Science* 253:146–152, 1991.

Meadows, D. H., Meadows, D. L., Randers, J., and Behrens, W. W. III, *The Limits to Growth*, Club of Rome and Universe Books, Washington, DC, 1972.

Pimentel, D., and Pimentel, M., "Land, Energy, and Water: The Constraints Governing Ideal U.S. Population Size," Negative Population Growth, Teaneck, NJ, 1991.

"Poor Pay a Big Price to Drink Clean Water," *Wall Street Journal* Jan. 15:B1, 1992.

President's Commission on Population Growth and the American Future, *Population Growth and the American Future*, New American Library, New York, 1972.

19. And Away We Go

Ahlburg, D. A., and Vaupel, J. W., "Alternative Projections of the U.S. Population," *Demography* 27(4):639–647, 1990.

Bancroft, A., "Immigration Expert Urges Crackdown on Illegal Migrants," *San Francisco Chronicle* Nov. 21:1, 1991.

Bouvier, L. F., State-by-State Projections of Migration from Foreign Countries in the 1990s, *Balance Data*, Population-Environment Balance, Washington, DC, 1992.

Carlton, J., and Marcus, A. M., "Undocumented Workers May File Discrimination Suits, Judge Rules," *Wall Street Journal* Feb. 25:B3, 1991.

Center for Immigration Studies, "In a Harsh Budget Climate, Is 'SAVE' Keeping Ineligible Aliens Off the Welfare Rolls?" *Scope* 9:1–3, Author, Washington, DC, 1991.

Ehrlich, P., "Opening Address," Symposium on Population and Scarcity: The Forgotten Dimensions, Smithsonian Institution, Washington, DC, April 20, 1990.

Kamen, A., "INS's Unofficial Open Door," *Washington Post* Jan.:1,7, 1992.

Smith, J. W. (ed.), *Immigration, Population and Sustainable Environments: The Limits to Australia's Growth*, Flinders Press, South Australia, 1991.

Urban Institute, "Immigration and Race," *Policy and Research Report* Winter-Spring:16–17, 1992.

20. Let Freedom Ring

Brimelow, P., "Time to Rethink Immigration?" *National Review* June 22:30–46, 1992.

Duncombe, L., *Immigration and the Decline of Democracy in Australia*, Kalgoorie Press, Canberra, 1992.

Ferguson, T. W., "The Sleeper Issue of the 1990s Awakens," *Wall Street Journal* June 23:A21, 1992.

Gibbons, A., "Rain Forest Diet: You Are What You Eat," *Science* Jan. 10:163, 1992.

"Hearing Date Set in $15 Million Free Speech Suit," *U.S. English Update*, May–June:1, 1991.

James, D., "Big Immigrant Wave Swamps Assimilation," *Wall Street Journal* July 2:A13, 1992.

"The Landless Landed," *The Economist* June 8:31, 1991.

Lynch, F. R., "Tales from an Oppressed Class," *Wall Street Journal* Nov. 11:A12, 1991.

Potter, D., *People of Plenty*, University of Chicago Press, Chicago, 1954.

President's Commission on Population Growth and the American Future, *Population Growth and the American Future*, The New American Library, New York, 1972.

Schlesinger, A. M., Jr., "A New Era Begins but History Remains," *Wall Street Journal* Dec. 11:Editorial page, 1991a.

Schlesinger, A. M., Jr., *The Disuniting of America*, Norton, New York, 1991b.

Wortham, A., "Multiculturalism and Immigration," Annual Meeting of the National Association of Scholars, Minneapolis, Oct. 1991.

Young, C., "Equal Cultures—or Equality?" *Washington Post* March 29:Editorial page, 1992.

21. Taking Hold

Alexander, C. P., "Gunning for the Greens," *Time* Feb. 3:50–52, 1992.

Bancroft, A., "Immigration Expert Urges Crackdown on Illegal Migrants," *San Francisco Chronicle* Nov. 21:1, 1991.

Bouvier, L. F., State-by-State Projections of Migration from Foreign Countries in the 1990s, *Balance Data*, Population Environment Balance, Washington, DC, 1992.

Bouvier, L. F., and Simcox, D., "Population Change in Meso-America: The Tip of the Iceberg," *Population and Environment* 10(4):206–220, 1989.

Briggs, V. M., Jr., *Mass Migration and the National Interest*, M. E. Sharpe, Armonk, NY, 1992.

Burke, B. M., "It's Just Getting Too Crowded," *San Jose Mercury News* June 2:7C, 1991.

Burtless, G., *A Future of Lousy Jobs*, Brookings Institution, Washington, DC, 1990.

"California Wakes Up to a Financial Hangover," *The Economist* Jan. 12:19–20, 1992.

Estrada, R., "Will Rising Tide of Immigration Lift All America's Boats?" *Dallas Morning News* March 25:Editorial page, 1991a.

Estrada, R., "The Impact of Immigration on Hispanic Americans," *Chronicles* July:24–28, 1991b.

Goshko, J. M., "Bush Urged to Admit 100,000 East Europeans," *Washington Post* Sept. 8:A11, 1989.

Holdren, J., "Population and the Energy Problem," *Population and Environment* 12(3):231–256, 1991.

Huddle, D. L., "Immigration and Jobs: The Process of Wage Depression and Job Displacement," Society for the Advancement of Socio-Economics annual meeting, Irvine, CA, Mar. 27–29, 1992.

"Letter to the Editor," *The Economist* Jan. 11:4, 1992.

Lucas, G., "Capital Bomb Linked to Wilson's Views on Immigrants," *San Francisco Chronicle* Jan. 3:A13, 1992.

Morris, F., "Testimony before the U.S. House Judiciary Committee Subcommittee on Immigration, Refugees, and International Law," *Congressional Record*, March 13, 1990.

Population-Environment Balance, "Conservation and Population," *Balance Report #70* (August), Author, Washington, DC, 1991.

President's Commission on Population Growth and the American Future, *Population Growth and the American Future*, New American Library, New York, 1972.

Rieff, D., *Los Angeles: Capital of the Third World*, Simon & Schuster, New York, 1991.

Smith, J. W., "Population, Immigration and the Limits to Australia's Growth," in J. W. Smith (ed.), *Immigration, Population and Sustainable Environments*, Flinders University Press, Bedford Park, South Australia, 1991.

Taylor, S., "Scribbling While Rome Burns," *American Renaissance* Nov.:7, 1991.

Whitmire, R., "When Living and Wages Don't Meet," *Tennessean* Jan. 5:1,4E, 1992.

Index